Privacy
in the
New
Media
Age

Withdrawn

UNIVERSITY PRESS OF FLORIDA

Florida A&M University, Tallahassee
Florida Atlantic University, Boca Raton
Florida Gulf Coast University, Ft. Myers
Florida International University, Miami
Florida State University, Tallahassee
New College of Florida, Sarasota
University of Central Florida, Orlando
University of Florida, Gainesville
University of North Florida, Jacksonville
University of South Florida, Tampa
University of West Florida, Pensacola

   Privacy

in the

New

Media

Age

Jon L. Mills

University Press of Florida
Gainesville
Tallahassee
Tampa
Boca Raton
Pensacola
Orlando
Miami
Jacksonville
Ft. Myers
Sarasota

Library of Congress Control Number: 2014949012
ISBN 978-0-8130-6058-3

The University Press of Florida is the scholarly publishing agency for the
State University System of Florida, comprising Florida A&M University,
Florida Atlantic University, Florida Gulf Coast University, Florida
International University, Florida State University, New College of Florida,
University of Central Florida, University of Florida, University of North
Florida, University of South Florida, and University of West Florida.

University Press of Florida
15 Northwest 15th Street
Gainesville, FL 32611-2079
http://www.upf.com

I dedicate this book to my wife, mother, and children. I thank Beth, Marguerite, Marguerite and Elizabeth Mills not only for their love and support but for the joy of living around their optimism, wisdom, and love for life. They inspire me every day.

Contents

New
Media,
Old
Conflict

The media and personal privacy are inherently in conflict. Although the degree of conflict has changed over time, the media have always thrived on publicizing exciting information, a pursuit that often reveals intimate details of the lives of people who may not want that information disclosed. The new media today are no different. While the media provide a critical function in our democratic society, they also commit intrusions into private endeavors for the sake of information gathering and news making. We want politicians, government, and other public figures and organizations to be subject to criticism, and we enjoy the satire that often ensues. We enjoy news. But when the new media overstep during the news-making process, real people suffer real harm.[1]

A decade ago, we were a different kind of society. Now, many of us work and live constantly wired to the Internet, seeking perpetual information updates. In current times that seems normal and even necessary. These new conveniences come at a price. The Internet, an easily accessible means for distributing information globally, is the primary engine behind the new media and its perils. In the span of an hour or less, a blogger can unfairly ruin your life. On July 19, 2010, Shirley Sherrod expected a normal day of work. However, that morning, the late Andrew Breitbart, a well-known conservative blogger, posted a deceptively edited video of a speech by Sherrod on his blog. Sherrod, an African American official in the U.S. Department of Agriculture, was shown describing how she discriminated against white farmers. Soon a video depicting her as a racist was all over the Internet. From there, the story picked up steam. It was posted on the Fox News Channel website, and then followed by the New York City CBS affiliate and the website of the *Atlanta Journal Constitution*. The mainstream media quickly joined in. CNN and the *New York Times* reported the story. Even the National Association for the Advancement of Colored People (NAACP) publicly condemned Sherrod. The Department of Agriculture quietly sought her resignation, and within twenty-four hours she was fired.

Twenty-four hours later, everyone started apologizing. In the span of a day, it became clear that Breitbart had deceptively edited the video to make Sherrod appear to be a racist. A full viewing showed that depiction to be false; in fact, the full video showed Sherrod discussing her joy in helping a white farmer.

This saga is a perfect example of how the new media have created a situation that breeds the wide dissemination of untruths. A complete lie can travel worldwide and savage an innocent individual in less than a day. Reporters and media are not inherently evil, nor do the vast majority intend to defame anyone. But the new media have created a world in which fast delivery of information seems to have become more important than checking facts and being accurate. Being the first to get a story now requires the story to be broken in a matter of minutes or seconds, not hours. The media are hypercompetitive, and the motivation to be first is strong. Since the new media now include instant Tweets, thousands of blog posts, and real-time, on-location video from citizen observers, a significant amount of information that we consider news is inaccurate—sometimes blatantly false. In the Sherrod case, some purveyors of information were malicious or negligent, while others just followed the pack. The savaging of Sherrod's reputation is a perfect symbol of how new media may cause harmful intrusions. Even the traditional media—more cautious from years of fact checking—were lured into making mistakes in the name of speed.

Basic and fundamental values such as personal autonomy, freedom, liberty, and the ability to be an individual are threatened by modern technology and new media. Sometimes the modern media are a vehicle for freedom, as in the recent examples of social revolutions broadcast by "iReporters" who were able to capture the scene in a more honest light than their government-controlled press would have been capable of doing. At the same time, some aspects of the new media can rend and tear lives and reputations apart with all the forethought of a rabid animal. In these attacks there is no conscience, no reason, and no noble purpose. These mindless intrusions do not represent the historic role of the press and should not be the ultimate by-product of the principles of free press and free speech.

Privacy and dignity matter. And although the law has identified them as protected rights, they suffer from the same disadvantage as other abstract assets like love and happiness. These concepts are hard to value using traditional metrics. When the values of privacy and free speech are pitted against each other, speech often wins in the name of freedom of expression. The United States has a well-established history of fighting against the chilling effect on speech that occurs by the mere threat of punishment.[2] Yet, the current state of the law does not explicitly protect against the same chilling effect on an individual's activities when his or her privacy is placed at risk. Particularly in the modern world, our society should have concerns about the chilling effect on a person's freedom of thought, freedom of choice, and even freedom of speech that occurs by the stripping away of individual privacy rights. Because freedom and liberty are equally at risk when privacy is left unprotected, protecting personal privacy is part and parcel of protecting free expression.

Competing Principles

The right to privacy and the right to a free press are bedrock principles that are fundamental to free and democratic societies. The principles are found in the texts of modern constitutions worldwide and were certainly part of the American Constitution, even though the word "privacy" is not in the text. Consequently, the conflict between the expression of the free press and individual privacy is particularly difficult because of the importance modern societies ascribe to each value. This book discusses the views of scholars who have tackled the conflict, its evolution and history, the new global nature of the conflict, and the role of technology in exacerbating the conflict. Ultimately, this book defines the role of law in resolving the conflict.

I personally respect and support the role of a strong and aggressive media. As a former elected official, I received from the media what I considered at the time to be unjustified criticism as well as unjustified praise. As a statewide official in a state that nearly twenty million people now call home, I remember reviewing the comments and coverage of seventeen different newspapers. Not infrequently, the same event generated very different views and even different "facts." Again, mistakes happen, and mistakes are a fair price to pay for a free and active press. In fact, some critics rationally argue that the new world has so many media outlets and online critics that we may be better off because mistakes are susceptible to attacks from multiple perspectives. But the blizzard of information also creates damage. Retractions and clarifications may not completely repair the damage done in a forum as vast and far reaching as the Internet. Once information is posted online, it can be seen, captured, obtained, edited, and controlled by anyone who can access it. Posting information on the Internet is tantamount to giving that information—and any rights to control it—away completely.

My other perspective of the press comes from my experience as a lawyer who has represented victims who were in the line of fire of free press principles. The families of the students murdered by serial killer Danny Rolling were innocent victims, but the press had a legitimate and important public interest in covering the brutal murders. Regarding a similar issue in a different case, the family of Dale Earnhardt had the right to keep autopsy photos of Dale from being displayed on the Internet, but the press had the right to investigate how he died in the fatal crash at the Daytona 500. In another case, I represented the family of Dawn Brancheau, who died in an encounter with a killer whale.

The family wanted to avoid the release of an underwater video that recorded the incident. Were it not for the judge's finding that the value of publishing the video was outweighed by the privacy rights of the family, it would not have been long before some blogger or news website would have enabled its public posting. In each of these cases I believe the family had a right of privacy that outweighed the media's right to publish. The press has a right to acquire information and a right to publish information. This book simply states that there must be limits, those limits must be legally enforceable, and the media should be held accountable when they exceed those limits.

An overview of the Constitution and the Bill of Rights demonstrates that the founders of our country clearly intended to protect individual identity, creativity, and personality. The founders also intended to instill strong protection for free expression and the press into the very first amendment to the Constitution. The First Amendment protects freedom of speech and press, as well as freedom of association, freedom of religion, and the right to petition government. All of these principles, including free expression, foster individuality. Constitutional individuality includes the ability to have a personal identity, personal property, and personal beliefs, and the right to be let alone. In more explicit codifications of the right to be let alone, the founders sought to protect private property against unreasonable search and seizure and the quartering of troops. They could not actually imagine the Internet, GPS surveillance, drones, and spike mikes, but they certainly demonstrated a strong and specific concern about the personal privacy and consequent freedom of our citizens.

The Globalized Conflict

Today, the forces of globalization and technology have expanded the scope and reach of privacy intrusion to a worldwide network of individuals. While the Internet is borderless, the world is not. Different nations, with different concepts of privacy and access to technology, attempt to solve the conflict between press and privacy in different ways. Those conflicts are increasingly global. In this book I frequently rely on examples that illustrate the difference between the policies of the United States and policies within the European Union. While I also touch on policies and laws of other nations, I view the E.U. approach as demonstrative of the direction in which the United States should trend its changes, and therefore I discuss it in greater depth. But by no means do I mean to suggest that the scope of this problem and any potential solutions to it are anything but global in nature.

The geographically borderless Internet is part of a globalized culture and economy. Since the Internet is nearly universally available in the developed world, it is an integral part of global culture. The Internet has developed its own digital culture and mores that are distinguishable from those in the analog world.[3] Still, digital values have not replaced the laws and values of the analog world. Press-privacy conflicts often revolve around clashes between these two worlds. Part of the challenge of evaluating these conflicts is to understand communication and intrusion in the new media age. Since an increasing number of individuals consume, produce, and share information digitally, understanding the modern technical capacity to intrude is elemental to understanding the potential for media intrusion. Perhaps even more critical is a true understanding of the need for individual privacy and human dignity.

Free expression is a critical global value, but in the expanded context of emerging technology and digital press, the sword of the free press cuts two ways. The media can communicate globally and instantly. They can also cut deeply into an individual's personal life. The goal of balancing free press with personal privacy is complex because the definition of the press is becoming ephemeral. Today, a single Twitter user with an Internet connection can accomplish distribution faster and on a larger scale than any traditional press outlet of the nineteenth and most of the twentieth centuries. In defining "press," it is important to evaluate the modern meaning of "news." Is a Facebook posting to friends considered community news? Moreover, how do we even define the term "community" in the modern world? Is it your city, your neighborhood, your Facebook friends, all worldwide fans of impressionist art? These are fundamental questions. Is the traditional press the best source of information? Or, in the modern world, is traditional press obsolete? And what is the value of the editorial filter in the traditional press? How has this filter been changed by the transition of publication to the Internet forum? How do we safeguard personal privacy when any individual can spread intrusive or slanderous information instantaneously, on a global scale? How has the capacity for instant communication changed the nature of news?

A twist to globalism is that local communications about a localized event can go global and be very important to worldwide news. For example, local Twitter users and bloggers—"web speakers,"[4] if you will—provided direct, current, and important information during the Boston Marathon bombing and the Arab Spring. How else would the world have had this important news if not for the technology that made their transmissions possible?

The right to free speech has not been uniformly embraced throughout history, even in contemporary societies. In the United States, free expression is highly protected, and there are even laws that punish baseless slander or libel suits (known as "strategic lawsuits against public participation" or SLAPP). American culture is protective of free expression, even at the expense of personal dignity and privacy. In some other cultures, such as in the European Union, the scales tip more toward protecting individual dignity.

Yet in other places, neither freedom of speech nor personal privacy is protected as a core value. Dictators, monarchs, and totalitarian governments require and thrive on control over the press and over the lives of their citizens. Press or media freedom is an inconvenience for totalitarian regimes. Such regimes control their citizens and routinely maintain surveillance that invades citizen privacy. For example, in China, press regulation and control over citizens is more important than free expression. The Chinese government does not embrace the same free expression principles as democratic states. Even in some democratic systems, such as parts of Latin America, members of the press are placed in jeopardy when they conflict with public figures or the government. In these nations, criminal defamation charges can place a journalist in jail for the mere criticism of government officials.[5] In contrast, criticism of government is a core mission of the U.S. press. U.S. courts protect even highly offensive actions if the issue involves political speech or criticism of the government.[6] Ultimately, press intrusions into privacy are an issue where both free press and individual rights are important. There is a natural tension. The more the basic rights of free press and individual liberty gain support, the greater the conflict.

Currently, cultural and national approaches to conflicts between the media and individual privacy vary widely. Although there are international treaties and agreements, most laws are still applied depending on the geography of the conflict. Multinational treaties are more effective when applied to globally shared values such as ending war. Such treaties are less effective with more localized values such as free speech and personal privacy, which vary widely among nations. Because laws on privacy are different in different countries, establishing where an invasion of privacy occurred is important, but that determination is not always straightforward in the Internet age. If a German citizen was slandered by a blogger in the United States on an Internet publication available in Ireland, which law applies? The laws and cultures are different, and the results of conflicts may be very different in different legal forums.

Because nations have varied responses to this natural press-privacy struggle, the media face increasing uncertainty in their distribution of information. The *Wall Street Journal* was liable in Australia for Internet defamation,[7] while the same conduct in the United States would have been protected speech. The varied approaches across jurisdictions create tremendous risk and uncertainty about rights and liability for individuals and businesses. This ambiguity creates an atmosphere where some are reluctant to speak or act and others recklessly test the limits. And because of advancing technology, cross-border intrusions will surely multiply into a worldwide Wild West of information.

The Future of the Media-Privacy Conflict

This book describes the evolution of the clash between press freedom and individual privacy and evaluates potential remedies for the increasing intrusions. The modern combination of anonymity, immunity, and technology creates a major hurdle for an individual harmed by false or intrusive media publications. Today, even the task of defining the news is a moving target. Over the course of writing this book, I have constantly had to return to previous passages to edit or add content based on the ever-changing nature of the way that people receive information. The constancy of this change illustrates the difficulty of remedying the problems that occur as a result.

Some options for remedies are expansions of classic privacy causes of action such as the traditional public disclosure of private facts or intrusion upon seclusion. But because law and the courts cannot always make old remedies fit new technology, newer policies and remedies are necessary. The fundamental importance of protecting personal dignity and protecting free press and speech will remain the same. However, with Wi-Fi tapping, drone surveillance, and other technological marvels, the facts will be radically different, and the law will need to adapt.

Effective remedies must take into account the future of new media. More information is available and distributed today than ever before. In some ways, we are a more informed society and are better off because of the increased availability of varied sources of information. In fact, some evaluations suggest the new media represent an advancement of more democratic and free speech principles than the old press. For example, the new press provides more democratic access to media publication and more direct public participation in and reaction to the news-making process. In the past, access to media was limited by high costs or government restrictions. The new media provide more varied and accessible opinions—a larger marketplace of ideas. The new media have few or no filters. Technology enables direct reporting of events that is then immediately published. Although there is more information, in the current age of Big Data there are also looming questions about the quality, accuracy, perspective, and analytical depth of this information.

While the proliferation of media, greater transparency, and openness foster certain democratic principles, the very same characteristics carry with them major risks for accuracy and privacy. The traditional press seeks accuracy as a fundamental goal. At least part of the new press trades accuracy for speed. The viewpoints presented by new media are so unfiltered, broad, and varied that even advocates of the flat-earth theory will have a forum and, no doubt, will also have followers.

Some scholars suggest the increased level of extreme and inaccurate publications will result in more litigation, more general distrust of the press, and more findings of defamation.[8] Quantity does not equal quality in terms of information and information sources. A larger marketplace of ideas is not automatically a better marketplace. A produce market is not necessarily enhanced by adding rotten fruit. Logically, the risk of privacy intrusions increases with the exponential increase of random and often unverified sources of information.

By the early twenty-first century, channels of information included blogs, websites, social media networks, Infotainment, and postings to sites like YouTube. Ambient news—a media environment that is saturated with information from multiple sources—is becoming the norm. More material is distributed through free expression than ever before, and the consumer has more information to consume. With the advent of microblogging sites such as Twitter, both the mainstream media and the individual are able to distribute more information instantaneously and worldwide. However, in this form of ambient journalism, it is unclear how individuals assign meaning and credibility to the information they consume. Additionally, as more information is made available, the general public is becoming more skeptical of the institutional press without becoming more confident in any particular alternative.[9] More information does not necessarily mean better or more reliable information. Today, information is widely distributed by many bloggers and other new media without the dogged fact checking of the traditional press. Therefore, more information, both true and false, is available through ambient journalism. However, either type of information can be intrusive to the individual to whom it pertains. In some circumstances, disclosure of an intimate truth may be more harmful than a lie. Some media outlets today opt for speed and take the approach to talk first and correct misstatements later. The result is the circulation and redistribution of bad information. Just ask Shirley Sherrod. In the Internet age, once information is released, the genie is most certainly out of the bottle.

Because intrusions are increasing and because information spreads globally, the law is struggling to keep up. Technology will always move faster than the law. While we desire to curb the intrusions caused by new technology, complete surrender to individual privacy is not an option. There must be a balance. Freedom of expression is no less important than it has always been, but individual dignity and privacy are not obsolete, either. This book pursues real answers and real remedies to a number of issues. Requiring media accountability for real misconduct and true harm is not unreasonable. Further, it is not enough to say technology has outstripped individuality; the choice between technology and individuality is a false one, and far from irresolvable. The quest for real solutions must be based on current realities of technology, globalism, and legal systems. The solutions must be based on the facts and circumstances of each intrusion, requiring that our theories must be able to produce real legal results—the core goal of this book.

Can Privacy and New Media Coexist?

Media and privacy have been in conflict for a long time, but most frequently the academic dialogue and theoretical discussions have occurred in isolation without confronting each other. That is, there is a series of free speech theories, and there is a series of privacy theories. Only recently have there been efforts to articulate a resolution of the two competing rights. A reason the principles of free press and right to privacy evolved in parallel are that their origins differ. Free press and free speech have been articulated as collective democratic rights that are a fundamental principle of democracy. Privacy evolved as an individual right against intrusion by the state or by others. At the core of the right to privacy are individual identity, freedom, individual dignity, and the right to be let alone. The phrase "right to be let alone" was coined by Samuel Warren and Louis Brandeis in their historic article on privacy and continues to be used by courts and commentators. On the other hand, the core principles in press freedom are to protect the marketplace of ideas, provide an open public forum, promote the free flow of ideas, and hold government accountable. Clearly both values are desirable.

The advocates for press freedom and for privacy each have substantial theoretical and practical justifications. For example, the U.S. Constitution provides a basis for each right, although the free press right is more explicit. America's founding fathers had both concepts in mind when they drafted the Bill of Rights, particularly the First and Fourth Amendments. An advocate for press freedom will argue that reporting newsworthy events and activities is critical to the public welfare and must prevail over an interest in protecting an individual from an embarrassing or harmful intrusion. A privacy advocate will argue that individual dignity and the personal right to be let alone should prevail unless the media intrusion serves a public purpose. Resolving the balance of these two rights is clearly a difficult and elusive task that should not be subject to absolutist or dogmatic resolution.

While the theoretical debates may proceed comfortably without resolution, the legal system must deal with the actual and real cases of alleged intrusion that have harmed real people. Cases such as the release of crime scene photos of the bodies of mutilated college students involve much more than an academic debate about the boundaries of free expression. Either the grotesque crime scene photos will be released to the press or they will not be released. Once the conflict is joined, real people and real harms are at issue. A judge in that case had to decide whether the public interest in seeing crime scene photos that most certainly influenced a death penalty sentence outweighed the potential trauma to family members of releasing pictures of their mutilated and dismembered children to the public. In the real world, people matter as well as theory.

The realities of new technology have dramatically affected the new world of media and the new world of privacy—leaving each set of scholars and theorists to plow new ground. Media have been redefined by technology. The Internet, Twitter, and the rise of social media networks have left media and journalism in a mode of reinvention in the glare of a new reality. Who is a journalist today? Privacy scholars are confronted with a new reality that facilitates intrusion into virtually all private activities. Does privacy exist in the world of contemporary technology?

The Principles and Values of the Free Press

In democratic nations, which characteristically enshrine free press and free speech principles in their founding documents, the media have a critical role in exposing matters that are deemed newsworthy—particularly those matters related to the government, its functions, and the effect of its functions on the populace. Several theories have traditionally supported the strong protection of press and media publication. The concept that the press fosters a "marketplace of ideas" is a well-accepted principle of media advocates and the courts. Another theory that has gained traction posits that the free speech right of the press is basically absolute. This view has been termed the "absolutist" theory. Each of these theories has become part of the legal structure that protects free speech rights in the United States and worldwide.[1] A more specific and widely applied legal test is the evaluation of a publication for newsworthiness. "Newsworthiness" presents a hypothetical requirement that information be qualified as a matter of public concern as a prerequisite for its publication. The reality, though, is that anything of interest to anyone is usually sufficient to pass the newsworthiness test. Finally, the broadest theory that underpins all of these principles is the fundamental right to free expression. Whether good or bad for public dialogue, or whether true, false, or offensive, the overriding desire to allow free expression may be the strongest argument for press freedom.

Marketplace-of-Ideas Theory

The English utilitarian philosopher John Stuart Mill is widely credited with furnishing the ingredients for the marketplace-of-ideas theory of free speech that was later developed by two justices of the U.S. Supreme Court. In the 1919 case of *Abrams v. United States*, two individuals challenged a federal law that prohibited forms of sedition that would impede the American effort in World War I. While the law was upheld and remained good law for forty-seven more years, Justice Oliver Wendell Holmes Jr. penned a forceful dissent in which he stated, "The best test of truth is the power of the thought to get itself accepted in the competition of the market."[2] More than thirty years later, Justice William O. Douglas used the phrase "marketplace of ideas" in *United States v. Rumely*, which overturned the conviction of a journalist who refused to divulge the names of his subscribers to a congressional committee.[3]

Under the marketplace-of-ideas theory, laws that limit the media's publication of information erect the same sort of barriers on the trade of information as tariffs do on the trade of goods. The ultimate goal in the marketplace of ideas is the open search for truth.[4] This theory encourages multiple views and opinions as part of the public debate. The role of individual privacy in the marketplace of ideas is simply not critical—perhaps even nonexistent. The test for valuing public disclosure in the United States and other similar democratic nations has been to assess its newsworthiness and to weigh that value against any countervailing privacy interest. Particularly in the United States, the privacy interest usually loses to the media interest.

Newsworthiness Principle

In principle, nothing could be more logical than to say that the media should be able to publish that which is newsworthy. Newsworthiness is the quintessential factor in the balancing test of privacy and the First Amendment. The basic question of newsworthiness in any public disclosure controversy is whether the matter is one of public interest or private concern.

Courts have long struggled to categorize matters that belong in the public domain versus matters that should be protected as private. Historically, the newsworthiness test as applied in the United States has skewed toward a liberal determination of free speech. Part of this rationale is that publishers are in a better position to gauge public interest than courts, and the judiciary should be deferential to media rights. In other words, the courts should not be censors. It is better to let the media make reasoned decisions. This rationale is compromised when technology allows thousands to be publishers. Today, almost any fact or rumor involving a tangentially public figure, no matter how private, is arguably newsworthy simply because it is a matter that sparks public interest. For a variety of reasons, the new media exercise less restraint than the traditional mainstream media.

The ultimate issue is the meaning of "newsworthiness." A city official accused of taking a bribe will always be newsworthy. But should a photograph, taken surreptitiously, of a celebrity seen leaving a drug rehabilitation clinic be equally considered news? Such personal details might be considered news in the United States—but maybe not in Great Britain, a jurisdiction that makes a stronger effort to strike some balance between privacy and the value of public disclosure. In the United States, the scales are heavily weighted toward defining almost everything as newsworthy. The threshold question for publication is whether there may be *any* public interest, not whether there is an *important* public interest. If a public interest of any kind is found, the harm of the disclosure to privacy interests is virtually always deemed irrelevant.

Absolutist Theory

"Nothing that I have read in the Congressional debates on the Bill of Rights indicates that the First Amendment contained any qualifications."[5] This sentence, written by U.S. Supreme Court Justice Hugo Black, aptly describes the First Amendment theory known as absolutist theory. Justice Black's approach may be appealing for its simplicity. Acknowledging Justice Black's interpretation as the correct one would completely eliminate any need for balancing and a detailed newsworthiness analysis. But even the absolutist theory does not eliminate accountability for outright defamation and lying, the traditional exceptions to First Amendment protection.

In *Mishkin v. New York*, an obscenity case from the 1960s, dissenting Justice Black argued that the appellants' punishment for directing the publication of "obscene" material was censorship in that it unconstitutionally punished the appellants for "expressing views" on sex.[6] Characterizing the material as expression of views would allow it to fall under the broad protections given to satire, opinion, and expressive conduct. Essentially, he argued for an outer limit for absolute press freedom, one that only stops at illegal conduct. Importantly, even this theory would not protect the media against an "intrusion upon seclusion" remedy because that tort is based on intruding into a space rather than publication of any information. Eavesdropping, trespass, and other forms of physical—or even electronic—intrusion are certainly punishable illegal conduct, not an expression of views.

The new media today publish widely varying opinions and even widely varying versions of facts. The combination of the absolutist theory with the marketplace-of-ideas theory certainly supports the widest range of views—whether they are accurate or not. One supportive view of new media is part and parcel of the marketplace-of-ideas theory: with so many competing views, the truth will be available, regardless of whether it is buried among falsehoods and misrepresentations or emerges as a result of competition among ideas. The practical problem with this theory is that it enables widespread dissemination of inaccuracy in the search for truth. The absolutist theory, at its most basic, posits that information, regardless of its content, should be free of restraint. Even the most outrageous and inaccurate statements are part of the debate. That means that the value of pi can be a debatable issue. It harkens us back to a time when the Indiana General Assembly almost passed a law dictating that pi would be equal to 3.14. Inaccuracy and outrageous opinions have always been a part of free public debate. With the enhanced ability to publish, the new reality is that we will have more bad information in the marketplace and a need for rational responses.

The strongest theory supporting the new media explosion of information may be the simplest—free expression. The media's right to publish does not exceed the right of individuals to communicate or freely express themselves. The media is no more privileged in the publishing of information or expression of opinion than is an individual citizen. This theory provides more flexibility for dealing with the new media because each new definition of press becomes anachronistic shortly thereafter.[7] The right of the media to publish is not dependent on the definition of a reporter. There are other issues such as reporter privilege that do require some definition of the press, but not regarding the actual dissemination of information.[8] While the marketplace-of-ideas theory supports multiple speakers and their differing points of view, free expression focuses on the right to communicate irrespective of the value of that communication to the general public.

Theories of media freedom are inherent in more general theories of government such as those expressed by John Locke and other classical Liberalists. In the United States, the constitutional protection of the media keeps the right of speech free from government control and free from attacks by individuals or corporations that may otherwise seek to suppress unpopular viewpoints. The free press holds a special status in the governance of the United States. But the practical evolution of the rights of the press—now the new media—trades losses of personal privacy for gains in available information. This book seeks to define rational limits for the media that will preserve the need for human dignity and privacy. Modern scholars have articulated an array of reasons that support individual freedom from intrusion.

Theories of Privacy

Privacy theories deal with freedom from intrusions by government as well as intrusions by nongovernment entities. The focus here is on private intrusions and particularly intrusions by the press, with the acknowledgment that the rationale at the heart of both types of intrusions—the reasonable expectation of privacy—is a critical piece of either analysis.

Being Let Alone

At the close of the nineteenth century, the landmark article on privacy was spurred by concerns with new media and new technology: the technology of photography. "The Right to Privacy," by Samuel Warren and future U.S. Supreme Court Justice Louis Brandeis, is cited as the theoretical birthplace of the right to privacy.[9] Extending principles of tort injury to the concept of privacy, Brandeis and Warren outlined a common-law "right to be let alone." Even then they recognized that new technologies would increase the capacity for individual harm through invasions of privacy. Recognizing privacy as a right was a ve-

Family Tree for Privacy in Contemporary U.S. Law

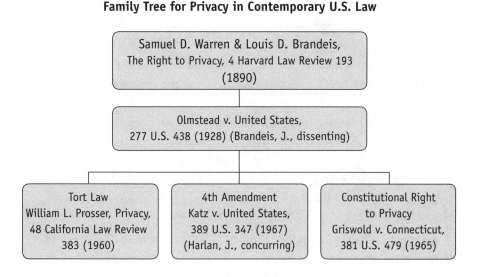

Samuel D. Warren & Louis D. Brandeis,
The Right to Privacy, 4 Harvard Law Review 193
(1890)

Olmstead v. United States,
277 U.S. 438 (1928) (Brandeis, J., dissenting)

Tort Law
William L. Prosser, Privacy,
48 California Law Review
383 (1960)

4th Amendment
Katz v. United States,
389 U.S. 347 (1967)
(Harlan, J., concurring)

Constitutional Right
to Privacy
Griswold v. Connecticut,
381 U.S. 479 (1965)

hicle to fashion legal actions in order to remedy these invasions. The privacy right to be let alone was grounded in the idea that each individual had the right to disclose or withhold his "thoughts, sentiments, and emotions" to the extent he so desired.[10]

It was fortuitous for the article's impact that its co-author would become a U.S. Supreme Court justice who could advocate privacy in the United States. Once the theorist Brandeis became the jurist Brandeis, the privacy theory became law.

Almost eighty years after Brandeis and Warren's article was published, and twenty-eight years after Brandeis retired from the Supreme Court, the Court articulated its concept of a right to privacy in *Katz v. United States*.[11] While contemporary scholars have since lamented that the right to be let alone is an overly broad definition of privacy, it is an instructive starting point for evaluating future theories.[12]

Informational Autonomy

Proponents of informational autonomy conceptualize privacy as the ability to control one's personal information. Personal information in this sense could mean anything from social security number and bank account information to cell phone data, records of consumer purchases, and photographs taken of or by a person. It could also refer to information contained in e-mail, online profiles, or other sources. Personal control may have a basis in the personal nature of the information, the ownership of information, and the privileged nature of information shared in certain relationships.

Personal control of information is made more difficult because today personal information is often a product of our interactions with others.[13] The Internet has only furthered such informational collaboration. For example, information disclosed between two or more users via e-mail, Facebook, or any online chatting function inherently belongs to, albeit not equally, both the sender and the recipient. In response, some scholars have proposed limiting protectable information about oneself to "intimate information,"[14] meaning information necessary to form and foster relationships based on concepts of love, respect, friendship, and trust. However, limiting the protection to such intimate information would not capture other essential information, such as financial information.[15] Even with this limitation, the problems persist. Intimate information may also be a product of more than one person; for example, an intimate sexual relationship's existence is known to two people.

As for other forms of personal information, courts have decided that sharing information such as bank records (with a bank) and phone records (with a phone company) means that the individuals to whom the information relates have no expectation of privacy in those bank or phone records because they willfully disclosed the information to the third party. In other words, there is a significant amount of information that, although personal, may not be legally private.

One well-established commercial version of a privacy right is the ability to protect a trade secret. The formula for Coca Cola and the recipe for Kentucky Fried Chicken are examples of some of the best-protected information in the world. The legal theory is focused, however, on the issue of commercial value of the secret to a commercial entity. The analogy to personal privacy is that the owner has control of the information it wishes to keep secret. It is irrelevant that the formula for Coca Cola is newsworthy; the formula is protectable because the law cares about its value. Trade secrets in the United States are protected by federal statute. The underlying theory revolves around the conduct of the secret holder and the conduct of a possible secret taker. To have a trade secret, one must act both to protect it and to use it commercially. Furthermore, the secret taker must take it knowingly. Freedom of speech is not a defense to the taking, because the secret is treated like property. Like other intellectual property, the one justification for protecting trade secrets is the promotion and protection of creativity. Perhaps the value of some personal information about individuals should likewise be protected to promote personal individuality and creativity.

Breach of confidence is another potential privacy remedy involving control of information. Where an individual has a duty to hold some information in confidence, the theory allows for enforcement against the person who breaches that confidence by revealing the information. Qualifying breaches include attorney-client and doctor-patient relationships. Great Britain uses breach-of-confidence legal actions as an alternative to the U.S. privacy torts.[16] These remedies are based on actual relationships as well as implied relationships. The theory gives individuals the right to limit distribution of information even though they have disclosed that information to other persons, because the information was only disclosed in confidence. A patient has the right to seek redress if a doctor violates the doctor-patient confidential relationship by distributing information. The theory in Britain has been expanded to an implied confidence based more on the sensitivity of the information than a specific close or professional relationship with a person. The expansion of this theory could allow for enhanced privacy protections of sensitive information.

Some scholars suggest that informational autonomy is akin to the right to think freely. Certainly, our publicly held positions, statements, and publications are subject to public scrutiny, and we are accountable for what we say. But we should be able to think without scrutiny. John Stuart Mill described freedom to think as part of liberty.[17] Clearly, we control our thoughts and our own private ability to think. Reading and performing research have always been a part of thinking. If someone reads, writes, and does research on the Internet, should all of that person's actions be considered open to public scrutiny? That information is discoverable. The concept of informational autonomy posits that "intellectual privacy" protections should guard against such informational intrusions.

Neil Richards describes intellectual privacy as a zone of protection that guards our "ability to freely make up our minds and to develop new ideas."[18] This right to generate our own ideas and come to our own conclusions without interference is rooted in America's oldest civil liberties. Richards believes that increased state surveillance further chills creativity and risk taking in favor of safer, mainstream thought.[19] Does not the same chilling effect arise whether the surveillance is performed by private individuals or by the media? Does the potential for a media report about the books a person has read online affect a person's reading choice?

Informational autonomy is a concept that strives to adjust traditional civil liberties to the realities of the modern world—which means protecting not only against government intrusions but also intrusions by private entities or individuals. Controlling personal information is part of individuality and elemental to privacy.

Privacy in Personal Space

The "right to be let alone" in certain spaces, such as the home, has been part of privacy theory for some time. At the time that the framers drafted the Constitution, they gave great consideration to the sanctity of the home and the importance of protecting individuals from government searches, seizures, and other invasions of a person's most private space. Rather than declare that citizens have an absolute right to privacy in their home, the founders phrased these protections as rights of the people to be secure against government action.

It is well established that private actors, such as members of the press, can likewise intrude on private space and be liable for their actions, but these are not matters of constitutional magnitude. Legal remedies such as trespass and intrusion upon seclusion are based on intrusions into physical space but may also include a technological intrusion such as electronic eavesdropping or wiretapping. Scholars are seeking to expand the intrusion-upon-seclusion theory to protect an individual's existence and personal presence on the Internet or cyberspace.[20] This theory has some definitional obstacles: can one analogize a photo taken through a window to capture a person disrobing with accessing a Facebook posting deemed private for some but public to others? In both cases the individual may have an expectation of privacy. But will a court consider the Facebook posting to be a *reasonable* expectation in today's world? The future definition of reasonable expectation of privacy is a key to privacy remedies.

Privacy as Free Expression

The First Amendment is a source of authority for press expression but also a source of authority to protect individual privacy. The freedoms in the First Amendment contain critical elements of privacy such as free association and free expression. Impairments of this private expression can and have been prohibited because these freedoms are protected. For example, a membership list for the National Association for the Advancement of Colored People (NAACP) was protected from disclosure because the right to associate freely could have been impaired by the general dissemination of that list at that time.[21]

In a case dealing with the protection of First Amendment rights of the press to publish a private conversation, Justice William Rehnquist's dissent stated that the greater First Amendment violation was the impairment of the individual's right to express his opinion in the private conversation that was recorded.[22] The issue was whether a statute that prevented the surreptitious recording of cell phone conversations was constitutional. The Court held the statute unconstitutional and thereby protected the release of a secretly recorded conversation. While the free expression rights of the radio station broadcasting the conversation were protected in the publication of the conversation, Justice Rehnquist lamented that the free expression rights of the private individual were not protected unless the recording itself was prohibited under such circumstances. Justice Rehnquist's recognition of the danger of chilling individual speech is unusual and important. His concept of "chilling speech" is part of our traditional First Amendment rubric and is often used to shield and protect the media. But the protection against chilling speech applies to individuals as well. The First Amendment is equally concerned with policies that suppress individual speech. The First Amendment is a strong source of authority to protect individual privacy and needs to be cited more often in that context.

Privacy as Dignity

In the European Union, as codified in many European constitutions, privacy is explicitly protected, as is personal information and personal dignity.[23] This difference from U.S. law is substantial and the approach and cultural context most definitely different. In the European Union, dignity is a personally held human right that is balanced directly against free expression. Unlike in the United States, free expression does not automatically win most conflicts based on the newsworthiness of the information involved.

Another aspect of the E.U. concept of dignity is the approach to hate speech. In the United States, we are willing to protect hateful speech such as a Ku Klux Klan member's racist remarks.[24] In Germany, anti-Semitic expressions or malicious slurs are prohibited and punished.[25] Again, the United States is willing to accept publication of distasteful actions and hateful speech, including burning the American flag, to protect the ability to express widely varying viewpoints.[26] European scholars sometimes wonder why Americans, at least in terms of legal enforcement, seem more concerned with preventing obscenity than with preventing hate speech. Indeed, although it rarely occurs, when speech is defined as obscene, it is not protected speech.[27] Oftentimes, harmful or demeaning speech that could be restricted by the European Union is nonetheless protected in the United States. Ultimately, U.S. courts value free speech far more than protection of personal dignity.

Pragmatic Privacy

Pragmatic privacy is less a theory to define privacy than it is a contextual analysis to understand it in practice.[28] Daniel Solove, who has championed this theory, examines the role privacy plays in specific circumstances, and suggests that a variety of solutions are appropriate in different sets of circumstances. Solove argues that courts need the flexibility in evaluating privacy that a uniform theory simply cannot provide.[29] In fact, pragmatic-privacy proponents blame the conceptualization of various privacy theories for the failure to solve today's most important policy debates.[30]

Under the pragmatic-privacy analysis, a particular definition of privacy does not hold any intrinsic value. Rather, its importance depends upon the practices to which it must be applied and the wrongs it must address.[31] As other scholars have pointed out, the time, place, and circumstance of particular privacy intrusions matter.[32] By evaluating the different sets of circumstances that give rise to privacy problems, those circumstances can be placed on a sliding scale from the most important privacy implications to the least important. By avoiding the singular formula many theories use to address disparate problems, these scholars suggest the importance of flexibility to address changing circumstances and different facts.

As an example, Solove argues that recent privacy cases regarding the collection and use of personal information by private-sector companies cannot be remedied by any existing privacy theories.[33] Courts that have attempted to compare data collection to the disclosure of private or intimate facts have failed to adequately protect our privacy interests because such companies often aggregate only nonsecret information such as names, addresses, and phone numbers.[34] Furthermore, the data are usually disclosed to some third party on a voluntary basis. Traditional notions of privacy do not offer protections for information the claimant has rendered nonsecret by disclosure. Pragmatic privacy is supposed to solve this problem by first identifying the practice in question and then crafting a solution specific to that problem. This approach is indeed more pragmatic than trying to force particular facts into an ill-fitting solution. Modern intrusions and modern media intrusions do not fit neatly into the traditional privacy remedy boxes. There is a need to redefine the old remedies and creatively seek new ones.

The Right to Be Forgotten

As part of their efforts to better protect dignity and privacy, the E.U. nations have sought to define what has been termed "the right to be forgotten."[35] The nations of the European Union have been working on establishing continental data privacy regulations that would redefine the relationship between users and Internet companies that harvest, store, and sell their data. Article 17 of the Data Protection Regulation (DPR) would require that "data controllers" delete all information about a user upon that user's specific request to do so. Because so much of a person's identity—both self-selected and not—is based on data and the contextual information that can be gleaned from the data, this right to be forgotten is seen as a clear benefit to consumers.[36] Three theories have emerged, all under the banner of the right to be forgotten: the ability to require that data are deleted, a blanket right to a clean slate, and the right to require one's data footprint to reflect only current reality.[37]

In the United States, a college student who is arrested for disorderly conduct will soon find his or her mugshot on a host of websites. The people who run these websites, adept at search engine optimization, ensure that a Google search of that person's name will have the mugshot at the top of search results. These sites have learned a truism of business: if there's money in the problem, there's money in the solution. For a fee of several hundred dollars, the companies will take down your mugshot, although the arrest itself may live on in public records. It is important to stress that we are talking about *arrests*, not convictions. A wrongfully arrested person, perhaps someone arrested wrongfully for a heinous crime, will struggle to shed those digital handcuffs. But without further legal redress, the imprint of the past will always exist, accessible to everyone with an Internet connection.

The Internet is a global force, while the privacy laws of nations are localized by jurisdiction. For global companies that traffic in digital data—Google, Facebook, and Amazon—the challenges of adhering to a patchwork of localized regulations concerning one's right to be forgotten will be considerable unless we enact global standards. Regardless, much of the information that an individual may wish to have forgotten is still relevant on a localized scale—for instance, to future employers. It is also hard to imagine that we could place an absolute statute of limitations on disclosures about our personal past. As a society, we may be perfectly willing to forgive past conduct, such as the fact that a person was a prostitute or a drug dealer twenty-five years ago. We forgive because the person may have changed, but we do not entirely forget. Some conduct, such as mass murder as a Nazi war criminal, we will neither forgive nor forget. Ultimately, though, in the current world it is difficult to erase anything permanently.

The Media-Privacy Matrix: Beyond Theory

Reality, standing in contrast to the theoretical world, requires workable solutions to privacy intrusions rather than merely interesting theories that may generate another law review article. On a practical level, the families of victims struggling to keep autopsy photographs of their loved one from being publicly displayed do not care whether the reason used has its roots in property law or privacy theory.

Privacy intrusions by media raise a very different set of legal and moral issues than intrusions by government. While the Fourth Amendment has traditionally been viewed as protecting the individual from certain government intrusions, the First Amendment protects the free expression of press and of every individual. Broad support and substantial legal authority protect an individual from search and seizures and intrusions by government. Despite the revelations of Edward Snowden, there are definable constitutional limits to the government's powers. By contrast, the First Amendment protects individual speech and free expression even if that expression intrudes upon the privacy of another. Privacy interests lack the explicit and expansive constitutional protection afforded to speech. Protecting the individual from governmental intrusion is pragmatically difficult but nonetheless provided for by the Constitution. In the case of the media, the Constitution protects the intruder, and the citizen is left to fashion a legal remedy based on a privacy theory.

Free expression can plant a clear and visible flag by asserting the right of the public to know and the right of the press to publish.

> **Media-Privacy Matrix**
> Questions for Analyzing Media and Privacy Conflicts
>
> 1. Where did the intrusion occur?
> 2. Who owns or controls the information?
> 3. How did the media obtain the information?
> 4. Is the information true, false, or an opinion?
> 5. Is the published information private and intrusive in nature?
> 6. How was the information actually disclosed?
> 7. Who was the target of the disclosure?
> 8. What is the intent of the target and of the media?

Privacy suffers from complexity of definition and a need for reasonable limits—these qualities make privacy a ripe ground for academics but a minefield for legislators. There is no viable privacy theory that is absolutist. The primary legal test to establish these limits has evolved into various iterations of what a person may hold as a reasonable expectation of privacy. Other privacy-related wrongs, such as defamation or trespass, do not require a showing of a reasonable expectation of privacy because the nature of the wrong focuses instead on the intruder's conduct.

The history of media-privacy conflicts has not been neat, tidy, or predictable. The results also do not necessarily reach consistently "moral" results. What some may view as an immoral intrusion on the private life of the Duchess of Cambridge by taking pictures of her topless at a private residence may be legal in some places and illegal in other places. Accordingly, the first stop on our press-versus-privacy matrix is the location or jurisdiction of an alleged intrusion by the press. Legal standards can shift and change, both between communities and across nations. Unraveling media-privacy intrusions requires a panoramic understanding of the facts and laws applicable to a specific situation.

In examining multiple conflicts there is a series of common issues. This decision matrix can help resolve press-privacy conflicts, or at least help regularize the decision-making process. The answer to these questions should form the basis for any legal resolution of a conflict in this context.

Where Did the Intrusion Occur?

"Where?" rather than "what?" might be the most important question when analyzing a media-privacy intrusion. Jurisdictional requirements regarding what constitutes newsworthiness, a public figure, a public record, or defamation are starkly different in different countries. Global communications symbolized by the Internet will often create a situation where an intrusion constituting a legal wrong might be pursued in several different jurisdictions.

When an Italian tabloid published topless photographs of Kate Middleton, Duchess of Cambridge, the actual intrusion occurred in the south of France, where paparazzi surreptitiously photographed her sunbathing. But once the photos were on the Internet and published in print in tabloids around the world, the intrusion was globalized. Was a legal action available in Great Britain, France, or Italy?[38] While the Internet allows for uniform global dissemination of intrusive information, there is no uniform law dealing with such media intrusions. As a result, a victim like the Duchess of Cambridge could sue the offending tabloid from a variety of jurisdictions. Victims of privacy intrusion are able to shop for the most advantageous forum in an exercise known as libel tourism. As an overt example, actress Halle Berry cited stricter French privacy laws as her primary motivation for moving across the Atlantic.

There is another important facet of location in addition to the global conflict of laws and jurisdictional issues. Did the alleged intrusion occur in a space in which a person is entitled to and can expect personal privacy? For example, did a reporter enter a private home to obtain information, or wiretap a personal telephone? The law has placed higher protections on intrusions into personal space such as the home for many years. The issue of personally protected space may even be redefined in a new technological sense. In the many ways in which it is defined, location is of critical importance in evaluating any particular intrusion.

Who Owns or Controls Information?

Another threshold question is the matter of who controls the information at issue. For example, in the case of Dawn Brancheau, whose family I represented in their effort to prevent the distribution of a video that recorded her death at SeaWorld in 2010, the video at issue was underwater video recorded and owned by SeaWorld. In the course of the public investigation, the video was given to the medical examiner and the local sheriff's department. The video was never in possession of the media, although the media sought to obtain it for publication. When the media sued for access, the judge held that the video should not be released because it intruded on the family's privacy and did not provide significant additional information to the public apart from what was already known in the investigation.[39] In other words, the court performed a balancing test in which it determined that, under these particular circumstances, the newsworthiness of the information was inferior to the privacy right of the Brancheau family. If the video had been taken by a private individual who then decided to release it to the media, this controversy would have ended differently. At the time of the litigation, only two entities were in possession of the video: the state and SeaWorld. SeaWorld did not want to release the video, and the state was ordered not to release the video by the courts.

In contrast, if the media are already in possession of information, the question of whether they can publish it becomes an issue of whether the courts may place a prior restraint on the publication. Prior restraints are strongly disfavored at law. Only in rare instances of imminent threat and national security have U.S. courts placed prior restraints on the media's publication of information.

In the new world, organizations such as WikiLeaks pride themselves on obtaining confidential information. In the most positive light these are whistleblowers disclosing the misconduct of government or private corruption. Viewed at their worst, they are traitors. The twist in dealing with disclosure of such information is that even if it was originally obtained illegally, the millions of media outlets and bloggers who republish that information are free to do so as long as they did not have a hand in the original illegal activity that captured the information. As for the original publishers of the information, they likewise may only be liable if they were complicit in the illegal act.

In sum, who owns and controls the information matters, because that person's willingness to disseminate it—even to one other entity—could make the difference in whether the information is legally deemed public or private.

How Did the Media Obtain and Disclose the Information?

While we most often think of privacy invasions of new media as publication of information, privacy intrusions may well occur when the media *obtains* the information and before it is ever published. The very same piece of information might be legally or illegally obtained. Home values are an apt example. The appraised value of a person's home is public knowledge on county property appraisers' websites, as well as third-party sites such as Zillow. When the media publish home value information from a public source, they are not subject to liability. But if they break into a person's home to obtain that information from personal files, criminal and civil liability would attach for obtaining the exact same information.

When obtaining information, the media are generally treated as any person would be. If a member of the media steals information, that act is illegal. If the media engage in an illegal wiretap or solicit illegal conduct, they are liable and accountable. The U.S. Supreme Court has stated specifically that "the First Amendment does not guarantee the press a constitutional right of special access to information not available to the public generally."[40] In other words, members of the media are no better than anyone else when seeking to obtain information. However, if a person who obtains information illegally then gives it to the media, that person may be prosecuted, but the media may be free to publish it without liability. Such is the high value given to providing information to the public. As a caveat to this scenario, information obtained in violation of U.S. law can sometimes give rise to liability both for obtaining and for disclosing the information.[41] The legality in each case is not clear-cut. A range of factors will govern cases in the gray area, such as whether the publisher who obtained the information knew that the specific information was illegally obtained or directed the action that caused it to be illegally obtained.

The disclosure of illegally obtained information can create further liability, although it is not a certainty.[42] If publishers disclose information they know was illegally obtained or they directed the illegal act undertaken to obtain the information, liability is likely to attach.[43] If, on the other hand, the information is of significant public concern, the fact that the underlying information was illegally obtained may not matter and liability may be avoided.[44] In situations where a publisher discloses legally obtained information despite a preexisting contractual obligation not to do so, liability may follow based on contract, rather than ordinary tort principles. Disclosure creates a more obvious form of liability, but the mere act of illegally obtaining the information is sufficient to create liability.

In *Desnick v. American Broadcasting Companies, Inc.*, Judge Richard Posner explained the distinct issue of trespass in the context of the media.[45] In *Desnick*, a television producer obtained consent from a doctor to shoot footage in his office but then surreptitiously dispatched actors posed as patients to record the actions in the office with hidden cameras. In evaluating the legality of the producer's actions, Posner reasoned that while the right of a journalist to enter upon another's property without consent stretches no further than that of an ordinary citizen, the law will often "give effect to consent procured by fraud."[46] In short, the court held that consent to enter the doctor's office, even though obtained under fraudulent grounds, was sufficient to insulate the producer from the tort of trespass.

In his analysis, Judge Posner drew parallels to fraudulent consent in the battery context, specifically sexual intercourse on the false premise of being in love versus intercourse by a medical doctor on the false premise of rendering medical treatment.[47] What makes the latter actionable battery while not the former are the interests the specific tort are intended to protect. The tort of trespass is intended to protect the "inviolability of [a] person's property," just as the tort of battery is intended to protect the person's inviolability.[48] In the case of a seducer claiming love, the seduced also wants to engage in intercourse. However, in the case of a doctor victimizing a patient, the patient only sought a medical evaluation and not intercourse. The subtle but important analysis focuses on the intentions of the parties and the offensiveness of the conduct. Ultimately, while the media are given great leeway to get a story and may use deception, the media are still not above the law.

Is the Information True, False, or an Opinion?

Once the threshold issues of location and means of acquiring information are established, the next step is to evaluate the nature of the information. Remedies for intrusive publication, such as defamation, rely substantially on whether the information is true. Normally a disclosure of the truth is not defamation. In rare situations disclosure of a misleading truth may be defamatory, or subject to another remedy such as false light. A classic example would be a true statement that a woman had sex with a man who was not her husband. However, the full story was that she was raped. Although true, the statement is terribly misleading.

The media's disclosure of a true statement is almost always deemed protected because true information is the kind of information that media are expected to disclose. Absent a need to prohibit publication based on a state interest of the highest order, information that is both true and newsworthy receives paramount constitutional protection from courts. In contrast, a false statement that harms an individual's reputation in the community will likely result in a defamation action. But if the false statement is minor, inconsequential, or unlikely to harm a person's reputation in the community, a court may not find liability.

Opinion is also protected by free speech principles. If the information is opinion and thus not stated as an objective truth, free speech principles will erect a nearly inviolable barrier to its regulation. An opinion, defined as a statement that cannot reasonably be interpreted as stating facts about an individual, is likely to be immune from legal challenge, no matter how offensive it may be. Still, something that may sound like opinion may nonetheless be treated as a statement of fact if the context of the entire statement suggests so or if the opinion strongly implies a false assertion of fact. There should be a note of caution on definable protections against defamation under U.S. First Amendment principles. Other countries and jurisdictions reach different results. Thus, the importance of matrix principle number one: location.

Under limited circumstances, it is possible that a true statement that is not misleading can give rise to tort liability. This scenario is rare in the United States. However, in certain contexts, a statement that discloses sensitive, personal facts about a person that are nonetheless true may give rise to liability under the traditional tort of public disclosure of private facts. The next matrix factor addresses whether certain information is so sensitive, or whether its discovery so inherently intrusive, that a mere disclosure of that information will be a tort.

Is the Published Information Private in Nature?

If information disclosed by the media is true and not misleading, there are only a few options remaining for remedial action. Determining whether specific information is private and worthy of heightened protection from the media is difficult, fact specific, and inextricably linked to geography. In the United States, the threshold inquiry is whether the victim had a reasonable expectation in the privacy of the information that is obtained or disclosed. Information that is available to the public, or that an individual voluntarily discloses to the public, cannot reasonably be considered private. In American jurisprudence, an expectation to the contrary would be absurd. However, there is a major distinction between American and European approaches to privacy law. The European Union's Charter of Fundamental Rights recognizes human dignity as an "inviolable right" that must be respected and protected.[49]

The theory behind dignity is a much stronger argument to protect disclosure of private facts than the American approach. For example, photos of the celebrity wedding of Michael Douglas were deemed private in Great Britain.[50] There is little chance those photos would have been private if taken in the United States, where courts have long considered paramount the protection of the right to disclose information even if it harms another. This determination hinges on social mores and a willingness to accept an individual's assertions that certain information is, and should remain, personal—regardless of whether it was disclosed to a limited audience or aired in a place in which onlookers who were not involved nonetheless had the ability to observe. The dignity approach relies much more on the intrinsic value of permission to share information than it does on the expectation that such information could possibly be involuntarily shared with a curious observer.

How Was the Information Actually Disclosed?

The medium of the disclosure matters. Courts have held that the disclosure of a written description of certain facts is permissible and not a violation of privacy as compared to the disclosure of an actual voice recording or picture, which contain more vivid or visceral depictions of the events. Courts have recognized the fact that the real impact of photos and a recording of a dead relative's voice were more intrusive and harmful than a transcript of the words or a written description as compared to photos.[51]

In my conversations with E.U. lawyers about the *Challenger* and *Rolling* cases discussed throughout this book, they have noted with interest that an American court has applied a test that balances the degree of intrusion against the value of the information to the public. It is important to distinguish that in these particular instances, American courts made these decisions before information was actually available to the press and public, and therefore their decision was not a prior restraint. In these instances courts looked for instruction at either Freedom of Information Act criteria that restricted an "unwarranted invasion of privacy"[52] or to state standards that protected against intrusive disclosures. Nonetheless, the acknowledgement that allowing a medium of disclosure that is less disturbing and visceral, such as a written autopsy in lieu of autopsy photos, is a compromise that gives weight to privacy as well as to freedom of information.

Who Was the Target of the Disclosure?

The key distinction in this aspect of the privacy matrix is whether a person is a public figure. In the United States, a public figure is analogous to a public record—someone who is open and visible in the public domain, even unintentionally. Unintentional public figures can include accident victims such as Dawn Brancheau or accidental heroes such as Carlos Arredondo, the cowboy-hat-wearing rescuer in the Boston Marathon attacks. The publication of private facts about a public figure will be actionable only in the event that it was published with malicious intent.[53] The same publication about nonpublic figures will be held to a much lower standard by which a plaintiff need not prove malice, only the offensive nature of the publication.[54] Consistent with the divergence in international approaches to considering what kind of information is private, American and European courts come to different conclusions regarding the public figure issue. For example, a European who is undoubtedly a public figure may still be considered a private individual when performing private activities, as a German court ruled about Princess Caroline of Monaco in 2004 when she was having lunch with her children in a public restaurant.[55]

A twist in the public figure doctrine in the United States is that courts have allowed evidence of violations of "reporting standards" as an indication of malice. Evaluating the standards of reporters may be troubling to journalists because establishing liability based on common standards may increase the potential for liability. Moreover, defining reporting standards in today's world with new media is not an easy task.[56]

What Is the Intent of the Target and of the Media?

Members of the media may generally publish intrusive information about individuals even with the intent of harming them, as long as the information is true. A reporter may despise an elected official or a corporate executive, but the reporter who accurately reports corrupt activity about that figure will be a hero, regardless. By contrast, a blogger who posts photos of a mutilated child with the intent to harm the parents may well be liable for the publication, regardless of how the photos were obtained—as would a traditional reporter under the same circumstances and with the same intent. However, in the United States the traditional tort remedy available in this situation is not one of the traditional privacy torts, nor does it hinge on the European idea of dignity. The possible remedy for such a victim in the United States is the tort remedy of intentional infliction of emotional distress. However, this tort requires that the publisher of the information acted with the formal intent of inflicting the distress upon the victim, which can be extremely difficult to prove.

Another issue may be the intent of the *target* of a disclosure. In other words, there are some disclosures that would be embarrassing to some but would be sought intentionally or even welcomed by others. If the intent of a young actress in disclosing nude photographs was to advance her career, then the publisher of the photos is not likely to be liable for disclosure of private facts, defamation, or any other intrusion. The disclosure of those facts was not an intrusion because the actress had no expectation that they would be private. In contrast to this example is a case filed by Jennifer Aniston in a Los Angeles trial court, in which she alleged invasions of privacy and violations of state law for the taking of unauthorized photos of her sunbathing topless in her backyard.[57] The photos were taken by magazine reporters who obtained them by peering over the fence of her yard. The suit ultimately settled out of court.

Jennifer Aniston is a public figure but clearly did not intend that her partially nude sunbathing image be disclosed. As her case illustrates, no single factor in the matrix is necessarily dispositive of a result. The use of multiple factors is necessary to define particular intrusions because no single theory is sufficient.

There is also a need to place particular intrusions in the context of a particular time, place, and circumstance. Privacy scholar Helen Nissenbaum writes that privacy should be defined with "contextual integrity."[58] She suggests that time and place matter; even matters in a public square may be private in a certain context. Privacy, with regard to the press, must be defined in a wide range of contexts.

Using the above factors, it is easy to construct scenarios where liability is virtually certain. For example, say a blogger decides to bug the home of a local school principal, recording the principal in his own bathroom. The blogger later publishes the footage to his local news blog, intending to embarrass the principal. Here, the matrix questions go quickly: it happened in the United States, the intrusion occurred in a private home, the means of intrusion were illegal, there was no consent, the harmed individual is not a public figure, the information is intrusive and true (that is, not defamatory), the intrusion is harmful to dignity, and the medium of disclosure is very intrusive. The intruder should be subject to several legal causes of action.

Sometimes applications of the matrix are more complex and challenging. Take, for example, the following hypothetical. Mayor Alex Jones of Chicago, a former globally known basketball player, was visiting London, England. Mayor Jones spent the night at the apartment of his female cousin. A Chicago blogger followed Jones. The next morning, he took a video of the mayor through the window of his cousin's apartment with a telephoto lens. The blogger says the video shows Jones in the apartment of a single woman with whom he spent the night and asks the question, "Is this a faithful husband?" He posts the video on his Chicago-based blog, and soon it is viewed all over the world.

This example presents multiple factors. Can defamation be proven? Is a rhetorical question that suggests something false an actionable false statement? In what jurisdiction did it occur? Does the fact that Jones is a public figure matter? Is he a public figure in Great Britain? Was taking the video intrusive? Were the blogger's actions sufficiently malicious to prove malice for defamation in the United States? These circumstances are not terribly farfetched. This example shows how straightforward facts require complex legal analysis and demonstrates the importance of keeping this matrix of issues in mind when evaluating various specific media actions.

An analysis of the eight factors in the matrix will determine the outcome of any particular case, and dealing with these factors is fundamental to dealing with solutions to the press-privacy conflict.

Bringing Theory and Facts Together: How the Law Tries to Prevent Media Intrusion or Provide Remedies for It

Individual privacy can be protected in several ways. The law can prevent the release of harmful information, punish intrusions, or compensate for harm—or any combination of these remedies. There are basic privacy torts, statutory causes of action, and varying actions for intrusions in different international jurisdictions. Moreover, some media intrusions can be classified as violations of basic criminal laws to which all citizens are subject. The media is not immune to wiretapping laws, trespass laws, or any number of other transgressions of the law.

Explicit Violations of the Law

Even though there have been theoretical arguments to the contrary, the courts have consistently held the media accountable for legal violations rather than exempting them because of their status. That is not to say that the media does not receive some privileges, such as those granted under press shield laws that protect the media's confidential sources. However, being a member of the media does not give a reporter the right to hack or wiretap to get a story.

In April of 2011, *News of the World* chief reporter Neville Thurlbeck, former editor Ian Edmondson, and journalist James Weatherup were all arrested on suspicion of phone-hacking charges. Further investigation into News Corp., parent company of the *News of the World* paper, revealed that News Corp. employees had hacked into databases containing thousands of phone messages. Targets of such hackings ranged from celebrities, including Hugh Jackman and Sienna Miller, to 9/11 victims, royal aides, families of dead veterans of Iraq and Afghanistan, sports figures, and even murder victims. Perhaps the most astonishing account was the phone hacking of Milly Dowler. After Milly went missing in March of 2002, her family held onto hope that she was alive for months based on information that her voicemail messages were continually being deleted during that time. Dowler's remains were found in September 2002. It was later revealed that a private investigator, working for *News of the World*, had been intercepting the cell phone messages and using them, then deleting them to make room for more messages. It was not until July 2011 that the hacking was reported. This example demonstrates a clear violation of criminal law in pursuit of information.

In contrast, a law prohibiting wiretapping was declared unconstitutional when it was applied to a journalist broadcasting a recorded cell phone conversation whose broadcast would have been illegal under an existing federal statute. In 1993, a teachers' union and local school board in Pennsylvania were engaged in heated collective-bargaining negotiations. A phone conversation between the chief union negotiator, Gloria Bartnicki, and the union president, Anthony Kane, was intercepted and recorded by an unidentified person. This person gave the recording to a local radio journalist who then broadcasted the conversation on his radio show. The union members sued the journalist, alleging violations of state and federal wiretapping statutes. However, the Supreme Court held that, as applied to the journalist, the wiretapping statutes were an unconstitutional violation of his free speech.[59] Since the journalist did nothing illegal in acquiring the conversation, his First Amendment right outweighed the privacy interest.

Violation of Contractual Obligations

In some cases, privacy rights are preserved by a contractual obligation rather than existing legal theories that protect that particular interest. For example, a patient with HIV sued his hospital after his doctor and the hospital allowed a newspaper to photograph him while he was being treated for his illness.[60] The photographer had promised the doctor that the patient would be unrecognizable in the publication. However, members of the man's family were able to recognize him based on the newspaper's photograph. The patient sued and won a judgment against both the hospital and the doctor. The doctor and the hospital, in turn, sued the newspaper for breach of contract, for causing a breach of the doctor-patient privilege, and for negligence, among other things. The court ruled that the First Amendment did not shield the newspaper from liability in light of the fact that the issue was governed instead by the contractual obligations of the parties.[61] Requiring the press to comply with its own promise did not infringe upon the freedom of the press. Thus a privacy interest was vindicated through contract theory.

Enjoining or Preventing the Release of Intrusive Information

The goal of preventing a media intrusion by publication is a difficult task. Prior restraint of information already in possession of the media is not favored, particularly by American courts. The value of free expression is seen to override other dangers unless there are severe national security interests. As has been demonstrated in the past in instances such as the release of the Pentagon Papers, even when there are matters that the government deems highly sensitive, the courts are reluctant to punish the media for disclosure. Where matters of national security do not justify prior restraint, few matters of personal dignity would be expected to give rise to that remedy. While some jurisdictions consider preventing publications that are intrusive, the U.S. courts will generally not. It is difficult to obtain a remedy for the disclosure of truly private facts, much less prevent their original publication.

Other jurisdictions have sought to control or prevent the release of sensitive information. One interesting example is the so-called super-injunction in the United Kingdom.

In May 2011, Ryan Giggs, a British soccer star, sought an injunction to stop U.K. tabloids from publishing rumors that he was having an affair with TV star Imogen Thomas. Seeking to prevent the press from publishing this damaging information, Giggs sought a superinjunction. Such an injunction would suppress both the information (that is, his affair) and the very fact that he was seeking the injunction. It involved (1) service on nonparties to the underlying suit; (2) anonymous proceedings; (3) limited access to court records; and (4) prohibition on the disclosure or existence of the order and its proceedings.[62] Although the media were bound by the ruling and could not report on it or the affair, individuals who found out about it were not. Unfortunately for Giggs, individuals did find out and posted to Twitter, where the information spread globally, virally, and quickly. Thus, although Giggs was successful in prohibiting the tabloid paper from publishing the information, he was not successful in his ultimate goal of keeping the information secret. The superinjunction failed.

Similarly, in 2008, a New Zealand judge issued a gag order preventing the publication of the names of two defendants in a murder case.[63] However, the names of the defendants were posted to the Internet from sources found to originate overseas and therefore outside the court's jurisdiction. Hence, the publication of the information was likewise immune from punishment.

These two examples show the futility of efforts to prohibit the distribution of information that is available, findable, or leakable in the new world. Prohibiting disclosure by a media source in one country may have no effect on other sources of information, such as bloggers and Twitter users. However, the release of information can be prevented if the information is not yet available to the public, as was the case with the video of SeaWorld trainer Dawn Brancheau's death.

The Traditional Privacy Torts

The majority of civil causes of action arising from a media intrusion into personal privacy come from tort law. An old French word for a "wrong," a tort is ordinarily a civil remedy, meaning that an intruder does not face a risk of jail time. The following are the traditional remedies derived from privacy theory.

Intrusion upon Seclusion

The tort of intrusion upon seclusion protects an individual's spatial privacy, and the commission of the tort, unlike the others in this section, does not require disclosure or publication. Like most torts, which are very fact intensive, the judicial application of intrusion upon seclusion is relatively inconsistent because many of the triggering elements are ill-defined legal standards: private space, intrusion, and reasonable expectation of privacy. Intrusion upon seclusion does not require a physical intrusion; one can satisfy this element of the tort with intrusions upon intangible spaces such as bank accounts. Whether this protection extends to digital spaces such as social media accounts remains to be seen.[64]

The intrusion-upon-seclusion tort provides a useful jumping-off point for the creation of analogous remedies that are helpful in the world of the new media because of its potential to avoid the pitfalls of other torts that are subject to defenses such as newsworthiness. This tort focuses on the intentionality of the intrusion and its objective degree of offensiveness rather than the value of the information gained by the intrusion.

Public Disclosure of Private Facts

The tort of public disclosure of private facts is a critical option in the age of social media. The "private facts" of this tort are typically true. The facts must be of such a personal and sensitive nature that a reasonable person would object to publication. One need not prove that an intruder intentionally disclosed the private facts, eliminating one possible obstacle to recovery. Another obstacle remains, though—proving that the facts disclosed are private. The zone of private information in one's life is shrinking rapidly, which threatens to further reduce the effectiveness of this tort. As with defamation, media defendants sued for public disclosure of private facts have an effective defense if the information published is newsworthy. The newsworthiness or free-expression defense severely limits the public disclosure remedy. Further, what is deemed private is often the result of social mores and other norms that can vary from jurisdiction to jurisdiction, depending on the strength of the dignity concept that the particular community is willing to protect.

False Light

False light is essentially an injury to dignity. A case of false light can occur when a person discloses information that makes a false impression and may even technically be true when taken at face value, but the information or its presentation distorts the actual attributes of a person, such that the distortion is unreasonably offensive. The focus is the misrepresentation of the individual by the offender. Similar to defamation, the tort of false light requires that a plaintiff prove that a publisher was either negligent (if the victim is a private figure) or acted with actual malice (as in the case with public figures). The newsworthiness doctrine likewise remains a significant obstacle to a successful case for false light. This is the only traditional privacy tort in which falsity is a factor.

Appropriation of Name or Likeness

The tort of appropriation of name or likeness is based on the property concept of an unjust taking. If a company takes the image of a well-known public figure and uses it in advertisements for a product, it has misappropriated that person's image. There are numerous cases dealing with similar misuses, but if an image of a well-known person is used in a news context, there is no liability for appropriation. This tort is focused on commercial and advertising uses of images (that is, instances in which the image itself is used to generate revenue). For example, if you use the image of Cary Grant in an advertisement against his will, you have taken something of value from him and he has a right to be compensated for your taking and for your insult. Setting aside potential copyright issues, the use of the image outside of an advertising purpose may be protected by free expression principles.

Defamation

Defamation is not classified as one of the four traditional privacy torts. However, defamation is a remedy for insults and attacks on personal dignity. A statement is defamatory if it affects one's reputation or dignity by lowering the esteem with which the individual is held by the community.[65] In order to create liability for defamation, the following four elements must be satisfied: (1) a false and defamatory statement concerning another; (2) an unprivileged publication; (3) at least negligent fault on behalf of the publisher, or, in the case of a public figure, actual malice; and (4) either independent actionability of the statement or special harm.[66] Throughout this book, defamation is discussed as a traditional legal remedy to punish false statements by the media. As a basic idea, defamation is simple. If you lie about a person in a way that harms his or her reputation, you have committed defamation. Defamation is a broad term that encompasses both libel, which is based on written statements, and slander, which is based on the spoken word. Based largely on efforts in U.S. jurisprudence to protect free speech, defamation has evolved into a more complex set of principles. Since the Supreme Court's decision in *New York Times v. Sullivan*[67] and the many cases that have built upon it, defamation is far more difficult to prove against a media outlet. Media outlets now have multiple permutations of defenses against defamation at their disposal. Those defenses are at least partially based on the identity of the defendant (media or not), the identity of the plaintiff (public official, modified public official, or private citizen), the nature of the communication (opinion, satire, nonfactual statement, or matter of public interest), damage caused to the plaintiff, and the conduct of the defendant (malicious or negligent in reporting). A combination of these factors can amount to a complete defense to a false and harmful statement.

In some jurisdictions, defamation is treated as a crime rather than a civil wrong. In 2011, the U.N. Human Rights Council ruled that the criminalization of defamation violates freedom of expression and is inconsistent with Article 19 of the International Covenant on Civil and Political Rights.[68] Treating defamation as a crime creates the risk of the government prosecuting journalists and sending them to jail for criticism. The sentiment of the United Nations and the prevailing view in the United States is that we would rather risk some inaccuracies than chill the media from communicating—particularly about government.[69]

In the new world of media, defamation is a difficult challenge because of the anonymity of blogs and other publications. Anonymity is an important element of free speech and has been an element of speech protected by the courts. Today a person who is defamed by an anonymous blogger must surmount several hurdles. A plaintiff must show that statements are likely defamatory to even obtain the identity of the writer. The test in U.S. courts is called the *Dendrite* test and is described in more detail in chapter 5.[70]

Legal decisions now specifically hold that bloggers are entitled to the same First Amendment protections as are the institutional media.

Moreover, the satirical, critical, or exaggerated nature of some blogs actually contributes to their defense against defamation because courts have held that an audience would not reasonably interpret such statements as assertions of fact. In other words, being hyperbolic and unprofessional expands free speech protections for blogs. Anonymity and exaggeration serve to protect bloggers from liability.

Other Remedies

Beyond the traditional torts and defamation, other remedies may be available to individuals who feel their privacy has been intruded upon by media. States and the federal system have independently enacted laws that provide the vehicles for statutory remedies. Also, the vindication of privacy rights through other torts, such as the intentional infliction of emotional distress, has been sought in media intrusion cases. Intentional infliction is a high standard, and facts would have to be outrageous in order to be successful.[71]

Media and privacy advocates each have credible and logical theories and principles supporting the importance of both free expression and privacy. Over history, real conflicts compelled the theories to become actual legal remedies or statutory policies.[72] An overview of that history reveals that there is a series of common factors in the press-privacy matrix that determine outcomes in each unique situation. To understand the evolution of the matrix, a discussion of the origins of media law is necessary. Therefore, the next question is how the new media evolved to bring us to today's conflict.

Information,
Power,
and
Intrusion

The contemporary press is an amalgam of print, broadcast, and Internet media. The common theme binding them is the fact that they all convey information. To truly understand the current law relating to modern media and privacy, it is necessary to understand the law's historical roots.

Obtaining and distributing information has been a part of civilization from the beginning of time. Advances in technology have taken information distribution from word-of-mouth transfer to global broadcast. Recognizing that information distribution can be harmful, the law has evolved to punish offending communication. But the law constantly lags behind the times, always nipping at the heels of shifting technology rather than preceding it. Consequently—as this chronology of the law, communication, and technology reveals—the law provides little guidance and much uncertainty in the modern world.

The History of Information: Prelude to the "Press"

Information is and always has been power. Those with the most information are often the most successful, whether they are our hunter-gatherer ancestors or the Wall Street investment bankers of today. For example, a nomadic village might survive because the villagers have unique information about the location of a water source, and a banking firm may achieve the greatest rate of return on an investment because the firm has developed unique information about particular stocks.

While information is valuable, its distribution can be intrusive and harmful. Examining the evolution of information and information sharing provides insight into how the world's media became so intrusive. Modern media are more intrusive now than at any other time in human history. The transfer of information has progressed from primitive speech and basic forms of writing to global and instant dissemination on the Internet. The implications for individual privacy are enormous and, unfortunately, ominous.

Following the handwritten records of scribes that began in 3200 B.C., civilization's abilities to communicate began to expand. Historically, information was shared among tribes, villages, and small communities. Today, the new media distribute information instantly and worldwide. And just like the harmful gossip of ancient times, the new media communicate insults and private information about individuals. But unlike ancient times, new media have a global audience.

At its core, gossip functioned as a news broadcasting system. One tribesman might reveal to another where rivals were camping or which crops were thriving. This type of information would be integral to the survival of that community. But there was no guarantee that the information was true or valuable. Thus, the listener's judgment was important, as was the credibility of the speaker. Because speakers and listeners were usually face to face, listeners used their personal discernment in filtering the information.

By the thirteenth century, most Europeans lived in small towns inside fortified walls.[1] Yet information was just as critical to these communities as to their ancestors. Sources of information included public sources, such as the town crier and postings in the public square, as well as private common gossip and conversation. Through these various sources, people learned group mores and reported wrongdoings. Communal information produced community standards, and continued information sharing was necessary to enforce those standards.

Fear successfully incentivized villagers to follow the community standards—those who did not abide by the standards were cast out of the protective town walls and left to fend for themselves.

Yet fear was not the only force that controlled people's conduct in thirteenth-century England. A series of acts known as the Scandalum Magnatum were put into place beginning in the year 1275.[2] The acts prohibited defamation and the invention or spreading of "false news" concerning the crown or "magnates of the realm."[3] Scandalum Magnatum was the first form of criminal libel because the publication of such false news was a crime rather than a potential tort action.[4] The publisher of false rumors was imprisoned until he revealed the original author of the false news.[5] While this was a powerful deterrent to spreading false information, there were limitations on the law's effectiveness.[6] The law only applied to false news, a phrase that eluded precise definition.[7] Medieval prosecutors also faced an early version of the plaintiff's paradox: efforts to prosecute someone under the Scandalum Magnatum led to further publication of the false news for which the person was being prosecuted, possibly undermining the original purpose of the prosecution—preventing the publication of criticism of the Crown.[8]

In the mid-1400s, Europe developed the printing machine,[9] and by the 1600s the first newspapers circulated.[10] With the advent of the printing press, mass distribution of the written word became practical. Books and newspapers became available to masses of readers, and this broader dissemination of information began to create new types of communities.[11] During the eighteenth century, the first mass printing press system was under the strict authoritarian control of the government.[12] Governments throughout history have asserted this sort of control over information, as instances from book burning to Internet censorship exemplify. When mass printing began in England, a printer could share only limited information. He could enjoy the privilege of publishing only by grant of permit or decree, and only so long as he published politically safe material.[13] From there, political controls evolved into economic controls—the government permitted only individuals who could afford to post a bond to publish.[14]

From the Enlightenment through the Romantic Period: Formalizing Freedom of the Press

It was not until the late-eighteenth and early-nineteenth centuries that the classic, liberal-democratic concept of freedom of the press began to form.[15] This period, known as the Enlightenment, introduced the notion that a rational being could best determine truth from falsity when ideas are available in the marketplace.[16] This tenet became the core of press "libertarianism" beliefs.[17] Justice Oliver Wendell Holmes later articulated the theory in his dissent in *Abrams v. United States*, where he suggested that competing ideas lead to the truth.[18]

A different concept of the press was incorporated into the First Amendment to the U.S. Constitution by its framers. When the framers drafted the First Amendment, journalism and the modern media did not exist. The press of the eighteenth century was a trade of printers, not journalists.[19] Thus, to the framers, the "press" meant the printing press.[20] The First Amendment referred to the technology of printing and the opportunities for communication that the technology created—freedom of the press meant freedom of the people to publish their views.[21] The 1776 Pennsylvania Declaration of Rights asserted that "the people have a right to freedom of speech, and of writing and publishing their sentiments; therefore the freedom of the press ought not be restrained."[22] Additionally, James Madison's original proposal for what became the First Amendment stated: "The people shall not be deprived or abridged of their right to speak, to write, or to publish their sentiments; and the freedom of the press, as one of the great bulwarks of liberty, shall be inviolable."[23]

In terms of privacy interests, protection against press intrusions was not a primary concern of America's founders. Rather, it was protection against *government* intrusions and abuses that was of great concern. This notion is apparent in the Third, Fourth, and Fifth Amendments, which prohibit government from intruding into our homes and private lives. Those concerns were products of oppressive practices of the British, including boarding soldiers in homes. Because the founders viewed the press as a check on government power, intrusions by the press against government or individuals was not a top priority then. However, in 1798, the government, still made up of many founders, became concerned with press abuses.[24] As a result, they passed the infamous Alien and Sedition Acts, which represent a dark moment in America's infancy. The Sedition Act, while short lived, specifically prohibited "false, scandalous, and malicious" writing directed toward the executive or legislative branches of the government.[25] While only fourteen people were ever indicted under the act, the debate that preceded its passage was one of the first true tests of the First Amendment.[26] Ultimately, free speech won the debate.

Concerns about press freedom continued during the Romantic Period, which spanned from 1820 to 1900. The public generally accepted the notion of valuing emotions and sentiment over rationality and reason,[27] as well as the notion of having concern for the "self" and the individual.[28] As a leading chronicler of that time, Alexis de Tocqueville approved of censorship for purposes of public morality, advocating the "tyranny of the majority" as a benefit to society if it prohibited anyone from publishing "licentious books."[29] De Tocqueville's view was entirely in conflict with the free speech and free press principles inherent in the formation and embodiment of the U.S. Constitution. It is not surprising then that when de Tocqueville wrote of the American press, he expressed concern about its absence of limits:

> Journalists in the United States . . . in general, hardly have an elevated position, their education is only sketchy, and the turn of their ideas is often vulgar. . . . The spirit of the journalist in America is to attack coarsely, without preparation and without art, the passions of those whom it addresses, to set aside principles in order to grab men; to follow into their private lives, and to lay bare their weaknesses and their vices.[30]

Similar commentaries on the twenty-first-century media have been made in far less elegant terms. Indeed, the conflict between vicious or intrusive personal attacks and freedom of the press is a continuing theme.

Early Recognition of Press Intrusions

Privacy as a concept received enhanced attention in the nineteenth century when writers began to recognize intrusions by the press.[31] In their classic *Harvard Law Review* article "The Right to Privacy," Louis D. Brandeis and Samuel Warren criticized the intrusion of the press on personal privacy:

> The press is overstepping in every direction the obvious bounds of propriety and of decency. . . . Each crop of unseemly gossip, thus harvested, becomes the seed of more, and, in direct proportion to its circulation, results in a lowering of social standards and of morality. Even gossip apparently harmless, when widely and persistently circulated, is potent for evil. . . . When personal gossip attains the dignity of print, and crowds the space available for matters of real interest to the community, what wonder that the ignorant and thoughtless mistake its relative importance.[32]

The historical event that spurred this article was the invention and use of photography to record and publish events. What would these authors think about blogs and gossip on the Internet? If Brandeis and Warren found the scope of nineteenth-century print circulation alarming, imagine how they would react to the scope of twenty-first-century Internet circulation.

At the time of its publication, the Warren-Brandeis article was unique not only for its discussion of media privacy invasions but also for its novel treatment of the overall concept of a legal right to privacy. Property and criminal law already recognized privacy-related issues such as trespass and assault, but privacy had not yet manifested itself in tort law.[33] Warren and Brandeis focused on a tort of the "right to be let alone":

> The intense intellectual and emotional life, and the heightening of sensations which came with the advance of civilization, made it clear to men that only a part of the pain, pleasure, and profit of life lay in physical things. Thoughts, emotions, and sensations demanded legal recognition, and the beautiful capacity for

growth which characterizes the common law enabled the judges to afford the requisite protection, without the interposition of the legislature. . . . The intensity and complexity of life, attendant upon advancing civilization, have rendered necessary some retreat from the world, and man, under the refining influence of culture, has become more sensitive to publicity, so that solitude and privacy have become more essential to the individual.[34]

The authors recognized that recent inventions—for example, photography—showed that current law was inadequate to protect individuals from privacy invasions that had become possible due to new technology.[35] Traditional contract principles were too narrow to be useful in guarding against privacy intrusions, protecting society only when an abuse could not have arisen without violating a contract or special confidence.[36] As photography became more widespread, opportunities to perpetrate wrongs without the participation of the injured party became more commonplace.[37] Warren and Brandeis lamented:

> The state of photographic art was such that one's picture could seldom be taken without his consciously "sitting" for the purpose, the law of contract or trust might afford the prudent man sufficient safeguards against the improper circulation of his portrait; but since the latest advances in photographic art have rendered it possible to take pictures surreptitiously, the doctrines of contract and of trust are inadequate to support the required protection, and the law of tort must be resorted to.[38]

Little did they realize that their concerns would continue to be predictive of modern technological intrusions and the inadequate remedies available at law.

Although Americans had always valued privacy, solitude, and individuality, the articulation of privacy as a legal concept was new. Alongside legal privacy emerged palpable anger at the press for "overstepping . . . the obvious bounds of propriety and of decency."[39] "Yellow journalism"[40] flourished in the 1880s and 1890s, and a surge in mass communication due to the newly renovated printing press and improved photography tools brought to the fore fresh privacy concerns unknown to prior generations.[41] Luckily, there was a swift evolution of American jurisprudence to recognize a common-law right of privacy, which stands as a testament to the importance of the Warren-Brandeis article.[42] In the early example of *Pavesich v. New England Life Insurance Co.*, the Georgia Supreme Court found that a right to privacy for Paolo Pavesich was breached when an insurance company advertised for life insurance by juxtaposing the photos of a well-known local artist and a sickly man, Mr. Pavesich.[43]

Not every state, however, recognized the newly evolved common-law right to privacy.[44] In reaction to this judicial refusal to include privacy in the common law, a number of state legislators enacted privacy statutes specifically aimed at protecting the individual against invasions by the media and advertisers.[45] In the early twentieth century, the media-privacy debate intensified further. Justice Henry C. Brown urged self-restraint of the media instead of censorship, but he criticized the press's "cruelty in assaulting character and invading privacy with sensationalism."[46] President Theodore Roosevelt countered that virulent language was an acceptable cost of the free discussion of public issues:

> If there is one thing we ought to be careful about it is in regard to interfering with the liberty of press. I think it is a great deal better to err a little bit on the side of having too much discussion and having too virulent language used by the press, rather than to err on the side of having them not say what they ought to say, especially with reference to public men and measures.[47]

These statements are characteristic of the strong split in viewpoints at the time. But Roosevelt's view was, and continues to be, the prevailing legal view. The Constitution will protect ugly and offensive communication, especially if that information informs citizens about public matters.

With the invention of the radio at the turn of the twentieth century and the first radio news broadcast transmitted in the 1920s, a new medium was formed, capable of transmitting information instantaneously and beyond the traditional walls of the community. Information transmission via television emerged in short order. Television, which was first introduced to the general public at the 1939 World's Fair and first manufactured on a large scale after the end of World War II, became a way to instantaneously transmit visual as well as audio information to a wide audience. Various government controls emerged, and understanding these controls sheds light on how the law operates with respect to the broadcast media and privacy intrusions.

In the United States, the Federal Communications Commission (FCC) regulates the majority of broadcast mediums. The agency regulates television and radio broadcasting as well as interstate wire, satellite, and cable transmissions.[48] The FCC even has the authority to punish television broadcasters for airing obscene content.[49] The agency's authority derives from the notion that the public owns the airwaves.[50] Interestingly, the FCC does not regulate fleeting expletives on the Internet. The U.S. government also controls some international communications, including global satellite communications and global television *if* these communications either originated or terminated within the country.[51] This is in line with one principle of international law that protects a country from subversive propaganda broadcast over its airwaves.[52] This regulation of the airwaves has substantial implications for both privacy and free speech. It imposes greater limitations on a speaker using broadcast media than one using print media. While there is no question that broadcast news is protected by the First Amendment, the print media enjoys greater First Amendment liberty than these newer and more regulated forms of media.

The New Media: 1980–Present

The evolution of the media has paralleled advancements in technology. The advent of the Internet in particular altered the consumption of media in two important ways. First, it has decentralized information sharing at the global level. Rather than turning to a single newspaper or television news network, the Internet has allowed consumers to scan numerous media outlets for vastly different types of news with the click of a mouse after one simple query. Personal web logs have the ability to be as widely consumed as traditional brick and mortar media products. This shift from the one-to-many delivery of news by self-termed professionals to a many-to-many delivery of news by citizen journalists has revolutionized the playing field in terms of media production.[53] In a way, freedom of the press has come full circle, with more and more people publishing their own views, albeit via computer rather than printing press.

Although citizen journalism may have rocked the foundations of the traditional media, it certainly has not changed its commercial nature. With an intensified supply of media production, speed has become the new metric for success. The primary risk of the new hypercompetitive market is that the urge to be first can displace the urge to be right. News organizations run with the story they have instead of waiting for the story they want. Publish-and-then-correct is the new standard.[54]

In the wake of tragedies such as the Boston bombing or the Sandy Hook shooting, this pressure to be first has led to news organizations sourcing each other, rather than obtaining independent and credible verification. With Boston, it is still unclear where exactly the confusion and misinformation originated. However, just two days after the bombing, the Associated Press (AP) reported by tweet, "Arrest imminent."[55] The *Boston Globe* followed suit just ten minutes later.[56] Shortly thereafter, CNN confirmed the report, citing its own law enforcement sources.[57] NBC, due in large part to veteran reporter Pete Williams, was the first organization to affirmatively deny the report that any arrest had been made.[58] CBS, Reuters, and NPR soon followed his lead. Finally, fifty-two minutes after the AP's tweet, the Boston Police Department confirmed that no arrest had been made.[59]

The urge to be first is not the only factor to blame. The increased supply of media production has caused a fractionalization of the market as a whole. There are simply so many consumers and so much competition that it makes more business sense to target small audiences. The reduced market share among media producers can lead to a focus on the fringes. By exploiting submarkets, Fox and MSNBC allow consumers to listen to what they want to hear. While such networks are not necessarily engaging in purposeful misrepresentation of facts, their previous demand for accurate reporting is simply not as stringent now when the networks are compromised by the demands of their respective audiences. Many networks' consumers are not necessarily interested in hearing the truth.

Second, the increased demand for multiple sources of media has exacerbated the problems Louis Brandeis and Samuel Warren first warned us about in 1890.[60] Today, the problem of surreptitious invasions of privacy persists—only with better technology. On one hand, the new media have the ability to bring us unprecedented access to far-flung events such as the Arab Spring uprisings in 2012. On the other hand, technological capabilities have heightened the prospect of privacy intrusions. The new media will need to be able to strike a balance between information and intrusion.

A central dilemma focuses on how to deal with the rise of the most prevalent new medium: the Internet. Is the Internet more like broadcast media or print media? How will it be regulated? Broadcast media, when compared to print media, exhibits a history of more extensive regulation and a scarcity of available frequencies on which to broadcast.[61] The Supreme Court, however, has found that the factors justifying regulation of broadcast media are not present with respect to cyberspace. In *Reno v. American Civil Liberties Union* the Court focused on the fact that the Internet has never been subject to the same type of government supervision and regulation as the broadcast media and that there is not the same issue of spectrum scarcity; therefore, it should not be subject to government regulation.[62] If the Internet is subject to less regulation, do First Amendment principles applicable to the traditional print media apply to the Internet? Is the Internet really like a newspaper?

In a recent case from the Fourth Circuit Court of Appeals, the court held that the action of "liking" a political candidate's Facebook page in a local sheriff's race could be protected speech if the facts presented on summary judgment were proven at trial.[63] In that case, multiple employees of the incumbent sheriff challenged his refusal to rehire them after he won the race and took office because they—in various ways—had expressed their endorsement of his challenger. While the court's analysis also depended upon the status of the employees, ultimately the court determined that the qualified employees had engaged in protected speech when they expressed verbal endorsements in public, put political bumper stickers on their vehicles, and used Facebook as a forum to post comments and to like the candidate.[64] Holding specifically that liking a Facebook posting can be protected speech, the court found that the conduct unambiguously conveyed a particularized message that constituted both pure and symbolic speech. Because it was political speech, the court acknowledged that it was entitled to the highest protection.[65]

This case presents interesting questions regarding the quality of the speech at issue: what if the employee had been fired not for liking a political candidate, but for liking a pro-choice campaign? A movie about a homosexual couple? A racist slur made and published on Facebook by another person? If the government is not going to regulate the Internet to the extent that it does broadcast media, where will the legal system set the standards?

Cyberspace cannot be a free-fire zone where any conduct is tolerated. While obscurity and anonymity make enforcement difficult, defamation committed online is still defamation. It must be punished. In order to be punished, the wrongdoer must be identified. Anonymity should not be legally protected when there is bad intent and harm. Bad intent and harm are legal and common-sense principles. Websites that are designed to facilitate such harmful speech are good examples of this remedial need. The website JuicyCampus.com solicited and received outrageously false, defamatory, and intrusive statements to be posted about college students. Further, the website encouraged the outrageous statements and encouraged anonymity. This type of website should be liable for its intentional conduct and for the foreseeable harm it caused and should not be protected by free speech principles.

Another contemporary problem is the ability of media, or for that matter, almost anyone, to track or publicize an individual's movements. Most of the time, actions in a public space are not considered private, particularly in the United States. If we walk down a public street and go into a pornography shop or an abortion clinic, the fact that we walked in that door is not considered private. These circumstances are a difficult and classic confrontation of free speech and individual freedom. Domestic courts undervalue individual freedom in these circumstances and allow publication. However, free association and personal choices have been upheld to protect the identity of individuals' participation in organizations where there is a perceived threat to political freedom, such as the NAACP. In fact, the ability to associate and move anonymously is a privacy protection, but one that is severely limited by the fact that it occurs in a public space. New technologies have made this issue more complex.

There is some hope that federal courts are beginning to evaluate more carefully the movement of individuals in public space, at least with respect to government surveillance. In a case involving the warrantless use of a GPS device to track a criminal suspect, the U.S. Court of Appeals for the District of Columbia approved the "mosaic theory," which holds that the aggregation of trivial information can lead to an intrusive, complete insight into a person's life.[66] Acceptance of the mosaic theory by a court of this stature is extremely significant. The judges embraced the notion that the intrusive impact of data in the aggregate is greater than the sum of small intrusions. The overall movements of an individual over a period of time present a complete picture of the individual's life and value as a mosaic. The court offered the example of observing a woman's single visit to an OB-GYN versus observing her continual visits to an OB-GYN and subsequent visits to baby stores.[67] Observing the former visit independently is indicative of little more than an annual checkup. However, observing all of the woman's movements collectively allows for the deduction of a most intimate life detail. This case admittedly stands in contrast to other cases that have held that the warrantless pinging of a cell phone to determine a criminal suspect's GPS coordinates does not intrude upon a reasonable expectation of privacy when exigent circumstances are present.[68] An important distinguishing factor in the pinging cases appears to be the amount of time over which the GPS data is collected.

Just like the government, the media, including paparazzi, have often tracked or stalked their targets. Technology will only continue to expand the media's capacity to gather all sorts of information including personal movements. GPS and other technologies are simply part of the continuing evolution of the ways to gather information.

The Future and Information Overflow
in the Modern World

Aristotle once posited that "all men by nature desire to know."[69] For this reason, two immutable forces will define the future of the media-privacy conflict: human nature and the drive to create new technologies. In fact, the drive for new technologies is part of the human drive to know.

New technologies for communicating and gathering information will continue to proliferate. All indications are that people want more news and information. They are getting it on their smartphones and tablets. They are utilizing any possible mode of connecting to the Internet and engaging in that forum in order to obtain more information. But are we ready for all of the implications of expanding technology? In 1980, general public conversation did not include discussions of drone surveillance, GPS tracking by police, metadata mining of e-mails, or the presence of surveillance cameras in public spaces. In the modern world, most members of the public would understand a conversation about any of those topics. Technology will move fast, and newsgathering sources will move with it. There is little doubt that if there are news helicopters now, there will be news drones in the future.

Certainly one can speculate about new technology. For example, facial recognition technology tied to CCTV may end up being able to locate anyone anytime. The ability to track the location of individual cell phones already exists. The latest version of the iPhone 5s includes fingerprint recognition technology in order to enable the phone to be unlocked only by its owner. These technologies are consistent with a society where individuals willingly disclose intimate details of their vacations on Facebook and Twitter.

There are positive implications for free speech and democratic principles from the new media. The new media provide multiple news sources, which expands the number of viewpoints and the concept of citizen watchdogs with cameras on every corner. For example, a local radio or television station can crowdsource a news story on a local disaster by simply reaching out to one of the bystanders to the disaster.

We live and exist in a society filled with ambient information. Information is everywhere—good, bad, comprehensive, inaccurate, laudatory, and inflammatory.

The human desire to learn is a hallmark of evolution and the advancement of knowledge. From a Darwinist's standpoint, the hunger to know more is good for the species. In the modern world, that appetite is being fed by an unprecedented capacity to obtain, organize, and deliver information. There are, however, risks and costs associated with the overflow of data. Human instincts that have served us well over the millennia have different consequences in the new world.

Craving information comes to us naturally. Anthropologically, the acquisition of more information helped both groups and individuals make better decisions, depending on the quality of the information and the rationality of the user. Successfully gathering information assisted in finding food, finding a reproductively valuable mate, and managing friendships, alliances, and family relationships. The pressures on early humans required them to develop means to gather information and social intelligence in order to predict and influence social behavior and increase their own success. This evolutionary need for information is characterized most simply as an instinct to know more.

Natural curiosity motivates humans to discover and innovate.[70] One of our more attractive characteristics is that of the inquisitive risk taker. Someone had to discover fire, invent the wheel, and conceive the iPhone. In all of these circumstances, humans needed to acquire more information. Those who acquired the most and best information and used it wisely were the innovators.

In addition to these positive instincts, there are elements of human nature that create dangers in the context of new media. Among the less attractive traits that are present in humans are selfishness, bias, enjoyment of the suffering of others, willingness to believe information that matches our bias, and the ability to lie. We humans are also more interested in learning about others than we are in revealing secrets about ourselves. We gossip about others, and we have an intense interest in the activity of others. That too is a historically based instinct. The successful use of gossip to gather and pass along information has been important in evolution. It is not a surprise that tabloid gossip and gossip blogs are popular.

We are susceptible to believing what we read—even more susceptible when it is something about which we have less direct knowledge. I participated in the Senior Executives in State and Local Government program at Harvard University, which included a class about the press that was given to a group of state public officials. We were asked to evaluate the credibility of a series of articles on professional sports and then some articles on politics. The group rated the sports writing as much more credible in a secret poll of the class. Presumably, we knew more about politics and public affairs than sports and were therefore more gullible or inclined to believe sports writers than political writers. Other experiments show the same sort of willingness to believe that about which the reader knows less.

We are also more inclined to believe opinions consistent with our own. This characteristic is called the "reinforcement bias." With so many potential options for news outlets, people tend to choose sources that fit their own political, personal, and social views. This type of bias affects a fundamental part of the marketplace-of-ideas justification for free press. The marketplace of ideas is supposed to provide multiple viewpoints to assist citizen decision making. Extremely biased and opinionated broadcast commentators work so well in this overwhelmed marketplace of ideas because they can obtain reliable and large niche followings. The new media is providing more options to satisfy not only our information addiction but also our personal preferences, which has the effect of excluding the consideration of other ideas in the marketplace.

In sum, the new and future technologies are fulfilling our desire for information, consistent with our biases and our desire to hear good gossip. Among the problems with the new onslaught of information is loss of credibility and accuracy. The amount of commentary and gossip available in the public forum has grown because of electronic communications and the Internet. Our craving for information and our infatuation with gossip make the new media a magnet for feeding these human interests. One problem with these new sources of information is that the consumer has no ability to observe the source of the gossip. We are not personally observing the credibility of the source, and we often do not even know its identity. Thus the growth of anonymous information and gossip presents a danger of spreading harmful inaccuracies.

There are other problems that exacerbate the decreased accuracy of the new media. One side effect associated with exponential growth of media outlets through websites, blogs, and individual iReporters is a phenomenon called "Internet disinhibition." The term was succinctly described in a 2004 abstract that appeared in the journal *CyberPsychology and Behavior*—"People say and do things in cyberspace that they wouldn't ordinarily say or do in the real world."[71] The producers of information are less inclined to be cautious on the Internet, partially because of anonymity and partially because of the absence of direct human contact. Researchers have proposed several factors for the behavior, including perceived anonymity, invisibility, and lack of recipient reactions. One benefit of Internet disinhibition is that Internet users express themselves more openly. This open discussion allows users to express opinions and viewpoints that they might not otherwise raise, producing a more varied and perhaps more honest picture of social and cultural thought.

At the same time, Internet disinhibition leads some users to express themselves in "rude, critical, angry, hateful, and threatening" and otherwise offensive or intrusive ways.[72] The craving for more information creates a demand that is sometimes filled with harmful speech because human nature enabled by the new tools that technology offers can generate a flood of information. Every person with a smartphone can anonymously post content to the Internet as a member of the new media, with no editorial filter. The potential harm is twofold: increased invasions of privacy and increased risk of inaccuracy.

Obtaining information used to be limited to what a person could personally see, smell, hear, touch, and taste. As the world evolved, more information came to people from other sources. Later, what professional reporters decided was relevant, reliable, riveting, or just interesting became a new source of information. Now, with the advent of Twitter, Facebook, and iReporting, virtually unlimited sources of information are easily available.[73] In today's developed countries, more people get their news from the Internet than from printed newspapers or radio programs.[74] In a 2010 study, three-fourths of Americans polled reported that they hear of news through e-mail or updates on social media sites.[75]

The overflow of information increases the dangers associated with misinformation. We are likely to believe what we see on the Internet. Even though the avalanche of information absorbs more inaccuracies, people's instinct is to believe what they see, even on the Internet. An example is found in a study performed at the New Literacies lab.[76] The study was conducted to test the ability of grade school children to critically evaluate information obtained on the Internet.[77]

The students were asked to do online research about the "Endangered Pacific Northwest Tree Octopus."[78] A website created specifically for the experiment provided pictures and articles about the tree octopus.[79] The students took no steps to analyze and evaluate the information contained on the website, but took it all as true.[80] Even after researchers told the students that the website was a hoax, some students insisted on the existence of the tree octopus.[81] Instead of evaluating information critically based on sources and context, the students determined reliability of online information based on the volume of information found.[82] These children are not unique.

If a person acts on bad information about another, both individuals may be harmed. A slanderous inaccuracy contained in a neighborhood blog that a person is a child molester can hurt not only the falsely accused person but also those who act on the bad information. Likewise, the fact that information is truthful does not mean it is not intrusive and harmful. The human ability for cruelty and the availability of anonymous distribution allows and fosters the worst of human behavior. When humans do not think they will be held accountable or even identified, they may hurt others. The cases where individuals harass or bully others utilizing new technology are tragic, such as when a freshman in college set up a secret webcam to spy on his roommate while the roommate engaged in private sexual activity, the recording and replaying of which subsequently drove the roommate to embarrassment and ultimately suicide.[83] Disclosures of a person's sexual orientation or the circulation of a video recording of an individual having sex are truthful disclosures but are terribly intrusive. The worst part of human nature creates these intrusions, and the curious part of human nature encourages their publication and distribution.

Certain addictions may result in legal sanctions. The use of illicit drugs or alcohol while driving and the viewing of child pornography are offenses that can send people to jail. Addictions can be punishable by law. However, our culture will not punish an information addict. In fact, an information addict with good judgment may be highly successful. But an addict with bad judgment can harm himself and others.[84]

The greatest overall risk is that this demand for information has supported or even provided an incentive for the increase in bad, slanderous, and intrusive information that is now a byproduct of technology and fueled by Internet disinhibition.[85] The demand has created the endless supply of bad, meaning false or damaging, information, along with good, meaning true and socially valuable, information. The desire or even the addiction to information is not new. But the volatile circumstances and multiple informational sources that feed the desire are new and toxic.

Predicting the future is never easy, but we know for certain what will drive it. The audience for information has been empowered with the ability to consume the exact type of media it wants to see, hear, and speak—the exact type of media in which it desires to be a participant. While it is impossible to pinpoint where technology is going, we know how it will be used. As we entrench ourselves as the aggregators of our own news, reliability will become less and less important for any single piece of information. Thus, the future press is on track to breed more inaccuracies, and in turn more litigation.[86] The most salient issue will be how law and society or journalistic professionalism will rise to meet technology's new incursions upon privacy. Social media has tended to erode many professional journalistic norms. Ultimately accountability for misconduct and intrusions are the province of the law.

The Globalization of Information

Understanding the global playing field is a prerequisite to dealing with new media and evaluating privacy conflicts. The laws and policies regulating media and privacy are dramatically different in various jurisdictions around the world. The new global press is not confined by any national or jurisdictional borders. Therefore, complicated issues of international jurisdiction and cross-border legal enforcement are an integral part of resolving many press-privacy conflicts.

Global Perspectives and Philosophy

All media are controlled in some way. Enforcement is therefore a question of *how* the media are controlled.[1] Typically the media are constrained or influenced by professional, economic, legal, and social standards.[2] Some media are more controllable than others. Broadcast media are usually heavily regulated and require substantial capital investment. By contrast, a global blogger has few expenses and few direct or binding regulations. Bloggers even receive fundamentally the same First Amendment protections in the United States as the mainstream media.[3]

Within the global context, nations have adopted different approaches to regulating the media. These choices are reflections of individual national philosophies regarding the role of the press. Generally, nations have adopted one of four approaches as the basis for regulation of the press. Fred S. Siebert, Theodore Peterson, and Wilbur Schramm's book *Four Theories of the Press* articulates these four approaches as libertarian, authoritarian, social responsibility, and soviet communist.[4]

The social-responsibility approach[5] was once thought to be the model that the United States would adopt. In 1947, the Commission on Freedom of the Press, headed by Robert Hutchins, met to address the growing concerns about the waning credibility of the press.[6] The commission reached two basic conclusions: (1) The press has a responsibility to society; and (2) the libertarian press the United States has embraced is not meeting that social responsibility.[7] The belief was that the media should be controlled by community opinion, consumer action, and professional ethics as opposed to the free marketplace of ideas.[8] The social-responsibility approach is also called glorified libertarianism. Its goal is to impose strict codes of journalistic ethics on the press, while simultaneously ensuring that the press continues to provide newsworthy information to the public.[9] This approach has been criticized as sacrificing freedom of thought and expression for a secure system enforced by authoritarian means.[10]

The United States never embraced the social-responsibility theory and instead adopted the classic libertarian approach. The policy that has emerged from case law and social norms holds that "an individual's right of privacy must yield to the greater public interest in the dissemination of newsworthy material. It makes no difference whether the person involved is a public official, a public figure, or a private individual. The subject matter does not have to be of political, public, or private concern."[11]

As a result of embracing the classic-libertarian approach, the United States places a higher value on open dialogue and the marketplace of ideas than on attempting to control or balance information flow, which stands in contrast to nations that have embraced other approaches.

Continental (European) law has embraced the social-responsibility approach of regulating the press. Its law emphasizes personal dignity, including protection of "consumer data, credit reporting, workplace privacy, discovery in civil litigation, the dissemination of nude images on the Internet, or shielding criminal offenders from public exposure to people accustomed to the continental ways of doing things."[12] In other words, individual dignity is considered more important than free expression when it offends European values. In comparison to the American model, where privacy concerns grow out of an aspect of liberty,[13] European law recognizes that a balancing test should be applied when evaluating conflicting press and privacy interests. In Europe, press policies and regulations are more a part of legislative planning and policy.[14] In contrast, the U.S. analysis begins from a constitutional premise that free expression prevails and leaves the decision to the courts. Virtually any assertion of a privacy intrusion by the media will result in a claim of First Amendment privilege.

Starkly different from both the European Union and the United States are nations like China, which have adhered to the "soviet communist model." Even though Soviet Communism is dead, its model for press control is alive and well. China's policy is to produce equality for its citizens by restraint and regulation. Consequently, the government tightly controls the dissemination of information and what the press may do. One major way it censors the new press is by controlling the nation's Internet service providers (ISPs). Similar to this model is the authoritarian model that is practiced in places like North Korea. The authoritarian model is predominated by state-controlled media and total censorship, as opposed to merely censorship of certain means of publication. Press-privacy controversies will continue to exist in a totalitarian state. A conflict with the state-owned or controlled media amounts to a conflict with the state and, for the average individual, is a losing proposition. Thus, divergent national philosophies regarding the press and privacy have produced very different national standards for regulating the press and protecting privacy. The conflicts are very different in jurisdictions that respect individual rights, such as the United States and the European Union, than they are where individual rights are subordinated to state-controlled media. Conflicting national standards and the lack of enforceable international standards create a complex and difficult problem for individuals harmed by media privacy intrusions.

Treaties

There have been some efforts to create international press and privacy policies. Treaties express respect and concern for personal privacy and the understanding that issues of privacy are a global concern. Article 12 of the Universal Declaration of Human Rights states, "No one shall be subjected to arbitrary interference with his privacy, family, home, or correspondence."[15] Article 17 of the International Covenant on Civil and Political Rights declares, "No one shall be subjected to arbitrary or unlawful interference with his privacy, family, home or correspondence, nor to unlawful attacks on his honor and reputation."[16] Implementation of these privacy safeguards is helped by the Organization for Economic Co-operation and Development. With the assistance of the United Nations, it developed "Guidelines on the Protection of Privacy and Transborder Flows of Personal Data" and the United Nations "Guidelines for the Regulation of Computerized Personal Data Files."

In 2005, the Asia Pacific Economic Cooperation (APEC) set out to provide the first comprehensive legal framework on the issue of global data privacy.[17] APEC is made up of twenty-one members, including among others Australia, Canada, China, Japan, Russia, and the United States. At the core of the APEC Privacy Framework is a set of nine principles that apply to "personal information" about a living individual whose information is possessed by a "personal information controller." This framework seeks to ensure the continued growth of online commerce by building consumer trust and confidence in the privacy and security of online transactions and information networks. In addition to the protection of information privacy, the framework also seeks to overcome regulatory systems that unnecessarily restrict data flow or place burdens on it because of possible adverse implications for global businesses and economies.[18] The framework, however, is not absolute, and nations can exploit the loose diplomatic language used by APEC to interpret it how they see fit.[19] In addition, the APEC framework is not binding on member nations unless the nation adopts it. At least one member nation, China, has not adopted the recommendations.[20]

Treaties of similar international scope have also sought to protect free press. The Mass Media Declaration, adopted in 1978 by the United Nations Education, Scientific and Cultural Organization (UNESCO), calls for a free flow of information from a balanced and diverse news media.[21] Western nations disapproved of the declaration, believing that it advocated for governmental regulation of the media. Although the declaration is not binding on any nation, the United States withdrew from UNESCO in 1984.[22] Currently there are no binding international treaties or standards that directly regulate the press.[23] Instead, organizations of professional journalists have published professional and ethical standards.[24]

Even when there is a basic agreement between nations as to the importance of protecting privacy, conflicts still arise when those standards are applied to particular cases. First, when national laws clash, whose standards should apply? The nation in which the information was accessed? The nation in which the information was published? And if those two countries have divergent positions regarding the freedom of the media, does one nation's shield of newsworthiness protect a publisher from a privacy invasion action in another country? The interpretation of what is illegal conduct and what is protected speech varies depending on which nation's laws are applied. Once choice of law is decided, what will be the effect of this judgment in a country that does not share the same standard when it comes to privacy or press? Will a judgment to enforce a privacy intrusion, such as a defamation judgment from Ireland, be enforceable against a newspaper located in the United States when the so-called defamatory speech would be protected speech in the United States? Uniform global standards on free press and individual privacy conflicts are not likely in the foreseeable future because the varying standards and cultural norms are locally important, powerful, and variable.

There are some overall evaluations of how nations protect privacy and how they treat media freedom. Institutions publish global rankings of nations on their press and privacy policies. Reporters Without Borders and Privacy International publish international ratings of countries based on their respect for the press and, separately, their respect for privacy. In 2008, Reporters Without Borders found that Iceland and Norway had the highest level of press freedom in the world. The United States ranked forty-eighth because of nondomestic violations of press freedom, such as the detention of Al-Jazeera's Sudanese cameraman at the Guantanamo military base.[25] In its 2007 privacy report, Privacy International classified Malaysia, China, Russia, Singapore, Taiwan, Thailand, the United States, and the United Kingdom as "endemic surveillance societies," entitled to the lowest ranking on the privacy scale.[26] These rankings show that privacy and press values are segregated by national borders and thus are analyzed separately by press and privacy advocates. However, these rankings alone are not particularly helpful in predicting the remedial outcome—if any—of particular intrusions by the media. There are no international rankings or standards dealing with intrusions by the national or global press on individual privacy. Individual media-privacy conflicts across borders are hard to predict. However, using the Media-Privacy Matrix (p. 28), one can evaluate a particular case based on its facts to assess both likely and ideal outcomes of the press-privacy conflict.

Defining National Legal Standards: Whose Standards?

Without effective and binding international rules, national standards will be the primary basis to resolve invasions of privacy by the media and determine protection of free speech. The ultimate question is whose national standards should govern. Because of differing laws, the determination of which jurisdiction's laws apply to a particular case will likely determine the outcome, although not necessarily its enforceability. Jurisdictions treat intrusions differently because their philosophies toward the press and personal privacy differ.[27] Thus, victims of the same privacy invasion will have different remedies available to them depending on where the intrusion occurred, where the matter is litigated, and the determination of which law applies.

In *Sipple v. Chronicle Publishing Company*, the *San Francisco Chronicle* published an article about Oliver Sipple's homosexuality.[28] Oliver Sipple had diverted an assassination attempt on President Gerald R.

Ford by striking the assassin's arm in the second before the shot was fired. Because of the *Chronicle*'s story about his sexuality, he suffered ridicule, mental anguish, embarrassment, and disassociation from his family. When Sipple brought suit in California against the *Chronicle*, the court dismissed the action. It concluded that Sipple was a hero, a public figure, and therefore his sexual orientation was newsworthy.[29] In comparison, a French man sued a newspaper in France for publishing a photo of him at a gay pride parade in Paris.[30] The photograph merely depicted the man as a participant in the parade. The French court held that the plaintiff had a right to oppose the photograph's publication. The court reasoned that mere revelation of oneself to the public does not mean that one has lost all protections before the larger public.[31] Clearly, the jurisdiction in each of these cases was determinative of its outcome.

Actions based on disclosures on the Internet can also lead to disparate results in different countries. An Argentinean court ordered Yahoo! Argentina to censor its search results for the famous soccer star Diego Maradona, to avoid invading his privacy. Finding the court's language to be broad,[32] Yahoo decided to remove *all* Maradona search results. A Maradona search on Yahoo now produced the following translated response: "On the occasion of a court order sought by private parties, we have been forced to temporarily remove some or all search results relating to it."[33] The court also ordered Google to censor its search results, but Google decided to continue returning Maradona results and stated it would block certain pages if a judge ordered it. The Maradona order is one of more than one hundred restraining orders relating to Argentinean names.[34] Had a famous U.S. athlete brought a similar suit in the United States, would the result have been the same? Definitely not—a public figure like Maradona would be considered newsworthy, and restricting access to publications about him would be antithetical to American jurisprudence. Additionally, the court order affects access through a search engine but does not censor the articles found in the search. The court seemed to emphasize the power of search engines to facilitate intrusions without dealing with the underlying inconsistency that the information still exists elsewhere.

The above cases illustrate that because national standards differ greatly, jurisdiction is often outcome determinative in privacy-related cases—although not necessarily effective at dealing with the global exposure raised by any particular claim. At the same time, because of the increasing number of cross-border intrusions, it is more difficult to ascertain which nation's law applies to a claim. An example of a cross-border intrusion case with unexpected results involved Joseph Gutnick, an Australian domiciliary, who sued the *Wall Street Journal* for publishing a defamatory article about him. Gutnick read the story on wsj.com from a computer in Australia. He sued in Australia; the court surprisingly denied the *Wall Street Journal*'s motion to transfer to the United States and applied Australian law. The court ultimately found the *Wall Street Journal* liable.[35] The article would have been protected speech in the United States, but Australia applies a completely different standard from that of the American First Amendment. Because the Australian court's conflicts of laws analysis concluded that the place where the person downloads the materials "will be the place where the tort of defamation is committed," Gutnick won his case. Thus, the procedural decisions determined the substantive outcome.

In another case, a Russian businessman, Boris Berezovsky, sued *Forbes* in a British court regarding an article appearing in the magazine titled, "Is he the Godfather of the Kremlin? Power. Politics. Murder. Boris Berezovsky Could Teach the Guys in Sicily a Thing or Two." The American-based magazine did not have many subscribers in either England or Russia, and the case was initially dismissed on the basis that there was no personal jurisdiction over the magazine. However, on appeal, the House of Lords reached a three-to-two decision in favor of letting the Russian plaintiffs proceed with their libel case in England.[36]

Another illustration of cross-border intrusions involves Laurence Godfrey, who sued a Canadian citizen, Michael Dolenga, in England. Dolenga allegedly posted defamatory messages about Godfrey on the Usenet news feed soc.culture.canada. Dolenga was a Cornell University graduate student, and Godfrey claimed that Dolenga was using Cornell as an ISP. Godfrey asked Cornell University to prohibit or block Dolenga from posting any additional messages, but Cornell denied this request. Several years after the postings had been made, Godfrey brought suit for defamation in England against both Dolenga (who had since graduated) and Cornell University. Godfrey won a default judgment against Dolenga, but Dolenga stated, "I'm not recognising the British court's jurisdiction and the hell with it."[37]

England found jurisdiction in a case concerning allegedly defamatory statements made by a New York attorney to a California-based website. *Lewis v. King*[38] involved an Internet defamation dispute relating to several postings made to boxing websites concerning the actions of Don King and even accusing him of being anti-Semitic. King claimed these comments defamed his reputation among the Jewish community in England.[39] The English Court of Appeals agreed and found that King could sue in England for his harm allegedly suffered in England, despite the fact that the postings were made by a U.S. citizen, about a U.S. citizen, to a U.S.-based website.[40]

The potential to be sued in any nation in which an Internet connection can be found has caused some mainstream media to use a more conservative approach in their reporting in order to meet the sensibilities of a global market. For example, the *Washington Post* and the *New York Times* management use very similar procedures and criteria when evaluating publications and broadcasts that will travel overseas as those they employ for the domestic market; these uniform standards are attuned to avoiding potential conflicts abroad, where the potential exposure to suits for defamation is riskier because of higher standards.[41] Additionally, Cable News Network (CNN) is now more likely to have lawyers routinely review its broadcasts prepublication in order to prevent defamation suits.[42] This caution shows that the threat of transborder liability could be hampering some speech in the United States. Without a clear indication of which nation's laws will be applied in any one press-privacy conflict, one result is greater uniformity among the global mainstream media.

Forum Shopping in Privacy and Press Cases

Because national laws are substantively different and each venue has varying degrees of willingness to exercise its jurisdiction, the determination of jurisdiction and conflicts of law are critical to the outcome of litigation. Two factors suggest that choice of law will be an even more important global issue moving forward. First, international laws vary substantially among nations. Second, the Internet and new communications technology allow for news to cross borders in a greater quantity and at a faster speed than ever before. These realities obviously create a great incentive to "forum shop." Logical plaintiffs will choose the most favorable jurisdiction for their claim. This tactic has been termed libel tourism and has received some public criticism. Lord Hoffman of the House of Lords, for example, cautioned courts against broadening personal jurisdiction because it would set a precedent for libel forum shopping.[43]

At its most basic level, conflicts of laws are about whether there is jurisdiction to decide a particular dispute. *The Restatement (Second) of Conflict of Laws* considers the following seven factors: (1) the needs of the interstate and international systems; (2) the relevant policies of the forum; (3) the relative policies of the other interested states and the relative interests of those states in the determination of the particular issue; (4) the protection of justified expectations; (5) the basic policies underlying the particular field of law; (6) the certainty, predictability, and uniformity of result; and (7) the ease in the determination of the law to be applied.[44] This is commonly referred to as the "interest analysis," and is followed in a majority of U.S. jurisdictions. However, other states still apply a territory-based test.

Many conflicts in the United States must be decided based upon whether there is an adequate basis for jurisdiction. The relevant laws are called long-arm statutes because they involve a state reaching beyond its territorial borders to invoke jurisdiction over an entity that may not be present in the state. However, the underlying logic is the same as with conflict of laws—is there sufficient contact within the state to justify bringing that entity to court; and is it fair in terms of notice and due process for the entity to be liable in that jurisdiction. The growth of Internet defamation promises that this issue will persist. Should a person who posts a defamatory comment on a Washington blog be liable to a person in Florida who is harmed by that post? The Florida Supreme Court believes the blogger could be.[45]

No matter the jurisdiction, national or international, this area of the law is highly unpredictable. The only certainty is that almost all jurisdictions consider publication within their borders sufficient justification for jurisdiction. With this open attitude toward cross-border litigation, American celebrities in particular are forum shopping. Many are taking advantage of greater privacy protections in Europe by suing American media industries in the United Kingdom and Ireland. Britney Spears settled a claim she brought in Ireland against the *National Enquirer* in 2006.[46] Kate Hudson, Cameron Diaz, and Justin Timberlake have all filed suits in European courts as well.[47] One aspect of these suits worth noting for the forum shopper is that the defamed person must have a reputation in the United Kingdom if a suit is to be successful. In other words, all of the listed celebrities have a U.K. reputation to protect, whereas low-profile citizens in the United States might not be able to avail themselves of the British courts.

According to an article in the U.K.-based *Times*, businesspeople and celebrities are now catching on to the plaintiff-friendly European laws.[48] In 2001, British supermodel Naomi Campbell sued the *Daily Mirror* for publishing a photograph of her at a Narcotics Anonymous clinic. The United Kingdom's House of Lords ruled that the publishing of the photos constituted a breach of confidence.[49] Although there is no express action for invasion of privacy in Britain, the judges did reference the "balance between the right to privacy and the right to freedom of expression."[50] The *Daily Mirror* would likely have carried the day in a U.S. court. The privacy right protected in the Campbell case would almost certainly lose to First Amendment rights to publish in the United States.[51]

Americans are not the only plaintiffs who have taken advantage of filing suits in jurisdictions abroad that offer more liberal libel laws. Americans are also being sued in foreign courts that render judgments against them for publishing speech that is considered protected in America but libelous elsewhere. In 2004, Saudi Arabian Khalid Salim A. Bin Mahfouz sued American author Rachel Ehrenfeld in British court for allegedly defamatory statements about his financial involvement with Al-Qaeda that she published in her book *Funding Evil: How Terrorism Is Financed—and How to Stop It*.[52] Mahfouz obtained a monetary judgment and an injunction against further publication of the book in the United Kingdom.[53] The basis for the U.K.'s assertion of jurisdiction over the claim was that twenty-three copies were purchased over the Internet in the United Kingdom and the first chapter of the book was available online for anyone to read, including British citizens.[54] In December of 2004, while the action against Ehrenfeld was still pending in England, Ehrenfeld filed an action for a declaratory judgment in a New York district court, seeking a declaration that the statements in her book did not give rise to liability for defamation under the laws of the United States or New York State and that the default judgment obtained from the British court was unenforceable in the United States.[55] Notably, the same jurisdiction issue that enabled the British court to render a judgment against Ehrenfeld became the basis of Bin Mahfouz's defense against her in U.S. courts.

Eventually, after the British court rendered a verdict against Ehrenfeld, the district court granted Bin Mahfouz's motion to dismiss the case for lack of personal jurisdiction.[56] Ehrenfeld appealed to the Second Circuit,[57] which in turn certified a question of state law to the New York Court of Appeals: whether New York's statute defining the limits of personal jurisdiction "confers personal jurisdiction over a person (1) who sued a New York resident in a non-U.S. jurisdiction; and (2) whose contacts with New York stemmed from the foreign lawsuit and whose success in the foreign suit resulted in acts that must be performed by the subject of the suit in New York."[58] The state's highest court answered the question in the negative, holding that Bin Mahfouz's actions in seeking an enforcement of the British judgment in the United States did not involve his invoking any privileges or protections of the state's laws and therefore the court lacked personal jurisdiction over him.[59] The New York Court of Appeals held that Ehrenfeld could not obtain the remedy she sought with the state courts; yet the story did not end with a judicial determination against Ehrenfeld's interests.

Ehrenfeld's case became so high profile that her cause—protecting from international affront the First Amendment right to report on newsworthy events like the funding of terrorism—garnered enough support that the legislature passed a law specifically enabling a New York court to assert personal jurisdiction in a case like Ehrenfeld's.[60] "Rachel's law" was passed in 2008, and since then California and the

U.S. Congress have begun drafting similar legislation.[61] The congressional bill, entitled the Free Speech Protection Act, modeled in part on the New York law, was introduced three times between the two houses of Congress in 2008 and early 2009.[62] The most notable difference between the state and federal legislation is that the federal legislation contains a "bite-back" provision that creates a federal cause of action and allows an American plaintiff facing a foreign libel judgment to sue in a U.S. district court and collect damages, including treble damages, and an injunction against foreign abridgment of that plaintiff's First Amendment rights.[63] Support for the bill, as evidenced in the media, was generally positive, as columnists championed Congress' attempts to safeguard the constitutional rights of Americans from attack by subversive terrorist organizations and overly wealthy, overly litigious types in other countries.[64] The support evidenced in the media should not be surprising, taking into account the highly emotive events triggering the legislation and the relationship of the press to the topic of limiting international liability for publishers. Unfortunately, both the House and Senate versions of the bill died in Congress after they were referred to committee.[65]

Regardless of the outcome of the legislation, the introduction of the bill shows that Congress felt a need to react to the forum-shopping issue because of the increasingly real possibility of litigation throughout the world. The global nature of new media and technology assures that this issue will continue to be important, and governments throughout the world will have to find workable solutions to all of the problems posed by varying international approaches to both substantive and procedural aspects of libel tourism. However, these solutions should not be created in a vacuum. The consequences of any country taking a myopic approach to the enforcement of its own laws could have destructive and undesirable international consequences.

Jurisdiction Wars

Suppose Congress had passed the proposed Free Speech Protection Act, including the provision allowing Americans to sue foreigners in the United States for obtaining libel judgments against them in other countries that would not be libelous under the First Amendment. By bringing suit in federal court, an American plaintiff could obtain a declaration in the United States that the judgment is unenforceable, a declaration that may or may not be necessary under existing law.[66] Additionally, the American plaintiff could obtain an additional judgment against the adverse party to a foreign judgment, who may or may not be a foreign citizen. Assuming the adverse party is a foreign citizen, the American plaintiff would now have a judgment he or she seeks to enforce against a foreign party in a foreign country and would be required to seek the aid of the foreign courts to obtain such enforcement. What would the party's luck be in executing this judgment? More importantly, what interest do foreign courts have in enforcing these claims, or even in adjudicating them in the first place?

There are three traditional bases for courts in any given country to assert personal jurisdiction over a foreign defendant: first, the subjective territorial principle, which allows a state to reach anyone within its territory regardless of the nationality of the individual; second, the nationality principle, which enables a state to reach its own citizens regardless of the immediate location of those individuals; and third, the objective territorial principle, which extends jurisdiction to acts committed outside a state's territory by non-nationals, on the basis that those acts have an effect in the controlling state.[67] International legal disputes that occur via Internet transactions will most often fall into the third category. Despite its similarity to the minimum-contacts requirements of most state long-arm statutes in the United States, this theory is highly controversial and yet increasingly in use as libel tourism gains speed.[68]

The proposed Free Speech Protection Act admittedly posed many of the problems associated with the exercise of extraterritorial jurisdiction. First, the proposed legislation might be unnecessary, as the current state of domestic law has consistently held that First Amendment concerns trump the general public policy of honoring international judgments.[69] Second, the act would unduly expand the scope of this country's domestic authority to enforce our substantive laws and norms against foreign parties and in foreign countries that have no interest in the litigation.[70] Third, the act did not contemplate the very real possibility that in some cases, it might be more appropriate for a U.S. court to enforce an international judgment, even against one of its own citizens, provided that the objective territorial principles of exercising jurisdiction weighed most heavily in favor of the foreign state's interest.[71]

Understandably, Congress would like to arm U.S. courts with new legal remedies in response to the growing threat of its citizens being subject to liability abroad that they could not incur in the domestic arena. However, as Linda Silberman admonished the House Judiciary Committee, "One need only be reminded of the possibility that an anti-suit injunction by a court in the United States may meet with the response of an anti-anti-suit injunction in the foreign court to realize that accommodation of competing policies is best achieved in other ways" than the new cause of action created in the proposed act.[72]

The broad and extreme sweep of Congress' proposed solution was likely inadequate to address the nuances of problems among competing international press and privacy standards. The international exercise of jurisdiction will continue to plague courts of all countries. Other ways to uniformly deal with this problem will necessarily be worked out as the problem progresses.

The global nature of the press-privacy conflict is only likely to escalate. The evolution and globalization of information are currently driven by a number of forces, but central to the state of the new media in the new world is the Internet. To be able to deal with the new and emerging press-privacy conflicts, understanding the Internet's profound effect on communications, information privacy, and the law is mandatory. Therefore, understanding the nature of Internet communications, use, and regulation is the next step in analyzing the press-privacy conflict.

5

The Internet
Defies
the
Gatekeepers

More than five and a half centuries passed between Johannes Gutenberg's invention of the printing press and the widespread adoption of the Internet as a medium for the broad dissemination of information. The printing press allowed the written word to spread across the world one book at a time and provided the technological underpinning to the subsequent Renaissance and Enlightenment periods. Printed books—as contrasted with the eBooks or streaming audiobooks of today—can only be consumed by one person at a time. Authors faced steep barriers to entry due to high production costs. For a while, it seemed that information was something that could only be produced expensively and distributed slowly. The Internet changed everything.

The Internet allows anyone with a computer—today, even a smartphone will suffice—to be his or her own editor, publisher, and broadcaster. For the institutional media, this development radically upgraded their existing capabilities. Problematically, it also created a level technological playing field for traditional media and the public at large. Before examining how technological advances have changed who qualifies as "the press," it is critical to understand the physical architecture of the Internet. As a common target of both judicial scrutiny and legislative regulation, the myriad networks that comprise the conventional Internet are a focal point for privacy analysis.

Regulation of the Internet

Most governments do not control access to the Internet and dissemination of information in a direct way, although some countries such as China have chosen to control the Internet directly. While policies differ from nation to nation, the United States allows Internet users to freely acquire domain names and establish their own websites. A user is not required to obtain a license from the FCC.[1] Additionally, an Internet address can be acquired anonymously,[2] which allows a user to post information anonymously on thousands of blogs or websites. Indeed, people are attracted to the Internet partially because of the increased potential to act and speak anonymously. Justice John Paul Stevens characterized the uncontrolled nature of the Internet as "a unique medium known to its users as 'cyberspace' *located in no particular geographical location but available to anyone* [emphasis added]."[3]

The Internet is conducive to chaos and free speech. Unlike broadcast television and radio, Congress has chosen to keep the Internet largely unregulated. Congress has stated that it is U.S. policy "to preserve the vibrant and competitive free market that presently exists for the Internet and other interactive computer services, unfettered by federal or state regulation."[4] However, the Federal Trade Commission (FTC) has stated that it is considering revising its privacy guidelines to compel Internet providers to notify consumers when their data is being collected by tracking technology, rather than only placing such notifications in the privacy policies of the websites.[5] Certain industry norms have developed independently over the years. Privacy scholars have suggested that the FTC is best suited to strengthen these norms by enforcing a uniform code of privacy policies.[6] Additionally, the Obama administration announced plans to create a special task force that will transform into policy the upcoming U.S. Commerce Department's recommendations about Internet privacy.[7] These recommendations would mark a major turning point in Internet policy from the traditional self-regulation to a more governmentally regulated media.

The ease of use and ready availability of this growing medium has changed the nature of information distribution and, as a consequence, the regulation and control of distribution including the press. The ability of Internet media outlets to offer free, instantaneous access to information worldwide has contributed to weakening subscriptions to traditional newspapers.[8] There are multiple impacts on the quality of information and the quantity of information. For example, Russell Weaver has noted that this shift to uncontrolled media largely eliminates gatekeepers, such as editors, who might provide enhanced accuracy and be concerned about avoiding defamation.[9] The nature of the Internet greatly enhances the likelihood of privacy intrusions. There are, however, substantial benefits to the absence of gatekeepers and the possibility of individual access to large audiences with otherwise unavailable information.

For example, during the 2009 reelection of Iranian president Mahmoud Ahmadinejad, the Iranian government barred journalists from covering "unauthorized demonstrations" protesting the election. However, citizens of Iran reported the demonstrations and protests via microblogging sites like Twitter.[10] The new media was able to do what the traditional media could not. The gatekeepers, in this case Iran's government, could not stop them. Demonstrations that the Iranian government sought to cover up made the news only because of Twitter technology. This new reality is a clear benefit to free expression but carries with it the risk of mass distribution of uncontrolled inaccuracies.

Internet Architecture: Physical Limitations and Controls

To understand the complexity of the application of law and policy to the Internet, one must have some understanding of how governments attempt to control the distribution of information on the Internet. The architecture of the Internet involves physical locations throughout the world that transmit information called network access points.[11] These points are owned by Internet service providers (ISPs). While no government controls all of cyberspace, each has the capacity to regulate ISPs that own access points found within its nation's borders. In fact, the government could own the ISP, which is the case in China.[12] So long as the ISP has network access points within the geographic space of a nation, the nation may place limitations on the information that flows through those points. As some countries have discovered, going after multiple ISPs to limit information contained on a single website is a bit like a child playing Whac-A-Mole. They keep popping up in different places.

For example, France has sought to enforce its laws against the selling of Nazi paraphernalia. But rather than targeting the ISPs that permitted access to the sales that were conducted on Yahoo Auctions, the government targeted Yahoo directly. Ultimately, Yahoo relented to the French, but not before an international set of legal cases dealing with free speech and jurisdictional enforcement was filed. This case serves as a prominent example of the difficulty of addressing cross-border Internet access.

ISPs are the distribution modes of the new media and serve as major conduits for distributing enormous amounts of information worldwide. Governments may impose standards on ISPs in order to control the type and amount of information they distribute. In the United States, the government may threaten an ISP with sanctions if it provides access to web pages that violate U.S. law.[13] Usually the sanctions result from a copyright or trademark violation such as a violation of the Digital Millennium Copyright Act, rather than a privacy invasion.[14] By encouraging a major ISP to deny access to a page that originates outside U.S. borders, U.S. Internet users are specifically inhibited from using those pages.[15]

The ability to access web pages varies from country to country.[16] China is perhaps the most rigorous in its monitoring; it "operates the most extensive, technologically sophisticated, and broad-reaching system of Internet filtering in the world."[17] The Chinese government not only regulates which domestic sites citizens view, but it also controls which foreign sites may enter its servers. Generally, Internet users who wish to obtain access to a site that has been filtered and blocked could do so through a proxy server, but China has limited the use of proxy servers as well.[18] It censors all Internet content by controlling the nation's two backbone ISPs: China Netcom and China Telecom. It conducts proxy censorship[19] through uniform resource locator (URL) filtering and domain name system tampering, which affects the ability of users nationwide to access websites like the *New York Times*.[20] Thus, while the Chinese government is not able to control the global Internet,[21] it attempts to control the distribution of information within its borders and has done an extremely effective job. Essentially, this firewall is the next Great Wall of China,[22] surrounding the entire nation with a cyberspace barrier. This centralized, authoritarian Internet architecture allows China to avoid the Whac-A-Mole problem faced by those nations with a decentralized ISP market.

The United States and the European Union take a more open approach to monitoring speech with respect to Internet users and their relationship to ISPs. But Western European nations control ISPs more strictly than the United States.[23] For example, the United Kingdom has historically taken a more rigorous approach toward regulating defamatory speech than the United States. In 2002, the United Kingdom passed the Electronic Commerce (EC Directive) Regulations, which gave effect to the European Electronic Commerce Directive (E-Commerce Directive).[24] Contained in this legislation is a provision delineating the liability of ISPs with regard to content posted by third parties on their sites, with the effect of articulating limits on the liability of ISPs as publishers that did not previously exist under the United Kingdom's common law. Under these circumstances, it is the act of publishing the speech, rather than writing or creating it, that is regulated.

Under the EC Directive, there are three categories of ISPs: (1) "mere conduits" of information posted by third parties; (2) ISPs that engage in caching information; and (3) ISPs that engage in hosting information. Mere conduits do not face liability for publication as long as the transmission of information is brief and not initiated or controlled in any way by the ISP.[25] Caching involves information transmissions during which the information is stored for a brief time in order to more efficiently transmit the information upon request of recipients of the information.[26] One example would be a temporary copy of a recently visited website, stored locally to facilitate more rapid access by the user. ISPs are generally not liable for caching as long as they do not alter the stored information and comply with any rules regarding access and updating of the stored information. In these cases, ISPs are essentially operating as electronic blackboards. They are erasable tablets upon which someone else writes. Additionally, where an ISP receives actual notice of the misuse of any cached information—which any Internet user could accomplish by utilizing the contact information for the ISP that it is statutorily required to provide—it has an obligation to take down the information or otherwise comply with a court order.[27]

In the third category, in which the ISP is hosting information, the ISP stores information provided by a recipient of the service—what we commonly think of as "posting."[28] An ISP is not liable as a host provided that it does not have actual knowledge of the unlawful activity or information on its site, the circumstances are not such that the unlawful activity should be apparent, and the ISP reasonably complies with any requests to take down or remove information once it obtains actual notice of such activity.[29] This statutory limitation of liability for Internet hosts is not procedurally dissimilar from that of the United States, but the substantive law underlying what constitutes illegal content creates very different results. For instance, in the recent case of *Google Spain v. AEPD & Mario Costeja Gonzalez*, the European Court of Human Rights held that an individual may, upon request, require an ISP to delete information from its search results that is "inadequate, irrelevant, or no longer relevant."[30] This result would be unlikely in a U.S. court. This holding represents an effort in the direction of "the right to be forgotten."

While the U.S. government regulates ISPs to a limited extent, it does not hold ISPs liable for slanderous or defamatory material posted on the Internet by third parties who transmitted the information through ISPs.[31] In the landmark case of *Zeran v. America Online, Inc.*, the Fourth Circuit Court of Appeals held that an exception to the Communications Decency Act of 1996 (CDA) granted ISPs immunity from liability for illicit acts of third-party users.[32] The exception provides, "No provider or user of an interactive computer service shall be treated as the publisher or speaker of any information provided by another information content provider."[33] The key is that the ISP will not be considered a publisher or speaker. This means that the ISP is again treated like a blank chalkboard that is not responsible for what another may write on it—not even for posted content that could give rise to liability under the EC Directive, the European analogue to the CDA.

Later, in *Batzel v. Smith,* the Ninth Circuit held that an "interactive computer service provider or user" includes "any information service, system, or access software provider that provides or enables computer access by multiple users to a computer server, including specifically a service or system that provides access to the Internet."[34] Under this definition, websites like Facebook and Twitter, which operate online services where users are invited to supply content, are granted immunity from civil liability when someone publishes defamatory comments on their sites.[35] Using similar reasoning, a more recent case from the Seventh Circuit declined to impose liability against the open-advertising site Craigslist for posts by users advertising housing that allegedly violated the Fair Housing Act.[36] The court held that because the ISP was merely a "messenger" rather than a publisher or speaker, and in no way caused the discriminatory content to be posted on its page, it could not be liable.[37]

However, two 2012 cases involving the website TheDirty.com resulted in clear procedural limits on ISP immunity.[38] TheDirty.com is a gossip website that solicits and subsequently publishes pictures and comments from its users. Its operator, commonly known as Nik Richie, also responds to the published pictures and comments. In the two aforementioned cases, TheDirty.com was sued for the publication of allegedly defamatory content, for which it claimed absolute immunity under the CDA. Out of these cases have arisen two types of limits on ISP immunity—participation and encouragement. The initial threshold issue is whether the site is a passive transmitter or an active developer of the information provided by its users.[39] Once an ISP moves from passive transmission of user-generated content into the active development of that content, it may lose CDA immunity.

The limits on the ISP are procedurally focused. Liability of the ISP is based on the conduct of the ISP in the generation of the illegal content at issue, rather than the substantive implications of that content. Thus, the first limit is on participation in the online posts. In *Hare v. Richie*, Nik Richie was actively creating the allegedly defamatory content.[40] His comments to user-generated posts about a Baltimore man were found to extend beyond "mere editorial functions" of publication.[41] The second limit is on the encouragement of defamatory online posts. In *Jones v. Dirty World Entertainment Recordings, LLC*, TheDirty.com was found to "specifically encourage [the] development" of offensive content regarding a Cincinnati Bengals cheerleader, thus resulting in liability at trial.[42] This decision was later overturned by a federal appeals court, which held that the scope of the CDA's immunity extended to protect the website operators, Nik Richie and Dirty World Entertainment, in circumstances where they were neither the creators nor the developers of the defamatory content, and therefore did not make a "material contribution" to its posting.[43]

Similar judicial holdings have resulted in cases decided under the CDA's European analogue. Consistent with the EC Directive Regulations, the United Kingdom has also held that ISPs may not be liable for defamatory statements of third-party users.[44] In a 2006 case, *Bunt v. Tilley*, the court held that "an ISP which performs no more than a passive role in facilitating postings on the Internet cannot be deemed to be a publisher at common law."[45] However, it also concluded that if the ISP was found to be a publisher[46] under common law, as it was in *Godfrey v. Demon Internet*,[47] then it could be liable in addition to the third party. In *Godfrey*, "Someone unknown made a posting [from] the USA in the newsgroup 'soc.culture.thai,'" hosted by the defendant ISP's news server in England.[48] The post, a forgery purported to be written by the plaintiff, was "squalid, obscene and defamatory" to the plaintiff. Although the plaintiff notified the defendant of the forgery and asked for its removal, the post remained. In the plaintiff's suit for libel, the ISP was held to be a publisher because of its active and informed role in the oversight of the publication. Because the defendant was not an "innocent disseminator" of the defamatory posting, each time a customer accessed that posting constituted a publication.[49] This standard provides for more ISP liability than the U.S. court's ruling in *Zeran*, which held that ISPs are not publishers.

In addition to the United Kingdom, other nations, such as Poland, hold ISPs more accountable than does the United States.[50] In Poland, an ISP may be liable without exerting direct control over editing and controlling the site.[51] Somewhere in the developing spectrum of ISP liability are the laws in South America. Brazil, for instance, has decided a variety of cases that come out differently on the issue. The Brazilian legislature debated a bill, informally known as the Marco Civil, that would codify a long-running practice: an ISP or website's duty to remove defamatory content upon request.[52] In April 2010, a Brazilian priest successfully sued Google after a defamatory message, accusing him of pedophilia, was put on Orkut, a Google social networking site that is popular in the country.[53] Brazil's hesitance to single out websites or ISPs, but instead leave both susceptible to lawsuits, is a common approach. The legislation requires ISPs to maintain a database of connection logs, which track the beginning and end of a user's Internet session. However, ISPs are forbidden from keeping Internet service access logs that actually track which websites a user visits.[54] Brazil's attempt to pass comprehensive legislation affecting the Internet will be challenging, just like similar attempts in the United States and the European Union.

In the famous Daniela Cicarelli case, a Brazilian judge ordered fixed-line telephone operators to block YouTube, preventing ISP customers from seeing any videos on the popular video-sharing website, after YouTube failed to prevent users from viewing a video of the celebrity having sex on the beach in broad daylight.[55] After a day, the order was modified to enjoin access only to the video contained on YouTube rather than the entire site.[56] However, in the interim, the video was uploaded to countless other sites, creating the exhausting task of seeking out each URL and pursuing takedown orders for the video contained on them. Undoubtedly, some of those are beyond the power of the Brazilian court, thus illustrating the problem with the instantaneous proliferation made possible by the Internet, one that is common to all nations. This case demonstrates the ephemeral nature of trying to control information once on the Internet and is a central issue in dealing with media intrusions on individual privacy.

In addition to using the law within its borders to control ISPs, a nation may even seek to control an ISP beyond its borders. This circumstance arises when a country believes an ISP has violated domestic laws. For example, Yahoo, a U.S. corporation, was found to have violated a law that prohibited the selling of Nazi paraphernalia within France.[57] A French court ordered Yahoo "to take all necessary measures to dissuade and make impossible visits by French web surfers to the illegal Yahoo Nazi auction site on Yahoo.com."[58] Yahoo, however, claimed that complying with the order was impossible, and there was no way to block only French Internet users from accessing the American website.[59] At the time, Yahoo refused to remove the site until an American court ruled on the issue.[60] It was not going to modify its practices in the United States because of a French court's order.

Yahoo brought a declaratory action in federal court seeking an order that the French order was unenforceable. The district court decided that the French order was not enforceable in the United States because "the principle of comity [was] outweighed by the Court's obligation to uphold the First Amendment."[61] Ultimately, the district court found that it is not "consistent with the Constitution and laws of the United States for another nation to regulate speech by a United States resident within the United States on the basis that such speech can be accessed by Internet users in that nation."[62] This case teaches an interesting lesson that applies throughout the privacy-press controversy. It is difficult or impossible to compel another country, in this case the United States, to enforce a law related to free press contrary to its own principles within its own borders. So, it is up to the country that wants to enforce its restrictions, in this case France, to figure out how to compel compliance.

While the appeal was pending, Yahoo concluded that it was in its financial interest to comply with the French court's order; otherwise, France would seize the company's assets held in France and impose a substantial fine.[63] Thus, France was able to persuade a cross-border ISP by threatening its corporate purse strings. However, the Ninth Circuit noted in its opinion that if a French court were to conclude that Yahoo had not conformed to the French order, then U.S. courts would have a ripe case before them, and a future case would not be dismissed.

There are multiple national means of regulating ISPs, including legal, technical, and economic powers. While China functions by exercising technical control over ISPs, the Yahoo case demonstrates the effectiveness of a nation's economic authority. Had the Yahoo case involved not France but rather a nation where Yahoo did not possess substantial assets, such as Fiji, for instance, then the practical result could be different. If a Fijian judge ordered Yahoo to take down its U.S. auction sites possessing Nazi memorabilia, Yahoo would have little incentive to do so if it had no assets in Fiji. Moreover, a U.S. court would likely uphold Yahoo's First Amendment right as it did in the French case; thus, Yahoo would be less likely to comply with a Fijian order because the order would not substantially affect its assets nor would the United States disapprove of its decision. This leaves countries such as Fiji with few options to control cross-border ISPs, short of installing a sophisticated firewall like China's.

Recent government attempts to stop digital piracy of copyrighted information raise doubts about the future of Internet regulation around the globe. While digital piracy is a different problem than online defamation, both share a common, enabling force: the Internet's decentralized architecture. In the United States, the entertainment industry has long pushed Congress to pass laws that encourage ISPs to report users who download pirated content. Congress seemed poised to pass such legislation in early 2012, but a groundswell of opposition prevented the passage of the Stop Online Piracy Act (SOPA). SOPA provides a teachable example of the politicization of legislative measures to regulate ISPs. To its supporters, SOPA encouraged accountability. The idea was that stronger enforcement of intellectual property rights was the best incentive for innovation and creativity.[64] To its opponents, SOPA violated the First Amendment. They claimed that the net effect of the legislation would be to censor those online platforms most conducive to free expression.[65] SOPA's defeat by the online activist community is a telling example of the challenges of imposing legal responsibility upon ISPs. Similar efforts in Canada and the European Union will likely face the same tenor of opposition, led by community-authored websites such as Wikipedia and Reddit.

This organized and durable opposition to government interference, or the appearance of it, combined with the hardware of the Internet, poses serious challenges to policymakers. For certain issues, such as France's use of economic power to persuade Yahoo not to display Nazi paraphernalia in auction results, it is likely that little will change. Such localized concerns do not implicate the same global issues that SOPA did. Both piracy and privacy are subject to country-specific laws; however, problems surrounding both are developing across the borderless Internet. Countries' attempts to regulate and control the new press will likely be as successful as their attempts at regulating digital piracy.

The laws relating to Internet information are in a state of flux. The reality of the Internet is central to the press-privacy controversy. The Internet and the new press provide massively expanded possibilities for improved public understanding and public access to information. At the same time the potential for unbridled harm to individual privacy is possible and more probable than ever before in our history.

There are established privacy theories and remedies that are the basis of holding the traditional press accountable for intrusions. New technologies and new realities have changed how these theories may apply. The question is: how do those theories work with the Internet and the new media?

Application of Traditional Media Principles to the Internet

The United States and Europe have a long history of applying free speech principles and evaluating issues like defamation or privacy intrusions by newspapers. In the last century electronic media have become part of this conflict. Now the Internet and new global communications technologies are challenging the capacity of the old laws to deal with new realities.

The legal and structural principles of the original concept of "press" were concerned with issues such as community, anonymity, and the gatekeeping role of press. First, the traditional press primarily distributed information to a defined community from a common geographic area and in a common language. Further, in legal terms, the press was penalized if it violated those community standards in terms of obscenity or invasions of privacy. The traditional press was held to the standards of the community it served. Second, anonymity was honored in order to protect sources and promote candor. Particularly in the United States, anonymous communication has helped those who are less powerful to criticize the government or other powerful institutions. Third, the gatekeepers of the press assured us that published information had some probability of being true. A newspaper editor or newspaper attorney would review a potential article to see if there were adequate sources or if the information might be defamatory. Further, sometimes editors simply decided not to publish something because it was too intrusive, even if they might have been able to do so legally. They were exercising judgment and discretion.

Many of these practices are still utilized today. While these issues are still important, they pose entirely different concerns with the new medium of the Internet. Do the changes in the press and the increase in new kinds and means of intrusions require new approaches for more accountability for the new press? While the original press was limited by the medium in that paper publications were limited by space and scope, the Internet is limited by neither space nor scope. It is a medium characterized by its lack of limits. Individuals have an endless amount of room to express their ideas and convey those ideas to a global audience. The questions are: how do these traditional issues apply with the advent of the Internet-based new media, and is the current law adequate to deal with the new realities?

The New Concept of Community

Location matters. One of the defining threshold questions in determining press liability for intrusion is where the intrusion happened. A newspaper publication in the United States is likely to enjoy greater protection than publications elsewhere because of the value Americans place upon free speech. The location issue is becoming more difficult with the evolution of the distribution of information from print to electronic distribution. Broadcast and Internet communications cross borders and complicate the application of the law even more, as illustrated in the previous discussion of ISP liability.

The fact that communications are now global raises an extraordinarily vexing problem for the law because the law has always been based principally on geography. Of course, there are treaties and multinational arrangements. But at the most fundamental level, cultures make laws and moral judgments for those who live together in nations, states, cities, and towns. These are geographic communities that make moral judgments in their statutes, ordinances, and laws. Communities communicate their own values. Further, the courts use community standards in defining legal boundaries and in defining reasonableness. The common term "reasonable person" naturally refers to a reasonable person in whatever community is defining the term. So the term "community" is a mutable yet fundamental building block of the law. Common community understanding is important in deciding whether one's expectation of privacy is reasonable. In the seminal search-and-seizure case of *Katz v. United States*, the U.S. Supreme Court found that one's Fourth Amendment rights have not been violated unless the person exhibits an actual, subjective expectation of privacy and that expectation is one that society is prepared to recognize as reasonable.[66] This analysis can be fairly simplified to state that if an intrusion violates both personal and community standards, it violates privacy.

The press-privacy conflict presents a direct conflict between values *within* any particular community as well as *between* different communities. Specifically, the conflict will arise when an individual asserts that the media has violated community standards and has published private information (public disclosure of private facts) or intruded into their private matters (intrusion upon seclusion). In order to establish such a violation, the violation must be offensive to a reasonable person. The common defense of the media to this attack is the assertion that their actions were consistent with the community values of free expression and free press.

Community standards may be a factor in determining whether a disclosure is newsworthy or an invasion of privacy. In the *Restatement Second of Torts* on public disclosure of private facts, two requirements are listed. A person publicizes private facts if the issue publicized is "of a kind that (a) would be highly offensive to a reasonable person; and (b) is not a matter of legitimate concern to the public."[67] Further, "in determining what a matter of legitimate public interest is, account must be taken of the *customs and conventions of the community*; and in the last analysis what is proper becomes a matter of the *community mores* [emphasis added]."[68] The *Restatement Second of Torts* further states that enforcement of public disclosure may be limited by free speech and free press rights. That limitation is, of course, the key to the media's defense of any disclosure.

Another privacy tort, intrusion upon seclusion, also includes language that says an intrusion is a violation if it is "highly offensive to a reasonable person."[69] Thus, an intrusion into a person's private matters or space is a violation. An unauthorized inspection of a hotel room, a person's wallet, or a private bank account is a violation. Since this kind of intrusion is not a matter of disclosure of information, free press or free expression is not a defense.

In a community that values free press more highly than personal privacy, such as the United States, the press will normally prevail. However, even in communities like the United States, certain media actions will not be protected. For example, if a publication is false, it will not be protected speech. If a member of the press trespasses or wiretaps, those actions are not protected. In other communities such as the European Union, where personal privacy and dignity are held in higher regard, the balancing of press and privacy interests will be very different. Since the Internet presents a situation where media cross into many different communities, what are community standards for Internet-based press-privacy conflicts?

The word "community" is a fourteenth-century term that has its origins in the Latin noun *communitas*. In the most primitive of societies, *communitas* signified the commonality of a group of people: common ancestors, common geography, common religion, and common values. The law has most frequently tracked geography as its unifying—and also delineating—community principle. In the past, geography also defined and limited communication modes that have a major role in defining common values. For example, geographic communities typically had a common language and received their information through a common newspaper or, before the press, by word of mouth.

Today, with two billion people using the Internet, should the law define community in terms of common communications, experiences, or ideas, rather than geographical limitations?[70] In 1996, a group of specialists in human-computer interaction considered the key characteristics of online communities and identified five: (1) Members have a shared goal, interest, need, or activity that provides the primary reason for belonging to the community; (2) members engage in repeated and active participation, and, often, intense interactions, strong emotional ties, and shared activities occur among the participants; (3) members have access to shared resources, and policies determine the access to those resources; (4) members engage in reciprocity of information, support, and services; and (5) there is a shared context of social conventions, language, and protocols.[71] None of the five factors relates to geographic proximity. Geography now has far less relevance to communications and publications in the Internet age, but it continues to define the scope of many legal principles.

The scope of distribution over the Internet is clearly affecting definitions of community standards because Internet publications may be viewed by and distributed to a vast number of communities and different legal jurisdictions simultaneously. Once information is released on the Internet, there is very limited ability to stop access to it in other geographic locations. Therefore, the distribution of information via the Internet will frequently, if not always, result in distribution to multiple jurisdictions.

The differences in jurisdictional norms on privacy will result in forum shopping. Recall from chapter 4 that the disclosure of sexual orientation in France and in the United States reached very different results when the plaintiffs in their respective countries brought suit to vindicate their privacy rights.[72] In those cases, the difference was that the French community standard was more protective of a person's privacy intentions. Community standards are still applied in the evaluation of defamation on a global scale. As a whole, the U.S. community forgives privacy intrusion to protect free press and free speech. But some other jurisdictions, such as the European Union, place a higher value on privacy.

Globally, different jurisdictions will likely continue to have different views on privacy and free speech. Global uniformity on culturally sensitive issues is very unlikely in the short term. Some common ground has been found to allow digital security and commercial communications. Treaties already cover some of these topics, in part because there are strong commercial incentives to reach compromise. But the issue of press intrusion on the personal privacy of an individual is a different matter. Even nations with similar free press traditions, such as the United States and the European Union, have distinctly different legal approaches to privacy and defamation. Searching for a friendly forum is not new for lawyers, and it is certainly used in defamation issues that cross international borders. "Libel tourism" aptly labels the search for the best jurisdiction for an injured victim of global or cross-border defamation.

Which community standard is appropriate when an Internet posting can be accessed from virtually anywhere? Does the inability to define a particular geographic community standard subject all Internet content to the standards of the least tolerant community?[73]

Interpreting Internet Community: The Example of Pornography
and Obscenity Cases

One category of cases that has compelled a struggle with defining community values is those involving pornography or obscenity. Community standards have been part of that test. The U.S. Supreme Court, in *Miller v. California*,[74] set forth a three-part test for assessing whether material is obscene and thus unprotected by the First Amendment: (1) whether the average person, applying contemporary community standards, would find that the work, taken as a whole, appeals to the prurient interests; (2) whether the work depicts or describes, in a patently offensive way, sexual conduct specifically defined by the applicable state law; and (3) whether the work, taken as a whole, lacks serious literary, artistic, political, or scientific value.[75] *Miller* adopted the use of "community standards" from *Roth v. United States*,[76] which repudiated an earlier approach for assessing objectionable material. The nineteenth-century legal analysis allowed English and American courts to evaluate material from the perspective of particularly sensitive persons.[77] However, *Roth* held that this sensitive-person standard was "unconstitutionally restrictive of the freedoms of speech and press" and approved a standard requiring that material be judged from the perspective of "the average person, applying contemporary community standards."[78] In *Miller*, the Court reemphasized that the use of community standards furnishes a valuable First Amendment safeguard: "The primary concern . . . is to be certain that . . . [material] will be judged by its impact on an average person, rather than a particularly susceptible or sensitive person—or indeed a totally insensitive one."[79] But the community standard still varies depending upon the norms and mores of a particular group; what is art in one community may be considered pornography in another.

Since the Internet is not geographically localized, should the community standards for the Internet be national? In fact, the United States has created national community standards in several fields where there is a national distribution of information. The FCC regulates television and radio stations with regard to inappropriate language.[80] The FCC may censor so-called fleeting expletives on the airwaves.[81] Those laws are applied nationwide and are justified by the conclusion that the airwaves are owned by the public and therefore may be publicly regulated. Films also undergo rigorous screening before their release to the public to determine whether content is appropriate for children under thirteen or under seventeen.[82] These national standards also focus on what could be considered obscene or pornographic.

There have been some efforts to regulate Internet content. One example was the Child Online Privacy Act. In *Ashcroft v. American Civil Liberties Union*,[83] the Supreme Court reviewed the constitutionality of the Child Online Privacy Act that sought to regulate material "harmful to minors" transmitted via the World Wide Web for "commercial purposes."[84] Previously, the community-standards criterion as applied to the Internet meant that any communication available to a nationwide audience would be judged by the *standards of the community most likely to be offended by the message*.[85]

The *Ashcroft* court evaluated earlier cases dealing with national distribution by mail and telephone communications in which the Court held that a statute requiring different messages to different communities was not a violation of free speech. The Court held in *Hamling v.*

United States, and reaffirmed in *Sable Communications of California v. FCC*, that a requirement that speakers who disseminate material to a national audience observe varying community standards does not violate the First Amendment because it does not require speakers to tailor their message to the least tolerant community.[86] In other words, speakers could use different messages for different communities because the means of communication could allow them to deliver different messages.

Internet publishers do not have comparable control on distribution. The fractured *Ashcroft* Court could not reach a majority over whether the standards applied in *Hamling* and *Sable* were applicable to the Internet, or whether there needed to be a national community standard when regulating obscene material on the Internet.[87] Justice Clarence Thomas found that the "unique characteristics" of the Internet did not justify adopting a different approach than that set forth in *Hamling* and *Sable*.[88] However, Justice Sandra Day O'Connor concurred separately in order to advocate for a national community standard for communications over the Internet. She felt that because Internet speakers are unable to control the geographic location of their audience, expecting them to bear the burden of limiting their communications based on the sensitivity of the wide spectrum of Internet recipients of their speech, as the Court did in *Hamling* and *Sable*, would be too much to ask and could potentially stifle an inordinate amount of expression.[89] Justice O'Connor conceded that asking jurors to apply a national community standard would lead inevitably to assessments based on the jurors' experience in their own local community. However, she found that the practice would lead to a lesser degree of variation than asking the jurors to apply a local community standard while further protecting First Amendment rights.[90]

Justice Stephen Breyer agreed with Justice O'Connor and wrote: "To read the statute as adopting the community standards of every locality in the United States would provide the most puritan of communities with a heckler's Internet veto affecting the rest of the Nation. The technical difficulties associated with efforts to confine Internet material to particular geographic areas make the problem particularly serious."[91] Additionally, Justice Anthony Kennedy found that the "difference in the characteristics of new media justify differences in the First Amendment standards applied to them,"[92] and he agreed with Justice O'Connor that a national community standard may be more appropriate for the Internet medium. It is possible that the new media will be treated more favorably and more leniently than a local newspaper with limited distribution.

Subsequently, the Ninth Circuit in *United States v. Kilbride*[93] applied Justices O'Connor and Kennedy's concurrences and found that a national community standard must be applied in regulating obscene speech on the Internet because Internet transmissions cannot be directed or contained in only one geographic area.[94] However, the *Kilbride* court did not define what a national community standard would be or how it would be applied any differently than a local standard, particularly where the judgment would still be determined by a jury of citizens from the same local community.

The Eleventh Circuit, choosing to read the concurrences of *Ashcroft* as dicta, declined to apply a national community standard to Internet obscenity.[95] Rather, the court in *United States v. Little* found that the *Miller* contemporary community standard remains the standard to be applied to the Internet.[96] Therefore, the court held that the district court did not err when it instructed the jury to judge the materials on the basis of how "the average person of the community as a whole—the Middle District of Florida—would view the material."[97]

Clearly this conflict among the circuits is ripe for resolution by the Supreme Court, but it may be awhile before a standard is set. Even if a national standard can be achieved, Americans face privacy invasions elsewhere, and citizens of other nations face privacy invasions here. The problem has become one of global standards.

Defining legal standards to apply to a media intrusion is hard enough in the United States, but it will become continually more complicated as a global issue as cross-border communications expand. Right now, the definition of community in legal terms will still be focused on geographic and physically definable jurisdictions. The struggle to define pornography in the U.S. courts indicates that, within a national jurisdiction, more national standards may overcome more local standards in the context of Internet publications because of the reality of Internet distribution.

Pornography and obscenity are categories of unprotected speech under the First Amendment. Therefore, the determination that something violates community standards and is pornographic allows liability to be imposed without violating the First Amendment. In the United States, being offensive in distributing information is still protected speech. Pornography is not protected speech. But the Internet is regulated differently than some other media. While the FCC regulates fleeting expletives in broadcast media, it does not regulate the Internet. The Internet is not treated as publicly owned, as are the airwaves. Yet there are some established limits to speech published on the Internet. Child pornography is illegal on the Internet—as it is if published or distributed in any other medium in the United States—and the international community broadly accepts that conclusion.

Anonymity on the Internet

The role of anonymity on the Internet is much more significant than anonymity in earlier publications because of the massive increase in access to publication and the fact that the Internet allows global access to virtually all publishers. The risks of the abuse of anonymous communication are now more substantial. The psychological implications of Internet communications are an important element of understanding the risks of anonymity in the new media. Some implications of Internet anonymity include dissociation, invisibility, asynchronicity, and the disinhibition effect. In other words, humans may act quite differently when communicating anonymously through a computer than they would if they were acting face-to-face in public.

Being able to remain anonymous in some situations has always been a part of individuality and in fact part of protecting our identity. While anonymity has been accepted and protected, the implication of anonymity on the Internet is a new problem. The vast reach and nature of dissemination over the Internet has allowed for greater abuses because those "speaking" are unknown and may be more prone to abuse that invisibility in the new world. Unlike traditional print media, and even broadcast media, the Internet does not have any major filter. There is no obstacle between the anonymous speaker and the receivers of the information. Therefore, there is little accountability.

The reality of mass distribution, particularly on the Internet, is the enhancement of an individual's ability to communicate information anonymously with a massive increase in impact and distribution. American law protects this anonymity so as to encourage free speech. But as journalism ethics professor Edward Wasserman has observed, anonymity on the Internet "is just the opposite of standing up and being heard. Instead, we have the rampant spread of a free-fire zone of wild, unattributed, unclaimed expression for which accountability isn't expected and, indeed, cannot even be sought."[98] Anonymity is not a new aspect of the media. Remaining anonymous is a well-established means of communicating cutting-edge issues. *The Federalist Papers* were published under the name Publius rather than Madison, Hamilton, and Jay. Free speech principles have also protected the right to be an anonymous critic.[99] The press itself relies on its privilege to protect the anonymity of its sources.

The founders desired to provide the media with sufficient rights to enable them to place an additional check on the power of the government, to act as the fourth estate.[100] In many cases, society welcomes this watchdog function. In other contexts, privacy expectations conflict with American notions of free speech and free press. Consider the whistleblower or the crime victim, each of whom usually has an expectation of anonymity that society has recognized through the passage of protective laws. Anonymity, whether of the writer or the source, is an element of free press. Yet the First Amendment protection of anonymity is not absolute. There is no right to slander anonymously.[101] And interestingly, anonymity is part of what many consider an element of their own personal privacy. Privacy in some contexts is almost synonymous with the term: if we are anonymous we have privacy. When we are identified, we lose some element of privacy. We lose some of our ability to be let alone.

Thus, some scholars fear that expanding the scope of libel suits will magnify the David-versus-Goliath effect of free speech battles.[102] Corporate plaintiffs eager to quell online criticism merely need to make out a prima facie claim for libel in order to unmask their dissidents. The easier it is for online anonymity to be erased, the more careful Internet users will be about asserting facts or opinions that may expose them to burdensome litigation costs. This chilling effect may well extend beyond curtailing Internet defamation to capturing "free-ranging debate and experimentation with unpopular or novel ideas."[103] The pendulum seems yet to have swung this far.

However, the ability to express anonymous opinions or to pretend to be someone you are not has reached new levels on the Internet. The Internet presents the possibility of taking on an entirely new identity in a second life. There are screen names and avatars, and then there are outright imposters. One nationally known example concerned a mother who posed as a young man specifically to torment a teenage girl. Her prosecution is known worldwide because the young girl committed suicide as a result of the digital harassment.[104]

Anonymity in the new press is also a staple of modern news communications. Sources of information and viewpoints are well protected, and some news mediums such as blogs do not disclose their authors. Anonymity is fundamental to criminal behavior on the Internet, enabling violators to engage in the distribution of child pornography, cyberstalking, and other cybercrime. Anonymity is a crucial tool that prevents unsophisticated targets from uncovering deception by pedophiles on the Internet. For example, MySpace made the astonishing admission that it had kicked ninety thousand pedophiles off its social networking site.[105] How did MySpace know that these people were pedophiles, and why did they wait until there was such an astonishing number to remedy the problem?

The battle to identify speakers, publishers, and editors on the Internet reaches concerns that are more mundane than finding and prosecuting child pedophiles. In a 2013 case, a prominent attorney sought to uncover the identities of two editors who changed information on her Wikipedia page to falsely allege that she had been sanctioned by a judge before whom she had never appeared.[106] The cases that seek to uncloak anonymity range from outing a whistleblower to tracking a pedophile. Thus, the two extremes of the benefits and harms of anonymity meet on the Internet; the well-meaning gadfly and the hated pedophile both share the anonymity of the medium. The cases of anonymity's harm are worth noting.

In *Carafano v. Metrosplash.com, Inc.*, the Ninth Circuit Court of Appeals found that the Communications Decency Act of 1996[107] immunized an Internet dating service against claims of misappropriation of the right of publicity, defamation, and negligence resulting from the online posting of the plaintiff's personal information without her consent.[108] An anonymous poster in Berlin, posing as a well-known American actress, created a profile on the dating service containing sexually suggestive statements and listing the actress' actual home address and telephone number in California.[109] The profile resulted in the actress receiving a flood of sexually explicit comments and threats by way of phone calls, voicemails, written correspondence, and e-mails.[110] The court characterized the act as "grant[ing] most Internet services immunity from liability for publishing false or defamatory material so long as the information was provided by another party."[111] It found that the dating service was immune because it had not acted as an "information content provider" in relation to the challenged postings.[112] The court reached this finding in spite of the fact that the contested information was provided in response to the dating service's questionnaire.[113] It noted that the dating service had no hand in connecting information to the questions, which was primarily the function of the third-party poster.[114] Importantly, the court went on to state that even if the dating service could be classified as an information content provider, the language in the act immunizing an Internet service provider for "any information provided by another information content provider" would require the dating service to have created or developed the contested information in order for liability to attach. This broad interpretation of immunity to Internet service providers under the act shifts most liability to the content providers; however, if the content providers can remain anonymous, they can avoid liability.

In the case of the Catsouras family in Orange County, California, anonymity became an issue, not in identifying the individuals who leaked official accident-scene photos of their daughter's horrific death, but in identifying those who obtained the photos and then e-mailed them to her father.[115] Two California Highway Patrol officers admitted to violating law enforcement policy by releasing the images of the nearly destroyed vehicle containing the badly mutilated body of eighteen-year-old Nikki Catsouras.[116] While one of the officers stated he only e-mailed the photos to his personal address, the other admitted to circulating the images to a handful of close friends and family.[117] Prior to the online circulation of the photos, the victim's family had not viewed the images. In fact, the crash was deemed so atrocious that the coroner avoided having the parents view the body for identification.[118] Before the Catsouras family even learned of the leak, anonymous individuals began e-mailing Mr. Catsouras, sending the images under innocuous subject lines.[119] One particularly egregious message paired the photos with the message "Woohoo Daddy! Hey Daddy, I'm still alive!"[120] The family filed complaints against the California Highway Patrol and one of the individual officers involved in the leak.[121] A California appeals court held that the officers violated their duty of care by placing the images on the Internet.[122] However, because the family was unaware of the identities of the parties responsible for the e-mails and the thousands of Internet postings of the images, they have limited, if any, relief against the anonymous posters and e-mailers. While the family hired a private company[123] that has successfully lobbied for the removal of the photos from a number of websites,[124] a Google search for the images almost four years after the accident revealed nearly seventy-five thousand hits.[125]

The dispute surrounding the now-defunct JuicyCampus.com website also demonstrated the viral nature of anonymous information dissemination on the Internet. The site welcomed "college gossip," and the comments it received from students across more than five hundred campuses resulted in a flood of legal debate regarding Internet privacy rights.[126] It officially shut down on February 4, 2009, citing lack of resources[127] and specifically refuting that the closure bore any relation to the shock waves that resulted from the numerous allegations of defamatory postings about college students across the country. Most interesting was JuicyCampus's terms and conditions and its interpretation of this policy. A post from December 2007 states that this policy "require[s] users to agree not to post anything that is defamatory, libelous, etc."[128] It goes on to state that any individual using the site has accepted these terms and conditions and therefore pledged that the postings are not defamatory.[129] JuicyCampus interprets this pledge as freeing it from any obligation to verify the facts of the posts, or perhaps more importantly, to remove the posts upon an allegation of defamation, absent a court order.[130] On the topic of anonymity, JuicyCampus reminded its viewers that "nothing is anonymous on the Internet" but essentially implied that it would not reveal user identity unless compelled to do so by law or by the site's own interests.[131] It stated, "If your school calls upset about some girl being called a slut, we're not handing over access to our server data. If the LAPD calls telling us there is a shooting threat, you better believe we're gonna help them."[132]

Despite the host of examples in which the unveiling of Internet anonymity is sought for a good purpose and frustrated by the obstacles inherent in this process, there remain some examples in which most would agree that anonymity was properly preserved. For example, few of us wanted to identify the individuals who Tweeted about the violence and abuses after the 2009 elections in Iran. They were the only source of information, and anonymity was critical to their safety. But clearly anonymity can protect both the good and the bad—at its worst, it can be highly dangerous and facilitate invasions of privacy in other settings.

Defamation and Anonymous Bloggers

Because of Internet anonymity, defamation cases are arising where a defamation plaintiff is seeking relief against an anonymous blogger.[133] Courts try to balance First Amendment rights with the right to pursue defamation. Generally, courts are requiring that defendants must have notice before their identifying information is disclosed. If they cannot be found, notice of the attempt to disclose is posted on the forum where the supposedly defamatory statement was made. The courts use various methods of deciding whether to disclose. The most dominant procedure is to determine whether there is a prima facie case for defamation and then balance the free speech right against the libel damage.[134]

The *Dendrite* case established the early benchmark for evaluating a defamation action against an anonymous blogger. The *Dendrite* test has four elements as described in *Doe v. Cahill*, a Delaware Supreme Court case on the same issue:

(1) To undertake efforts to notify the anonymous poster that he is the subject of a subpoena or application for an order of disclosure, and to withhold action to afford the anonymous defendant a reasonable opportunity to file and serve opposition to the application. In the internet context, the plaintiff's efforts should include posting a message of notification of the discovery request to the anonymous defendant on the same message board as the original allegedly defamatory posting.

(2) to set forth the exact statements purportedly made by the anonymous poster that the plaintiff alleges constitute defamatory speech; and

(3) to satisfy the prima facie or summary judgment standard.

Finally, after the trial court concludes that the plaintiff has presented a prima facie cause of action, the *Dendrite* test requires the trial court

(4) to balance the defendant's First Amendment right of anonymous free speech against the strength of the prima facie case presented and the necessity for the disclosure of the anonymous defendant's identity in determining whether to allow the plaintiff to properly proceed.[135]

Based on this test, a person who wants to pursue defamation against an anonymous blogger has several hurdles on the way to relief.

In some circumstances, the nature of the anonymous defamation is so extreme that it rises to a level of verbal assault akin to criminal threats or fighting words, becoming what appears to be an easy case for determining that a speaker has forfeited anonymity by publishing unprotected speech. One example is the Auto-Admit case in which a number of anonymous posters on a message board designed for law students to share their student and prospective career experiences posted incredibly offensive allegations and threats against two young women they identified by name.[136] Not only did the posters allege crude and outlandish sexual behavior and characteristics of these women, but they also threatened to force sodomy on them and stated that one of the women "deserved to be raped."[137] Arguably, these comments at least approach, if not amount to the prima facie case required to unveil Internet anonymity.[138]

Another recent example applying this standard to determine whether to unveil an Internet speaker comes from the *Krinsky* case out of California.[139] In that case, an anonymous poster on a financial message board insulted a number of officers of a Florida corporation, calling them names that included "cockroach," "mega scum bag," and "boobs, losers and crooks."[140] Specifically, this poster accused the plaintiff of having "fat thighs, a fake medical degree . . . [she] 'queefs' and has poor feminine hygiene."[141] The issue in the case was whether the subpoena that the Florida corporation had issued to uncover the poster's identity should be quashed. The court found that quashing the subpoena was proper in light of First Amendment principles that protect the right to anonymous speech.[142] The court articulated the balance it had to strike as one "providing an injured party a means of redress without compromising the legitimate right of the Internet user to communicate freely with others."[143]

The court found that the statements, taken in context, could not possibly be viewed as "asserting or implying objective facts," because the nature of the forum was one that encouraged venting and hyperbole and conveyed scorn and contempt rather than authoritative assertions, the language of the assertions was crude and ungrammatical, and such speech was merely offensive opinion rather than actionable allegation.[144] The most interesting aspect of the *Krinsky* court's analysis is its focus on the context or location of the speech, suggesting that perhaps the reputation of an Internet site could become a factor in Internet defamation analysis.

The *Krinsky* court's characterization of the Internet forum was that since message boards are less formal, readers take messages posted on them less seriously. This is dangerous logic: conveying a message to millions may not be grounds for libel or even obtaining the speaker's identity if the words appear on a trashy website, but the same words printed in a newspaper might be libel. In effect, the lack of credibility of the defendant becomes a litigation defense, and the rights of the plaintiff become dependent on the defendant's choice of medium.

Taken to the extreme, this context-dependent approach could potentially give rise to recognition of Internet forums with such widespread disrepute that no speech published on the sites could be actionable. Using the Internet as a location for publication has caused courts to struggle with finding where to draw the line when the speech itself is recognizably unprotected to the degree that the anonymity of the speaker may properly be stripped away to pursue liability. While it is not a settled factor in Internet libel analysis,[145] taking this distinction into account is exclusively a function of American law.

Proponents of the conclusion reached in *Krinsky* argue that the court simply applied current libel law to the message board context. However, the application of defamation to such a new and completely different situation is problematic. First, by extending the analysis from libel in a printed tabloid to libel in an anonymous message board, the court erected barriers to the original intended remedy. While a plaintiff may not prevail in her defamation claim against a columnist at the *National Enquirer*, at least she knows whom to sue. Second, a locational test exacerbates the multiplicity effects of the Internet. The combination of a greater ability to defame with a lesser ability to seek redress unquestionably increases the potential for harm. In the new Wild West, everyone is armed, and the sheriff has no bullets.

In a case popularly dubbed "Blonde v. Blogger," a New York trial court reached a different conclusion when it ordered Google to release to the petitioner "the identity of the Anonymous Blogger(s), specifically that person's or persons' name(s), address(es), email address(es), IP address(es), telephone number(s), and all other information that would assist in ascertaining the identity of that person or persons."[146] The petitioner, Liskula Cohen, sought a defamatory action against the party responsible for unflattering comments and photos posted about her on a blog entitled "Skanks of NYC."[147] The blog referred to Cohen using various derivatives of the words "skank," "ho," and "whoring" and posted group photos taken of Cohen in sexually suggestive positions.[148] The blogger, represented anonymously by counsel after receiving e-mail notification from Google regarding the suit, challenged the petition for disclosure on the basis that the petitioner failed to allege a proper cause of action for defamation.[149] The blogger's central argument regarding the text concerned the hyperbolic nature of the statements and the unlikelihood that any "reasonable viewer of the Blog" would consider it to present factual statements. The blogger also pointed emphatically toward the ubiquitous use of blogs as a medium for "trash talk" and venting, arguing that the nature of the medium negated any potential defamatory effect the words might have.[150] Notably, both of these factors—the location of the statements and their hyperbolic nature—were considered dispositive by the *Krinsky* court.

In the Blonde v. Blogger case, the trial court decided to grant the petition for disclosure in light of its finding that the statements contained assertions of objective fact capable of grounding a claim for defamation.[151] In making this determination, the court considered (1) whether the specific language at issue has a precise, readily understandable meaning; (2) whether the statements are capable of being proven true or false; and (3) whether either the full context of the communication in which the statement appears or the broader social context and surrounding circumstances are such as to "signal . . . readers or listeners that what is being read or heard is likely to be opinion, not fact."[152]

The New York court offers the sounder reasoning. The *Krinsky* court would allow bloggers and commentators to make outlandish statements on the premise that most readers might not believe them simply because of the medium. This logic allows the credibility of the source to come in as a defense, which ultimately rewards shady characters. The best practice is to recognize a cause of action where a person's safety has been threatened or pure slander is apparent, regardless of the medium of dissemination.

To place the *Krinsky* case in an international context, compare the *Keith-Smith* case out of the United Kingdom.[153] In that case, the plaintiff was Michael Keith-Smith, a former Conservative party member who engaged in a discussion on a Yahoo Message Board regarding the state of the Iraq war.[154] The discussion grew ugly; Keith-Smith was moved to sue when a college lecturer with whom he was debating began calling him names, including "lard brain," "Nazi," "racist bigot," and "nonce," a British slang term that translates roughly to child sex offender.[155] Finding the speech actionable as libel, a high court judge awarded ten thousand pounds in damages as well as attorney's fees, deeming the Internet chat room to be a forum indistinguishable from traditional forums for publication.[156] The court also required Yahoo to unveil Keith-Smith's defamer in order to bring suit, dispensing with the pseudonym that enabled her to vent anonymously on the chat board.[157] Despite the fact that the plaintiff was a public figure, that his character and qualifications for office were of public concern, and that the defamation occurred on a site designed to foster venting, the high court held that the statements were nonetheless actionable because they caused damage to the plaintiff's reputation. Therefore, the defendant could not hide behind the shield of Internet anonymity but had to come forward to be sued. The *Keith-Smith* case is a good example to illustrate how the substantive law of each respective country is developing to protect its principles and values against the pragmatic changes in operation posed by technological advancement. Clearly, the United Kingdom is willing to draw a line much more definitive than the United States.

Undoubtedly, the Internet has vastly expanded the media and the capacity of any individual to widely publish protected or unprotected speech. The threshold issue is whether the law should protect the anonymity of users. New programs designed to find lawbreakers, hackers, and pedophiles can also be used to find the anonymous blogger in some cases. Despite this advance in technology, both good guys and bad guys find ways to remain anonymous. They go to Internet cafés or libraries and use anonymous sites. If they are sophisticated, they route e-mails and communications through proxy servers, rendering themselves difficult to find. The challenge to the law is to figure out how to deal with offensive and slanderous communications in the age of mass communication while still protecting those who should remain anonymous.

Gatekeepers

Before the Internet, individuals had limited options to communicate their opinions. They could tell everyone they knew in their community, write a letter to the editor of the local newspaper, or send out a letter to everyone in the town. All these options are limited in scope or limited by the intervention of others. In the modern world, communicating information happens with little or no reflection and is instantly available to the entire world with one click of a button. There is no obstacle standing in the way of free communication.

Prior to the invention of the printing press, the average person was limited to oral communication and isolated written works.[158] These forms of communication were very limited in that oral communication was constrained by the size of community and the level of interest in the gossip, and written works were very time consuming and costly to mass produce. The printing press, however, allowed the private market to quickly create books, newspapers, flyers, pamphlets, and other documents and distribute them to a wider audience.[159] But this new technology was not available to average persons, who were unlikely to have enough money to buy or operate their own printing press. Additionally, market forces were a barrier to entry, even for those who could afford to use the printing press, because few communities could support more than one newspaper. Another limiting factor of the printing press was that some governments required licenses to operate a press and imposed censors who had to approve the content of the paper prior to publication. Therefore, in order to publish their ideas, average individuals were faced with high printing and distribution costs. The larger the audience, the larger the distribution costs. In sum, even though the printing press revolutionized communication, only government officials, newspapers, universities, and the wealthy—who were capable of owning and controlling the presses—benefited from the new technology. Market forces and economic realities were still an impediment between the communicator and his audience. Those who did not have access to the new printing press could try to publish their ideas in the newspaper. However, this ability was limited by the gatekeeper, the editor of the newspaper.

With the advent of radio and television, the number of people who could receive information greatly increased, yet private gatekeepers retained control of the medium. These new forms of technology had limited value to average persons who could passively receive the new media but could not easily generate or transmit their own content.[160] Access to television and radio was limited by the number of airwaves available, the requirement of broadcast licenses, and the expense of acquiring and operating radio and television stations. Those who had the means and the license became the gatekeepers of this new technology by deciding what to broadcast and what not to transmit.

During most of the twentieth century, the average person had few affordable or effective means of mass communication.[161] One could give a speech or compose an idea using a typewriter, then photocopy that document and mail it to the intended audience. However, the ability to reach others was limited by practical and technical considerations such as distribution costs and logistical difficulties. The Internet changed all of that because for the first time the traditional gatekeepers played a less prominent role in information dissemination.[162] In the 1970s the personal computer was created. The personal computer enabled everyone to have access to the new technology and allowed individuals to quickly and easily produce high-quality printed content at home using their own equipment.

Historically, individuals who created a printed work would have to distribute that work themselves by paying postage costs, or try to disseminate their ideas through existing newspapers, radio, or television. However, the Internet allows the average person to distribute information directly to the reader with no added cost. Individuals could disseminate their ideas all over the world and could do so instantaneously. Additionally, the access barrier was low—involving only the relatively small cost of obtaining a personal computer and an Internet connection—which allowed a wider audience to use the medium. Compared to the printing press, television, and radio, the Internet and the personal computer allowed for greater access and the potential for a greater audience without the financial or editorial impediments of the more traditional media. Although a victory for free speech advocates, it is also a potential tool for defamatory and intrusive publications.

In addition to the lack of impediment in the form of logistical and economic barriers, the Internet lacks an editorial barrier, which was a defining factor of the press when the First Amendment was drafted. At the time the First Amendment was ratified, the press was understood to be an institutional speaker, a crucial player in a democratic society.[163] "The institutional quality of the press reflects, in part, the typical process of judgment that accompanies the press's speech, which is governed by the ethic of disseminating material deemed important for a public readership and selected by a process of reason and audience-oriented (and thus not strictly personal) judgment."[164] Editorial judgment is the "independent choice of information and opinion of current value, directed to public need, and borne of non-self-interested purposes."[165] On the Internet, there is no requirement of independent editorial judgment. No gatekeeper stands between the scorned lover and the entire global community.

Russell L. Weaver has pointed out that the Internet is a new type of media, different from the traditional press, because it is less controlled by traditional gatekeepers.[166] These gatekeepers have traditionally limited the ability of the average person to use new technologies to advance their ideas or political agendas by acting as an impediment between the speaker and the audience. Without the economic, logistical, or editorial barrier, the free flow of information on the Internet can occur without reflection or independent judgment. Free speech advocates would argue that more speech is good, while others would argue that without gatekeepers, the Internet's potential for abuse is vast. Both sides are correct.

The WikiLeaks controversy illustrates how information can be spread through the new media, not just in lieu of gatekeepers but also in defiance of them. On July 25, 2010, more than seventy-five thousand classified military documents were posted on the WikiLeaks website; four months later, more than a quarter-million confidential diplomatic cables were published. While leading gatekeepers eventually published these confidential diplomatic cables, the controversy shed light on the rival forces that will dominate the future of media: traditional media, governments, and anti-gatekeeper organizations like WikiLeaks.

The differences between the Internet and more traditional media have direct legal implications on distribution and publication of information. Traditional legal theories about community and anonymity do not reflect new realities of the Internet and global communications. Because Internet publication is not confined to one community or jurisdiction, the issue of what law applies to privacy intrusions by new media produces complex, multicultural, and multijurisdictional disputes. The natural progression of these events indicates that more communications will be crossing borders. Anonymity, while still an important right for the watchdog role of the press, has taken on new meaning with the unlimited number of people who communicate via the new media—including those who are irresponsible or vicious. Further, as global distribution and anonymity expand the risks of privacy intrusions, the traditional gatekeepers and editors who tempered the media with professional judgment are disappearing from the scene or losing their importance.

6

Is
Everyone
an
iReporter?

Clearly, new technology increases access to information and vastly expands the ability to publish it. Anyone with a camera and a computer can be an iReporter. The traditional images of the lonely pamphleteer and the reporter with his pad and pencil are obsolete. So too may be the concept of editors and limitations on publication—at least for the vast number of individual bloggers and other web speakers. The new media are different. Erik Schonfeld, a blogger and former editor of a news magazine, describes the new-media philosophy of today as "You post now and ask questions later."[1] That approach has obvious dangers when speed becomes more important than accuracy.

The new media have provided unique insights, a wide range of views, and valuable first-person accounts of ongoing events. But at the same time, the vast increase in new media outlets, such as blogging, has also increased irresponsible, defamatory, and intrusive publications.

This chapter discusses these implications in five parts. First, it examines how the free press principles apply in the age of new media; second, it explores how the law distinguishes between the press and the public in free speech issues; third, the chapter discusses how courts have defined the press; fourth, it considers whether and how shield laws, which protect journalists from disclosing information they would otherwise have to reveal, protect Internet journalists; and fifth, the chapter concludes with a discussion of criteria one might use to distinguish reporters from the public in an era with an increasingly nebulous dividing line.

Free Press Principles for the New Media

First Amendment jurisprudence in the United States developed over centuries before the dramatic evolution of new media in the last twenty years. While it is true that as a result of these recent changes, today's marketplace of ideas is flooded with inaccuracies, bias, and misleading information, it is also true that the same changes have enabled the publication of truths that previously would likely have gone undiscovered.

Sometimes the anonymous blogger is the best, fastest, or perhaps only source of information—the only witness to a newsworthy event, for instance.[2] News from a disaster site or political uprising may be available only from individuals who are present on site. Surely this information adds value to the marketplace of information, but only as long as that information is accurate. However, we know from experience that on-site reporting that is not subject to scrutiny might be completely deceptive and inaccurate. As the publisher of *Harper's Monthly* ironically gibed, "Who needs fact-checkers when we have crowdsourcing to correct the record?"[3]

The larger number of news sources adds another dimension of complexity to the discussion. The emergence of new technology creates new news sources. Before the Internet, anonymous reporters could distribute information only by physical means—distributing self-printed reports or posting information in public places. One could send an anonymous letter to the editor of a newspaper, but the newspaper, as gatekeeper, could decline to print it. Now, anyone can use the Internet to instantly distribute information to a worldwide audience of millions. If a goal of the First Amendment is to achieve "the widest possible dissemination of information from diverse and antagonistic sources,"[4] then the new world's multiple strident, competing, and misleading voices seem to meet that goal. But to some, this cacophony looks more like the Tower of Babel than the Roman Forum. The easy distribution of information facilitates the spread of facts, lies, and defamation at the same time. The spread of information is now instantaneous, ubiquitous, and persistent. The "market" is flooded with half-baked ideas, knee-jerk reactions, gossip, and inaccuracies with no real limits. Can this be the marketplace that advocates and framers of free speech envisioned?

Does the new reality of global information chaos mean that we should think about free speech rights differently? The new media, by virtue of its propensity for collection and redistribution, often puts a global spotlight on traditional displays of free speech. In other words, a communication that would have reached a few hundred people is now seen by millions. This change has had unanticipated implications in the private sphere that the judicial system is now struggling to address.

In *Snyder v. Phelps*,[5] the father of a marine killed in Iraq sued the Westboro Baptist Church and its founder under several tort law claims including intentional infliction of emotional distress after the founder and church members picketed his son's funeral. The picketers, situated at a distance from the funeral, displayed signs reading, "God Hates the USA/Thank God for 9/11," "Thank God for Dead Soldiers," "God Hates Fags," and "You're Going to Hell," among other messages, reflecting the church's view that God is killing U.S. soldiers as punishment for Americans' tolerance of sin.[6] The Court declined to impose liability for intentional infliction of emotional distress under these circumstances because the protesters were physically situated on a public sidewalk and were engaged in speech on a public issue—regardless of the fact that some of their expressions of the issue were arguably "outrageous."[7]

At oral argument, Justice Breyer, who concurred in the opinion, suggested that the new media might require a new First Amendment precedent with respect to intentional infliction of emotional distress.[8] Justice Breyer suggested that these messages might exceed free speech protection when communicated over media with intent to harm. It is clear that merely holding signs in protest would not reach that level of intent to harm. This case is just one of many cases that will help to define the parameters of the First Amendment in the new information age. As Justice Breyer has remarked, "[Justice] Holmes said [the First Amendment] doesn't mean you can shout 'fire' in a crowded theater. . . . Why? Because people will be trampled to death. And what is the crowded theater today? What is being trampled to death? It will be answered over time in a series of cases which force people to think carefully."[9]

Perhaps the new and greater potential harm by new media requires evaluating what the equivalent of shouting fire in a crowded theater might be on the Internet.

One example in which the judicial system has treated the new media differently occurred when application of First Amendment principles protected a blogger from the consequences of publishing comments that would have been defamatory speech in a mainstream newspaper. This case, *Krinsky*, was discussed in chapter 5 in the context of the difficult issues raised by Internet anonymity. It is relevant here because the new media was held to a lower standard than the traditional press. The free-expression principle at issue is that slander does not occur if the statements are made in a satirical way that is clearly not intended to convey a true statement.[10]

In *Krinsky*, the court determined that a message board posting of otherwise defamatory statements about a company CEO was protected because the statements were made in a forum where hyperbole was expected. The rationale was that the message board was not viewed as a source of truth but rather exaggeration. Under this reasoning, a blog is not liable for harm that might be caused to readers who do not understand its statements as hyperbole or who may read the statement once it is republished and taken out of context. This reasoning is not embraced by all courts. In the popularly named case Blonde v. Blogger (see chapter 5), a New York trial court focused on the slanderous content of the statement, rather than the medium used, and arrived at a different result.

In the case of *Obsidian Finance Group, LLC v. Cox*, a federal appeals court decided two issues of first impression regarding defamation claims brought against noninstitutional media defendants, that is, bloggers.[11] At trial, a jury found and awarded presumed and punitive damages against the defendant blogger Cox for defamatory statements she made in an online blog. The trial court did not require the plaintiffs to prove fault or actual damages because the defendant "failed to produce evidence suggestive of her status as a journalist."[12] Relying on other nondefamation cases in which the Supreme Court had held that there was no distinction between the First Amendment rights of the institutional media compared to a private person, the appeals court held that the defendant blogger was entitled to the same protections against a defamation claim as an institutional media defendant, meaning that the plaintiff would have to prove fault and actual damages in order to recover. The court also affirmed the trial court's ruling regarding other defamation claims that were dismissed prior to trial because they were opinion and hyperbole and could not reasonably be understood as assertions of fact.

The *Obsidian* case demonstrates a court's attempt to fold the new media into the traditional press for purposes of the First Amendment analysis used in defamation claims. But the new media is also more likely than the traditional press to benefit from its form, which is more commonly associated with hyperbole and opinion, and from the protection afforded by the anonymity of the Internet. The court specifically held that Cox's strident and nonprofessional approach made her blog less likely to be considered factual and therefore actually accorded her more protection.

Free speech principles will continue to be tested by the ever-changing realities of the new media. At some point, courts may have to reassess whether such claims against the new media should be analyzed under the same old legal standard.

Free Expression Privileges: The Press versus the People

In many instances, the law treats members of the press no differently than ordinary citizens. For instance, a journalist who violates the law will receive the same treatment as anyone who violates the law. Common sense tells us that carrying a press card does not entitle the holder to break and enter a private home, for instance. The Rupert Murdoch wiretapping scandal provides a relevant example. In July 2011, Murdoch came under fire for a phone-hacking scandal involving the tabloid *News of the World*, a subsidiary of his company News of the World. *News of the World* journalists allegedly hacked into the cell phone of a thirteen-year-old murder victim, deleting voicemail messages in order to make room for new messages. The journalists' actions "confused and agonized" the victim's family and the police. Since then, Scotland Yard's investigation of phone hacking by *News of the World* journalists has led to at least twelve arrests.[13] All of these intrusions are punishable. The wrongful acts are not in the realm of distributing information but in *gathering* it.

WikiLeaks' August 2011 disclosure of uncensored U.S. diplomatic cables provides another example.[14] If WikiLeaks breaks the law by disclosing national security issues, the law will treat the company the same as any person or entity who commits the criminal act of revealing national security information. The issue in WikiLeaks is different from the *News of the World* case. The hacking case involves a crime in obtaining information. WikiLeaks involves the rare case where distributing information is illegal. The similarity in each case is that the media will be treated the same as a citizen for violating the law.

In gaining access to information, the press and the public have certain protected rights. Beyond the disclosure of information, this equal treatment extends to access to information as well. Members of the press have a limited First Amendment right of reasonable access to news concerning the operations and activities of government.[15] Journalists are likewise entitled to facts relating to the public's interest.[16] As a general rule, public-records laws treat the media and the public equally. Under narrow circumstances in a case decided in Florida, the court gave selected journalists special access to sensitive photos used in a trial concerning the murder of eleven-year-old Carlie Brucia.[17] Carlie's family had requested that the photos be sealed against public disclosure. Four news organizations requested that their reporters have access to the photos but not the right to reproduce the photos. As a compromise the court accepted this option. Selected members of the press organizations seeking access were granted it. The fact that the press organizations were actual parties to the case was likely part of the reason they were granted access; they had already been identified as specifically interested in the case. However, the decision was also protective of the family's privacy because a public release would surely have resulted in Internet disclosures and wide public dissemination. The ruling nonetheless raises questions about interpretation of public access. What if a member of the public had sued for access as well?

While the press does not ordinarily enjoy greater access to information than the public, members of the press may receive special access preferences in certain circumstances. The press may have greater access to prisons than ordinary citizens, increased freedom to travel to foreign countries, and increased access to emergency and disaster scenes.[18] Members of the press may receive government-issued press credentials to report on proceedings of Congress, the White House, the Supreme Court, and state-level proceedings. One might characterize these special preferences afforded to the press as access to a physical space, rather than access to information. But the access to that space allows the gathering of information not available to someone else. Scott Gant has noted that while such preferences may run afoul of the Constitution's equal protection guarantee, courts have found no equal protection violation in the few cases addressing the issue.[19] Selective press preferences are increasingly problematic in the era of new media, in which our definition of the press continues to expand. As Gant asserts, "It is far from clear . . . that the government may permissibly extend preferences to only those employed by certain news organizations or engaging in journalism for financial gain, while withholding those same benefits to those undertaking precisely the same activities on their own or without the objective of monetary enrichment."[20]

Just as the press does not enjoy greater access to information than the public, the press also does not seem to enjoy any unique or greater protection to publish information.[21] There are defined limits on each, such as defamatory speech and certain inflammatory or harmful speech. These protections are more limited in direct proportion to the degree to which the subject matter at hand is deemed to be a private matter rather than a matter of public concern. Because the act of publication was historically more difficult without modern technological means, matters of private concern were historically more likely to stay private. Now, what were once private matters have become mundane items that nonetheless reach a wide audience by their routine publication on Facebook and Twitter, thus exacerbating the problem of defining what is news. At some point, the distinction between matters of private versus public concern may prove unworkable. Courts will need to adopt a new framework in order to preserve defamation as a remedy for intrusions based on false publication.

Contrary to the law established in more recent cases, there is some support for the idea that the framers intended a special privilege for the press. The Speech clause reads: "Congress shall make no law . . . abridging the freedom of speech or of the press."[22] Written in the disjunctive, the decree seems to promise two rights—freedom of speech for the people *and* freedom of the press. Surely, the framers would not repeat themselves.[23] James Madison's initial draft of the First Amendment sheds some light on intent: "The people shall not be deprived or abridged of their right to speak, to write, or to publish their sentiments; and the freedom of the press, as one of the great bulwarks of liberty, shall be inviolable."[24] The original use of a semicolon indicates a distinction between the general right of the public to express themselves and the separate right of the press, charged with a duty to uphold democracy. It is particularly relevant to the instant discussion that Madison ensured the right of the people, as well as the press, to publish. He could not have imagined how easy it would become for the people to publish and for the "press" to become almost indefinable.

Ignoring the textualist argument, the Supreme Court in *First National Bank of Boston v. Bellotti* silenced any suggestion that the Speech clause afforded the press rights that were different from the rights granted to all citizens.[25] In that case, the Court dismissed the notion of a separate right for the press and found that "the First Amendment does not 'belong' to any definable category of persons or entities: it belongs to all who exercise its freedoms."[26]

More recently, the Court in *Citizens United v. Federal Election Commission*[27] reaffirmed the notion that the right of the press to speak is no different from that of other individuals. The Court deemed unconstitutional a federal statute that barred independent corporate expenditures for electioneering communications because it violated the First Amendment in part by exempting corporations that were considered the "press" from the statute.[28] The Court found that it was a violation of the Constitution to treat corporations differently based upon the identity of the speaker, even if the speaker was the press.[29] Therefore, presently the only distinctions between the rights of the press and the rights of all citizens are the right of certain press to gain access to selected spaces, and second, the right of the press to keep their sources confidential. The shield laws that protect journalists' confidential sources are important because enforcing such laws requires a definition of "journalist." Media have long resisted definition, licensing, or any means of narrowing or restricting the definition of "press." Of course, other countries license, certify, or define the press, but such definitions make American media uneasy. Who then may call herself a member of the press, entitled to the journalist's privilege?

Defining the Press in the United States: The Traditional Test

Defining the press in the United States has come as part of determining entitlement to press privilege. Press privilege is an important element of the press-privacy conflict because defamatory or intrusive information may have been obtained by a media source. The identity of that source is relevant to vindicating privacy interests.

In *Branzburg v. Hayes*,[30] the U.S. Supreme Court recognized that journalists have a qualified privilege under the First Amendment that protects them from compelled disclosure of confidential material and sources.[31] The Court rejected an absolute privilege but held that the privilege will generally exist except when a journalist is called to testify before a grand jury about evidence of criminal conduct.[32] Since this 1972 ruling, the definition of journalist is getting fuzzier.

Fifteen years later, in the case of *von Bulow v. von Bulow*,[33] the Second Circuit Court of Appeals designed a test to determine who would be entitled to the privilege. The test, later adopted by the Ninth Circuit, states that membership in the protected class "must be determined by the person's *intent at the inception* of the information-gathering process [emphasis added]."[34] Under this test, "an individual may successfully assert the journalist's privilege if he is involved in activities traditionally associated with the gathering and dissemination of news, *even though he may not ordinarily be a member of the institutionalized press* [emphasis added]."[35] The *von Bulow* test can be used for both traditional and nontraditional media because it focuses on the timing of and existence of the author's *intent* while newsgathering and not the dissemination *method*.[36] This standard is imprecise at best.

The Third Circuit purportedly adopted the *von Bulow* test in *In re Madden*.[37] The World Wrestling Federation (WWF) alleged that the World Championship Wrestling (WCW)'s 1-900 telephone hotline purposely disseminated false information.[38] The WWF attempted to discover WCW's source of the information by deposition; however, Madden (who gave the wrestling reports) invoked the journalist's privilege.[39] The court concluded that professional wrestling did not qualify as news but was instead creative fiction, and because Madden received the information from his executives, he did not act as a journalist.[40] In effect, the court drew a line between Madden's publication of statements from inside sources regarding the upcoming wrestling drama and true investigative reporting, stating, "As we see it, the privilege is only available to those persons whose purposes are those traditionally inherent to the press," further stating that what Madden disseminated was "hype, not news."[41]

This is an example of how the *von Bulow* test can be interpreted, particularly in regard to nontraditional journalists—although it is interesting to note that the district court below also applied *von Bulow* and reached a different result, determining that Madden did have an investigative intent.[42] The court in *von Bulow* emphasized that "the primary relationship between the one seeking to invoke the privilege and his sources must have as its basis the intent to disseminate the information to the public garnered from that relationship."[43] The test does not demand an inquiry on the method of newsgathering but asks, rather, whether the author intended to disseminate news.[44] The court analyzed Madden's *method* of newsgathering because the court seemed to disapprove of Madden's speaking to his executives. It also concluded that he intended to disseminate entertainment, not news.[45]

Furthermore, the court focused on the content of Madden's reports and found that the reports were not news. The reports dealt with the business dealings of the sport. It is at least questionable whether reporting on business dealings is "creative fiction."[46] Declining to bestow upon Madden the status of journalist is disturbing to some. It is particularly disturbing because the court considered the nature of the content produced by Madden.

The general trend of U.S. courts has been to expand the class of persons who are considered to be the press.[47] The Supreme Court stated in *Lovell v. City of Griffin*, "The liberty of the press is not confined to newspapers and periodicals. . . . The press in its historic connotation comprehends every sort of publication which affords a vehicle of information and opinion."[48] This 1938 definition could not contemplate the panoply of what now might be a "vehicle for information and opinion." There are three common elements in the courts' different analyses of the journalist's privilege:[49]

> First, the courts seem to require that the class in question [the journalist claimant] serves a public interest. Second, they balance the law's traditionally narrow view of privileges and the need to expand the protected class in order to maintain consistency in applying the journalist's privilege. Finally, the courts' determinations are often driven by the unique facts of each case.[50]

Even though the courts have generally expanded the definition of press, they have expressed reservations over permitting Internet journalists these privileges.[51] In a case out of New Jersey, the court declined to extend the statutory privilege to a journalist who posted comments to an online message board regarding information she received in her investigation into the online adult entertainment industry, determining that Internet message boards were too dissimilar from traditional journalism to be encompassed by the legislative intent behind the state's statute.[52] The focus was on the method and context of the dissemination: an online message board to which anyone could post. The courts' concerns about broadening the privilege have developed as a result of a low barrier to entry into the profession.[53] "It is possible for any number of people to transmit information, much of it unfiltered and possibly dangerous."[54] In fact, control and oversight of journalism as a profession is very limited or nonexistent in the United States. While there is a journalism code of ethics, the profession has no procedure to remove a journalist's professional credentials. There is no licensing analogous to the legal or accounting professions. Also, there is no degree requirement or entry exam. Nonetheless, if the intent test is effective, "Internet journalists of all kinds can likely depend on coverage wherever the privilege is recognized, so long as they can show that they acquired the sought-after information with the intention of publicizing it."[55]

The definitions of journalists and media continue to evolve rapidly. The blurring of entertainment and news has increased with the advent of the Internet and the growing presence of bloggers. In addition, the increasingly competitive nature of the media marketplace has contributed to the media delivering news and information together in what has been termed Infotainment.[56] Matt Drudge, the online blogger of the Drudge Report, would not typically be considered a traditional journalist. The Drudge Report, which does not create original content but instead aggregates content, has been considered a mix of news and tabloid journalism. Still, the court recognized that Matt Drudge could invoke a journalist privilege.[57] This approach follows the *von Bulow* test, but it would not follow the approach taken in the *In re Madden* decision or the decision of the New Jersey court in *Too Much Media, LLC v. Hale*. Following that rationale, "a court would grant Matt Drudge's privilege claim if he worked for the *New York Times*. However, because he reports on the Internet, *In re Madden* would permit discrimination against Drudge's reporting style."[58]

Based on these available tests, how will bloggers or other new-media-based speakers and publishers be characterized for purposes of privilege? Internet bloggers are not only more common than ever before, they are also becoming part of mainstream media. They are employees of the *Washington Post* and the *New York Times*. They are members of the White House press corps. They have won major awards for excellence in journalism.[59] CNN has opened the door for anyone to report on the news and become a special iReporter. During President Obama's inauguration, CNN and Microsoft encouraged witnesses to take pictures and post the stories online.[60] Following *von Bulow*, the iReporters should be considered part of the press because at the inception of the newsgathering process they *had the intent to disseminate information to the public*. Conversely, *In re Madden* and the New Jersey case *Too Much Media, LLC v. Hale* suggest that iReporters would not be considered part of the press for purposes of journalists' privilege because they are individuals who post on an Internet site and disseminate information from their cell phones. The law is not settled on the entitlement to journalistic privilege for bloggers. Courts will determine the issue where it is not specifically delineated by statute, and the law will continue to evolve with the reality of the new media.

Defining the press is central to determining press privilege. However, with regard to publishing information, the critical question is not "Who?" but "What?" That is, what is the nature of the content involved rather than who created or disseminated the information. If the content is newsworthy, should the reporter receive less protection because he recorded or observed something and *then* decided to disseminate it? For example, someone took images of a natural disaster or an accident and later decided to distribute those images. Since there is no discernible legal difference between the press and individuals regarding free expression, identity would not matter in publication. However, based on existing tests, identity and intent might matter in defining press privilege—as would the content and the mode of publication.

The issue of "Who is the press?" has several dimensions.[61] A person designated as the press may qualify for protection under shield laws. The liability of that individual for the information he or she publishes or distributes is a separate issue. At least in the United States, the broad interpretation of the First Amendment's right to free speech will likely protect an Internet reporter or blogger if the information falls in the broad definition of newsworthy. The expansive definition of newsworthiness should protect bloggers from liability, but the issue of extending press privilege is also important to privacy interests because privilege limits access to discovering press sources in the course of litigation regarding privacy intrusions. If privilege extends to all bloggers, it will be harder to hold them accountable, as well as their sources of defamatory and inaccurate information.

Shield Laws and New Media

State shield laws expand the federal interpretations of the privilege that protects journalists from disclosing information they would otherwise have to reveal. Thirty-two states and the District of Columbia provide such laws.[62] State shield laws are more protective of the press than the First Amendment interpretations, and most include language that leaves open the question of whether bloggers are covered.[63] As of this writing, some states require an affiliation with traditional media and some do not.[64]

Even when affiliation with traditional media is required pursuant to a state shield law, a state court may find that an Internet journalist falls within the statute's protection. For example, California has a shield law requiring affiliation with a traditional form of media. However, an appellate court found that an online author's source of information for the name of a new piece of technology fell within its shield statute because the author's website qualified as a "magazine" and "other periodical publication."[65] This result would have likely followed under the federal *von Bulow* test, since the author had intended to disseminate information. Although both the federal and California tests would have led to the same result in this case, the California test seems to focus on the dissemination method rather than the author's intent, as did the New Jersey court in *Too Much Media, LLC v. Hale.*

There is currently no federal shield law for journalists beyond the qualified privilege accorded under federal case law. Congress proposed such a law in 2009 entitled the Free Flow of Information Act of 2009. The Senate's version stated that "a Federal entity may not compel a covered person to provide testimony, or produce any document, relating to protected information."[66] A covered person was defined as "a person who is engaged in journalism."[67] Journalism was defined as meaning "the regular gathering, preparing, collecting, photographing, recording, writing, editing, reporting, or publishing of news or information that concerns local, national, or international events or other matters of public interest for dissemination to the public."[68] The House version of the bill had the similar purpose of protecting "covered persons" from compelled disclosure.[69] In defining a covered person, it included the additional requirement that the dissemination to the public be "for a substantial portion of the person's livelihood or for substantial financial gain."[70]

The additional language contained in the House version of the bill was more restrictive than the Senate version. For example, it is possible that all Internet bloggers would have been covered under the Senate's version, as long as they were engaged in the regular activities associated with journalists and they blogged about matters of public interest. The House version of the bill would seemingly have protected only a category of bloggers—those whose livelihood depended on blogging on the Internet or who received substantial financial gain from blogging. The inability of Congress to pass the federal shield statute is indicative of the trouble in defining a reporter as well as concerns over the ramifications of extending these protections to too broad a category of speakers.

Defining Journalists in the New World

Is it possible to define a journalist in the context of new media and the new world? As Justice Byron White noted nearly forty years ago in *Branzburg v. Hayes*, defining what a journalist is presents "practical and conceptual difficulties of a high order."[71] The rapid development of technology has made this task all the more convoluted. Today, various criteria might be taken into account in defining a reporter. For example, membership in professional journalism associations, education, and affiliation with a traditional news outlet might set professional journalists apart from amateurs. However, memberships are never required, education is not necessary, and the advancement in technology may one day make traditional media obsolete. Employment, as suggested by the House of Representatives and many state shield laws, is a significant criterion. But this too would draw razor-thin distinctions between unpaid bloggers and those with paid advertisers, and freelance writers and those on a payroll.

Erik Ugland has urged courts to adopt a functional test, such as the test suggested by the Senate, that would be based on newsgathering, rather than characteristics, credentials, or professional affiliations. That is, a journalist would be anyone serving a press function, "seeking out news of public interest for the purpose of disseminating it to an audience."[72] Ugland goes on to define those serving a press function as those (1) engaged in the process of gathering information of public significance, (2) for the purpose of communicating it to an audience, (3) with the intent at the start of the newsgathering process to distribute the information to others, and (4) whose compliance with the government's demand would pose a legitimate risk of impairing their *future* expressive or newsgathering activity.[73] The functional test could be subject to a very broad interpretation. What if an individual blogger obtained a deliberately inaccurate tip that a city commissioner took a bribe? What if that blogger was intent on harming the commissioner involved and made no effort to verify the bribery charge? Is the blogger's source protected by shield laws? Or should there be a similar requirement for discovering the identity of an anonymous source under the CDA, namely, that the plaintiff make out a prima facie case for defamation before the privilege is removed?

The concept of control over the content published is another viable option in defining the press. In *Kaufman v. Islamic Society of Arlington, Texas*, the Texas Court of Appeals reasoned that a writer for an online magazine was not a "member of the electronic or print media" because the writer did not own or publish the magazine, nor did he have editorial control over his articles.[74] He was just a writer. Under this control test, any blogger without a gatekeeper is not a journalist. This is an interesting approach because it would allow for some form of accountability. Following *Kaufman*, our hypothetical blogger intent on harming the city commissioner would not be protected by shield laws. By using the lack of gatekeepers as a threshold test, we can then determine whether or not reporters deserve the journalistic privilege and whether they can be held accountable for potentially harmful statements.

A third option is licensing. Journalists, unlike other professionals such as lawyers and doctors, are not currently required to submit to regulation. The issue with journalist shield laws is defining who will receive protection based on status as a journalist. Licensing is a way to define the category, but it also raises the issue of restricting access.

However, many of the complications in defining a reporter might be remedied by a stringent admission process to the profession.[75] Requiring a passing score on a national ethics exam, membership dues, or a certain education or work history would set professionals apart from amateurs. And although this may sound like an extraordinary measure, it is certainly not a unique concept.

The press was regulated through licensing as early as the seventeenth century in England.[76] As an adverse reaction to this practice, the framers of the First Amendment intended to prohibit the practice of requiring a license to publish. Much has changed over the past two centuries. The concept of licensing and regulation has become routine in certain areas of the press, such as broadcasting. The primary dangers of a licensing test are that it could impair press liberties or violate the Equal Protection clause. The framers wanted to assure press freedom and avoid government control over communications. One important necessity for avoiding these dangers is to ensure that the licensing party—whether professional organization, government agency, or private group—consciously disregard the content of an applicant's work in deciding whether to issue a license. Protecting content is the touchstone of constitutional free expression, and licensing should not be a means of controlling free expression.

Comparing these three options—the functional test, the control test, and the licensing test—requires us to return to the rationale for distinguishing the press from the public. Preserving the journalist's privilege to keep sources confidential is essential for ensuring First Amendment freedoms. But if everyone is a journalist, and everyone can invoke the privilege, the potential for intrusions on a person's fundamental right to privacy is significant. The modern ability to intrude and the incentive to intrude are too great to extend press privilege to everyone. Context is also an important variable. Whereas the functional and control tests may help courts decide whether a defendant can be held liable for harmful statements, the licensing test may help a government agency decide which reporters should receive access to certain information. Clearly, casting too wide a net in defining "journalist" will increase the potential for privacy intrusions. Selecting the appropriate test will require balancing press liberties with privacy rights.

There is no question that defining journalists today is difficult. Ultimately, the licensing option is not viable in the United States. Tradition, constitutional barriers, and basic practicalities are too high a bar. While defining a journalist for purposes of press privilege is a worthy goal, and important for limiting an overbreadth of the claim of privilege, the definition will have no effect on the citizen's right to publish.

7

New
Media,
Old
Law?

The legal conflicts between media and privacy are more complicated every day. Technology enabling intrusion has evolved rapidly but the law to deal with intrusion generally has not.

While some jurisdictions, such as the European Union, have aggressively sought to define the limits of privacy, others, such as the United States, have taken a more segmented and incremental approach. U.S. laws and policy target specific intrusions, as narrow as protecting video rental records, rather than sweeping grants of general privacy rights. The U.S. Supreme Court has haltingly entered the era of information-versus-privacy disputes and has been reluctant to draw any bright lines on the Internet, technology, and new media. Some of the justices have admitted to the Court's wariness in addressing privacy and technology issues.[1] Even though Justice Breyer has expressed concern about the impact of new media and the use of established legal principles,[2] press freedom still generally prevails in conflicts with privacy. But in a criminal case dealing with privacy in the search-and-seizure context, the justices made a great leap forward in recognizing that new technology may provide access to unprecedented amounts of intrusive information. In a unanimous decision the Court determined a warrantless search of a cell phone was unconstitutional.[3] The Court acknowledged that a warrantless viewing of the accumulation of highly personal information such as search history, phone calls, e-mails, and personal location data was a major invasion of privacy. While this decision does not bear on the media-privacy conflict directly, the landmark case demonstrates a major step forward in evaluating technology-related privacy issues.

Freedom of expression is still an overriding legal principle for democratic governments, and privacy is an important individual right. The harms of privacy intrusion are harder to quantify than limits on the freedom of the press. This chapter analyzes the law in the two most basic areas of media-privacy conflict: first, the gathering of information; and second, the publication and distribution of information. These two separate functions of the media each enable different kinds of intrusions into individual privacy.

Legal Perspectives on Gathering Information in the New World

The press is prohibited from trespassing, wiretapping, or otherwise obtaining information illegally. Neither the new media nor the old media are exempt from the rule of law.[4] If members of the media engage in robbery to get their story, they can go to jail. If they engage in the crime of video voyeurism, they are culpable. The press is not above the law. The tort remedy at issue in gathering information is usually intrusion upon seclusion, in contrast to the issue of wrongly *distributing* information.

The media, as well as the public, may acquire information lawfully from numerous public and private sources. Information may be obtained from public records or gathered from observing public space. In the United States, if the media obtain information contained in a public document or from a public space, then the media's actions are generally considered lawful and they are allowed to acquire and distribute the information with few exceptions. By comparison, some nations limit the disclosure of information acquired in public spaces if it is deemed intrusive or harmful to personal dignity.

Public versus Confidential Information

In addition to wrongly obtaining information, another legal issue is the unavailability of information that is held by the government. The issue with this type of information is access. Democratic governments hold the principle of governmental transparency in high esteem, making the central legal question in this debate: what are the proper justifications for withholding the public release of information? Determining whether a document is to be considered a public record may require analyzing whether the information, if disclosed, would be intrusive because of what it would reveal about a person or entity. This determination is exactly what certain exceptions to the public records laws attempt to address. If the document is too intrusive by virtue of its content, then courts may impose a limit to its disclosure.

One example is the attempt of certain news organizations and media representatives to gain access to the autopsy photos of NASCAR driver Dale Earnhardt, who died in a crash at the Daytona 500 in 2001.[5] As a result of his family's lawsuit, a court blocked access to the photos, and soon after, the Florida Legislature passed the Family Protection Act. The act required that persons seeking access to autopsy photos must show an appropriate reason for seeking access.[6] The media argued that the photos were public records. It was true that a few years earlier, pursuant to the Florida public-records law, the media were able to publish the autopsy photographs of another driver, Neil Bonnett. The Earnhardt facts, however, compelled the court and the legislature to change the public-records law by creating an exception that limited access to autopsy photos. In other words, because the legislature was offended by the pending disclosure of Earnhardt's autopsy photographs, it changed public policy to favor privacy over public disclosure. A similar line is drawn pursuant to federal law in the Freedom of Information Act. The act contains an exception to disclosure where production of the document "could reasonably be expected to constitute an unwarranted invasion of personal privacy."[7]

As a matter of practicality and public policy, the issue of preventing disclosure is very different from the issue of punishing publication of intrusive information. In the United States, exceptions to open government and the Freedom of Information Act preclude access of the public and the press to certain information. Hence, certain information is not considered public information. But if the information is made public—either inadvertently or even illegally—the very same information will almost always be freely publishable with impunity.[8] The Dale Earnhardt case illustrates this point. There was no real difference in the intrusion of publishing Mr. Bonnett's autopsy photos and the potential intrusion of publishing Mr. Earnhardt's. The only difference is that one photo was a public record and one photo never became a public record because of the change in the law.

Courts have also decided that some forms of a record can be made public while more intrusive forms will be exempted from release. These cases have involved releasing records that are captured in a less intrusive medium, such as the written transcript of a voice recording of astronauts during the Challenger crash;[9] Dale Earnhardt's written autopsy reports but not pictures;[10] and the written description but not the video of trainer Dawn Brancheau's death caused by a killer whale at SeaWorld.[11] In the Rolling murder case, Judge Stanley Morris used another approach to releasing sensitive information while limiting the impact of its disclosure. He limited the release of crime scene photos and autopsy photos by allowing viewing of the photos at a single controlled location and disallowing any copying or publication of the images.[12] These cases demonstrate a willingness of courts to be creative in limiting intrusive access to public records.

The law has usually treated the press the same as the public regarding access to information because the information itself is deemed either public or private. This means that generally, the same piece of information is not public to some groups and private to others.[13] All of the cases described above treat the press the same as the public. There is one outlier case that shows an effort to limit intrusive disclosure by treating the media and the general public in a disparate manner.

The Brucia case was a highly publicized child murder case in which an eleven-year-old girl was kidnapped near a car wash and brutally murdered. The prelude to her abduction was caught on camera at the car wash, the footage of which is still available on the Internet. The litigation, however, was not over the car wash video but occurred when the media sought access to a number of photographs of Carlie Brucia's tortured corpse. These photographs were introduced and admitted into evidence during her murder trial, an event that was open to the public in accordance with constitutional dictates.[14] After examining a number of exceptions to the general obligation under Florida law to disclose public records, the court concluded that the photographs could be made confidential only to a degree that would not unduly sacrifice their newsworthiness.[15] Setting aside the trial court's outright ban on disclosure, the appeals court held that the media, and only the media, were entitled to view and write about, but not publish, the actual photographs.[16] This case is an outlier because it treated the press differently than the public for purposes of viewing a document. However, the result is consistent with the purpose of preventing publication of the most intrusive information—in this case the photos.

The Danger of More and More Accessible Public Records

Beyond the issue of determining exemptions from public records is the trend toward the expansion of what records are considered public. At the same time, there are efforts and legal restrictions to protect private information that is held in public records, such as social security numbers and tax records held in government files.

Public records are more easily accessible and searchable than ever before, due primarily to advances in technology. Search engines can now assemble a profile in seconds that would have taken a reporter months of digging through old files to compile. This has been termed the "aggregation effect."[17] What was previously inaccessible or at least difficult to find is now at the fingertips of any Internet user, publisher, or blogger. In other words, anyone, including an inquisitive media person, may do a search of public records and find a thorough profile of almost any individual. They can find property records, arrest records, car ownership records, and utility usage records, just to name a few. This aggregation of information is a direct analogy to the mosaic effect that the D.C. Circuit Court found disturbing with the use of GPS. In that situation a GPS could provide a mosaic of a person's life by tracking their every movement in an automobile. Here, a researcher can track a person's life by the trail of public records he or she leaves. Information that used to reside in practical obscurity is now instantly available. Here again, progress and efficiency create a new issue.

Governmental transparency is a necessary tenet of democracy and has long been protected and promoted under the laws of the United States and other countries. The technological innovations of recent decades have changed the nature of public records. This circumstance has positive effects but also elevates the risk of intrusions based solely on the discovery of information. A blogger trying to determine the fitness of a candidate for public service might quickly uncover arrests and personal history that may be important in assessing that person's character. Some public records are necessarily intrusive and must be collected in order for the government to properly do its job. But the fact that the government makes a record of autopsy photos and crime scene photos of a horribly mutilated young woman does not mean those images should be available on the Internet for the world to see.[18]

One emerging area where public records are being put online is the court system. Court systems across the country have moved their entire docket systems online, now able to appreciate the convenience of online indexing and the compact nature of server space.[19] Most state court systems have moved all or at least part of their records online, although the degree to which entire documents are available electronically still varies.[20] However, potential problems arise with the ready availability of such information. Courts lose a measure of their control and protection, especially related to who may have access to the information. However, these protections can still exist. In a recent movement, states are working to change their online docket policies to favor systems where private information is not so readily available to the public.[21] In these states, even though a document may be public, and evidence of that document's existence can be located online—the case number, for example—the actual document itself must be obtained by contacting the custodian of records and putting in a request for a hard copy, subject to any rules governing redaction of sensitive or private information. These limitations are not universal and are not evenly applied in all jurisdictions.

As chair of the Florida Supreme Court's Task Force on Electronic

Records, I learned of the dangers and advantages of increasing online access to records. Advantages to keeping the records public do exist. Indeed, the availability of court records online has led to greater public oversight. In a Florida scandal, for instance, when a court failed to post records online, it was accused of keeping multiple secret records. The judiciary contested the accusation and attributed the error to a computer glitch.[22] However, one of the unposted records was the divorce record of a judge in the circuit, which, in turn, raised public suspicion surrounding the alleged glitch. The upshot of a scandal like this is that it proves that the public is paying attention and that online access has enabled the public to play its role in the oversight process.

The decisions of courts that determine which public records will be widely available are critical because they deal with the most sensitive and personal information concerning human conduct and personal tragedies. The courts deal daily with intimate details of a family's divorce, the details of a child's abuse by a relative, the painful details of a rape of a young woman, and the description of the ruined life of an accident victim. Consideration of these details by courts is critical to a fair justice system, but must they always be made available to public and media?

Privacy concerns still loom large, and the appropriate compromise between the public nature of court proceedings and the need to protect intimate details disclosed in these proceedings is yet to be firmly established. Protecting certain public records is a realistic option to protect the privacy of individuals. The Freedom of Information Act (FOIA) and all state public records laws have exceptions. The FOIA has an exception for an unwarranted invasion of privacy. In evaluating what constitutes an unwarranted invasion, U.S. courts have balanced privacy interests against the value of public disclosure. Because the FOIA applies prerelease, free press is not implicated, and the court is free to balance privacy interests. Once the information is public, the entire analysis changes; the issue becomes about public disclosure of private facts, which overwhelmingly loses to free press or free speech. Therefore, early-stage protection of private information is critical.

Public Conduct and Public Places

Separate and distinct from public records law is the rule that when conduct is actually committed in public, the actors do not have a claim for an invasion of privacy because they lack a reasonable expectation of privacy.[23] Because of this lack of a reasonable expectation of privacy, if the media disclose information about an individual's conduct committed in public, then generally they are not considered to be disclosing private facts, and there is no violation. Indeed, American courts have traditionally held that the press may publish stories about events that occur in public. An early example involved a couple that sued a magazine for publishing a photograph of them embracing in front of an ice cream stand.[24] The court dismissed the case because the couple "had voluntarily exposed themselves to public gaze in a pose open to the view of any persons who might then be at or near their place of business."[25] The court explained that "the photograph did not disclose anything which until then had been private, but rather only extended knowledge of the particular incident to a somewhat larger public than had actually witnessed it at the time of occurrence."[26] Can the publication of anything conducted in public ever be prohibited or limited?

In *Moreno v. Hanford Sentinel*, a case involving a teenager publishing her opinions about her hometown on MySpace, the court held that the publication was not private.[27] Anyone with a computer could read her article; thus, the court held that the teenager had no expectation of privacy regarding her published opinion. This case demonstrates that a disclosure on the Internet may be tantamount to disclosing that information in the public square. It also returns to the question of who may publish: should the opinions of a teenager contained in MySpace posts be evaluated differently than the news blog of an adult? The problem here is that regardless of the speaker, the disclosure was both public and voluntary.

The media have generally been free to disseminate information freely obtained from a public source to a larger audience because a person has no reasonable expectation of privacy and therefore no protectable interest in information available to or observable by the public.[28] U.S. courts generally do not recognize plaintiffs' claims for limited disclosure but hold instead that once information is disclosed, even if the disclosure is inadvertent, privacy is effectively waived.[29] This theory has been termed the "Public is public" approach.[30]

In the *Sipple* case, the press disclosed to a large audience information about Oliver Sipple that was previously known by only a few people. Because his homosexuality was a matter known to some members of the public, the court found there was no invasion of his privacy when the *San Francisco Chronicle* published a story about his sexuality.[31] Anita Allen examined this particularized tension between the LGBT (lesbian, gay, bi-, and transsexual) community and privacy interests in a *California Law Review* article published in 2010.[32] Selective self-disclosure of sexual orientation has been a necessary safeguard from the vitriol of society's most intolerant individuals. Allen argues that the courts' "expansive [and] optimistic assumptions" regarding the newsworthiness and publicity of individuals' sexual orientation should be tempered by the realities of this persisting intolerance.[33] Until such dangerous intolerance gives way to meaningful equality, LGBT individuals will continue to have a special privacy interest in their sexual orientation. This important realization has tangible consequences for remedies. As long as society remains intolerant generally, a disclosure of sexual orientation, if false, could be considered defamatory because of harm resulting from an intolerant society. Of course, defamation has to be an accusation of a falsity. If the statement about a person's sexuality is true, defamation is not a remedy. However, the disclosure could be considered a public disclosure of private facts. Even in a tolerant society, personal issues should be protected. Increased tolerance should not decrease the ability of an individual to control private facts. Thus, there is a continuing need for a viable remedy dealing with public disclosure of private facts.

Compare this result with cases in the European Union that focus on the *nature of the intrusion* and the wishes of the person, rather than where the information was obtained. The easiest comparison is another case involving a man at a gay pride parade in France. There, the court found that although information about the complainant's homosexuality was known, the disclosure of the information in a newspaper would be intrusive. The difference in the focus of the analysis is stark and determinative of the outcome of these types of disputes.

Trends in the United States continue to demonstrate that the interests of free speech in a public place are deemed to be of greater public importance than the right to privacy. In *McCullen v. Coakley*, a case that determined the state's ability to establish a buffer zone around abortion clinics in which protestors could not intrude, the Supreme Court held that the state statute unconstitutionally infringed on the First Amendment rights of the sidewalk counselors.[34] Focusing on the fact that the regulation prohibited speech on a public sidewalk, the Court reasoned that the State's legitimate interest in protecting the reproductive health and privacy rights of its citizens seeking access to clinics was not sufficiently important to justify such an infringement.

It is clear that the focus in the United States has been on protecting speech. However, the E.U. logic is definitely worth analyzing. Placing more value on the nature of the information than simply assessing its location is rational. In other words, an individual may have a right to prevent or constrain unlimited distribution of information even though it may have been viewed by some or may have occurred in public space.

Limits on Publication and Disclosure

There are several wrongs that may result from media publication of information,[35] including defamation and other torts associated with wrongful publication. Those include public disclosure of private facts, false light, and appropriation of personality. The emphasis of this section is on prohibiting the disclosure of information and the punishment of the disclosure of sensitive information. Those issues are treated very differently in different jurisdictions.

The issue of *limiting or prohibiting the distribution* of information is viewed much differently than *limiting access* to information. In the United States, once information is available to the press or in possession of the press, prohibiting publication is viewed as prior restraint or censorship. But there are a number of U.S. cases that have denied *access* to information. The courts prohibited access to certain information while allowing the distribution of less intrusive modes of the same event or information. Conceptually, this type of limitation is different from the European Union's punishing or prohibiting the publication of information *already in the possession of the media*. The tort at issue in the United States is public disclosure of private facts. The elements of this tort are different from the intrusion-upon-seclusion tort that is at issue when the intrusion is one of access to information. Here, the analysis asks whether information was newly disclosed and whether the disclosure itself revealed something private in nature. The most important issue, however, is the defense that media will always offer to any disclosure—that the disclosure was newsworthy.

In previous chapters of this book, I have discussed other global examples where the media has been prohibited from distributing or making available information that has already been "outed" to the public, such as the Yahoo case dealing with Diego Maradona and the superinjunction sought by Ryan Giggs. These cases demonstrate how the new world of communications and the Internet makes censorship harder and harder. Perhaps if the law were more effective at punishing such harmful disclosures, the incentive to commit these intrusions in the first place would be reduced. But effective remedies are needed on a global scale.

In regulating distribution of information, global philosophies differ as to whether personal privacy and dignity can justify limiting media publication. In the European Union, privacy and dignity are clear considerations when evaluating media intrusions. Princess Caroline of Monaco successfully fought to prevent the publication of unauthorized photographs taken of her engaging in private activities with her children; the European Court of Human Rights balanced the right to expression by media alongside her individual right to privacy, and her privacy rights triumphed.[36] One could hardly anticipate this result in an American court.

U.S. courts give substantial weight to the value of the First Amendment in cases involving public access to information, struggling to determine which test should be employed to determine newsworthiness and whether there can be liability. Courts consider numerous factors, including (1) whether the person is a public figure; (2) whether the method of accessing the information is lawful; (3) whether the action occurred in public; (4) whether the disclosure is intrusive; (5) whether the suit is brought prior to disclosure or after; (6) whether the medium of the publication is particularly intrusive; and (7) whether the information is relevant to the public.[37]

In California, for example, courts ask whether an intrusion into the private affairs of a person is justified by the "social value of the facts published." They also ask whether the person "voluntarily acceded to a position of notoriety." This approach is closer to the E.U. approach than other U.S. courts. The California test is best illustrated in *Diaz v. Oakland Tribune*.[38] The plaintiff, the student body president of a college, sued the *Oakland Tribune* for publishing information regarding her sex change from a man to a woman. She alleged that the newspaper invaded her right to privacy, and as a result, she suffered numerous harms, including the inability to return to school and the onset of insomnia and depression. On appeal, the court held that the plaintiff had the burden of proving that the article was not newsworthy. It concluded that the plaintiff was a limited public figure; therefore, the public only needed to know about her fitness to serve as the student body president. The court remanded the case with instructions to have a jury determine whether disclosure about her sex change was socially valuable.[39] Notably, this case was decided thirty years ago, when social mores about the private nature of issues regarding gender and sexual orientation were more conservative across the board.

The usual test in the United States is far more generous in defining newsworthiness. A newsworthy story will virtually always fall under the First Amendment's protection of free speech, even if the story is private and offensive.[40] In the Fifth Circuit, for example, matters of legitimate public interest (that is, newsworthy matters) include "information concerning interesting phases of human activity and embrace all issues about which information is needed or appropriate so that individuals may cope with the exigencies of their period."[41] Information may be disclosed even when it involves persons who have not sought publicity.[42] This test is different from the California approach, and more in line with the general U.S. view of newsworthiness[43] because it does not require that social value be derived from the information.

Despite the difficulty in suing the media because published information is usually newsworthy, people are suing the new media for privacy intrusions and are seeking the same traditional remedies. Bloggers and others who engage in web-based speech have been sued for defamation,[44] intentional infliction of emotional distress,[45] appropriation of name or likeness,[46] false light, and libel.[47] As of July 1, 2008, 160 criminal and civil court suits had been filed against bloggers in the United States.[48] Of those 160 suits, only seven resulted in judgments against the defendant blogger.[49] The traditional standard of newsworthiness and consequent defense to liability will likely continue to apply to bloggers as it does to traditional media.

The case of *Kono v. Meeker* exemplifies the possible liabilities of a blogger.[50] Larry and Carole Meeker were California residents who bought and sold antiques. Dana Kono was a hairstylist who collected antique woodworking tools and scientific instruments. After Kono and the Meekers argued over an antique transaction, the Meekers posted a web page, the Dana Kono Watch Page, that claimed Kono was a "liar," "thief," "cheat," and "drunk." The page also urged others not to use his services as a hairstylist. Kono filed for defamation, false light, invasion of privacy, and intentional infliction of emotional distress. The defamation and false light claims were based exclusively on the web page. The jury awarded Kono compensatory damages of $150,000 for defamation, $50,000 for invasion of privacy, and $50,000 for intentional infliction of emotional distress. The jury award was then affirmed on appeal.[51]

Although bloggers often receive the privilege of being treated as the press and thereby avoid censorship and prior restraint, they will still be accountable for transgressions that other members of the press (and any private person) can commit. The issue of Internet anonymity adds a degree of complication: what if an unnamed blogger posts information that was illegally obtained? What if the presentation of the information is susceptible to an interpretation of hyperbole or opinion and there is no way to pursue a remedy for the privacy intrusion? Although the law has attempted to limit the collection and dissemination of information when it is intrusive, the law itself is bound by the doctrine of free press, the rise of new technology, and the complexity of issues surrounding new media. The issues remain unclear, and courts today must apply innovative solutions to protect privacy. As the nature of information keeps shifting, so too will the form and content of media, a constant shifting that will force the law to continually adapt in order to keep up with media.

The
Future
of Dignity
and Privacy

The new reality is that there is more of everything. More information is collected, more information is demanded, more media outlets exist, and more sensitive and inaccurate information is available than ever before. The media—good, bad, informative, and malignant—operate in the permissive and technologically wide-open modern world. The new media have the ability to cause immense personal harm very swiftly. As a result, many people are intimidated, inhibited, and afraid. Values we cherish—identity, creativity, free expression, and privacy—are diminished.

Pervasive intrusion works to choke the exact human characteristics that free press itself is intended to foster—free thought and open expression of ideas. The individual right to be let alone is an important right for important reasons. This book does not suggest a Luddite reaction to modern technological advances. Curbing or eliminating technology is not a realistic response. A sensible response requires an acknowledgement of the harms of intrusion and an understanding that accountability for harms is in the best interest of our society, our citizens, and the modern media.

First, the law must give value to protecting individuality and personal privacy. The beginning point is the Free Speech clause in the U.S. Constitution. The First Amendment protects individuals' right to speak, to be silent, and to express themselves. It also protects religious beliefs, the right to petition, and the right to be an individual. While the framers were protecting against potential tyranny of government, they were also supporting principles of individual liberty and dignity. Second, the law must give meaning to the basic principle of justice that there should be no unjust harm without a remedy. While the new media cause real harm to personal dignity and liberty, there are few effective remedies to address these grievances.

Free speech is critical to modern societies. There is no doubt that new media provide more information than has ever before been available. At the same time, there is no doubt that there is more bad information coming from more sources than ever before. More individuals are being harmed and will be harmed. There is an alternative. Accountability for wrongful and harmful intrusions is possible.

The Good and Bad Consequences of the New Media

While there is a need for increased accountability for harm caused by new media, there are also great benefits of the new media. The convergence of circumstance that provides more technological means to gather and distribute information and facilitates the vast increase of reporters and publishers is both an asset to our society and a risk. With greater ability for a single blogger to assemble information and publish it, there is an increased ability to assemble more information, publish more easily, and increase the number of voices in the marketplace of ideas.

For example, a Boston citizen can witness the shoot-out that occurred in pursuit of the Boston Marathon bombers and report accurately where and when it happened. There was no other reporter present. The eyewitnesses to history in the Arab Spring of 2012 could report on demonstrations and send film of crowds even when there were few mainstream reporters on site. A citizen can take a video of police brutality and publish it. An anonymous blogger can criticize the city and its police department to expose inefficiency or waste. Even the disclosures by Edward Snowden that contained violations of American security laws opened the door to discussion of government surveillance. A blog that normally traffics in smut may end up disclosing true information that becomes news. For example, it was the notorious site *The Dirty* that initially disclosed Anthony Weiner's continued affairs during the New York mayoral race of 2013. Despite its nearly exclusive reputation as a tabloid, the gained national recognition when it broke the story on John Edwards' extramarital affair—particularly while major, established news sources declined to cover something they originally viewed as below their newsgathering integrity.[1] In these circumstances, sources dredging for smut happened to stumble upon real news about important political figures while simultaneously divulging the salacious details the public expects from such sources. The details disclosed related not only to sexual conduct but also to misleading the public and therefore ended up being relevant to criticism of a public figure.

While this new world of the new media has many benefits, there is also a dark side. Harm occurs because many of the same characteristics that provide advantages also provide more access, more reporters, and more publishers. These new circumstances mean there are more risks of inaccuracy today and more potential sources of malicious disclosure. This book has enumerated many intrusions that provide vivid examples of the dangers of new media.

1. THE MEDIA HAS A NEED FOR SPEED. The race to be the first outlet with the story creates a danger of spreading false and defamatory material because accuracy is sacrificed for speed. For example, the Shirley Sherrod case involved the broad spread of a deliberately incomplete and defamatory video in twenty-four hours. News distributors are under substantial pressure to be first or at least not lag behind competitors. The pressure is greater when there are more and faster sources than ever before.

2. TECHNOLOGY ALLOWS NEW INTRUSIONS THAT COULD NOT HAVE HAPPENED YEARS AGO. Once technology is available, it is likely to be used. The telephoto lens was an intrusive device when it was used to take photographs of the Duchess of Cambridge topless while she was

clearly in a nonpublic space. Now, cameras are devices small enough to fit into any cell phone or even the tip of a pen, enabling a new wave of video voyeurism. China Central Television captures more of our moves in the public arena than any of us would like to know. Google Earth has been forbidden from showing satellite camera footage around the world in real time, but that does not mean that the capacity to do it is not at someone's fingertips. What will the news drones of the future be capable of capturing?

3. TECHNOLOGY MAY FACILITATE ILLEGAL AND CRIMINAL INTRUSION. As noted in chapter 2, News Corp. tapped the phones of several celebrities as well as the phone of a young murder victim. Wiretapping is a crime, and so are other forms of technological intrusions.[2] It is illegal to take surreptitious pictures of private areas, such as the view up a woman's skirt.[3] However, the means to commit most of these crimes are inexpensive and readily available for public use.

4. THE MEDIA HAS AN "IF IT BLEEDS IT LEADS" MENTALITY. The belief that spectacular tragedy attracts readers and viewers has induced reporters and media to record or seek intrusive images of the injured or dead. In California, a production crew filmed and broadcast the extrication, helicopter transport, and accompanying medical care given to two vehicular accident victims who were in agonizing pain.[4] The medical crew was acting in concert with the television crew, allowing them to follow at close range and even mic a nurse who performed emergency care in the helicopter, but at no time did the plaintiffs give—or waive—consent to be filmed by the television crew.[5] While the court found that the media could produce and broadcast the newsworthy aftermath of the accident, it also held that the victims had a cause of action for the intrusive means by which the press pursued the material.[6] In so holding, the court stated:

> To allow liability because this court, or a jury, believes certain details of the story as broadcast were not important or necessary to the purpose of the documentary, or were in poor taste or overly sensational in impact, would be to assert impermissible supervisory power over the press. The intrusion claim [however] calls for a much less deferential analysis. In contrast to the broad

privilege the press enjoys for publishing truthful, newsworthy information in its possession, the press has recognized constitutional privilege to violate generally applicable laws in pursuit of material.[7]

There are other examples where new media and blogs actively seek autopsy photographs. In the case involving Dale Earnhardt's autopsy photos, one of the media outlets seeking publication was a blog that specialized in displaying celebrity autopsy photos.[8] The Learning Channel's now-defunct show, *Tales from the Morgue*, went to great lengths to broadcast graphic crime scene footage and autopsies.[9] Originally billed as a documentary series on medical examiners and their investigatory tactics, the show was cancelled after public outcry and litigation from victims' families.

5. BLOGS PLAY LOOSELY WITH THE FACTS. There are numerous instances where bloggers either engage in outright defamation or dramatically alter or omit facts. Recall the Sherrod case, where a falsified video posted to a blog generated completely false global reports of Sherrod's alleged racism. Blogs can be anonymous and lack editorial supervision, only enhancing the risk of abuse. In addition, blogs that have mounted vicious attacks have been defined as "unreliable and unbelievable" and have escaped liability for defamation because they were not credible. Yet, the content of blogs is still considered speech, entitling bloggers to the same protections from suit as the institutional mainstream media.[10] Ironically, it seems the more irrationally and unprofessionally a blog is written, the more likely it is to be viewed as not factual and therefore not defamatory.

Even where a blogger's conduct does not rise to the level of defamation, the ability for a single intrusion to spread across the country in a matter of minutes exponentially magnifies the harm that the intrusion causes. In the infamous Washingtonienne case, an aide to Senator Mike DeWine was discovered to be the author of an anonymous blog that discussed her sexual escapades with various men in the Washington, D.C., area.[11] One of the men she blogged about, a high-ranking staff member for the Senate Judiciary Committee, sued her for public disclosure of private facts, false light, invasion of privacy, and intentional infliction of emotional distress. Unfortunately for him, the suit caused more tabloid publicity than legal remediation. Even deeply personal, arguably offensive material is newsworthy under the modern standard.

6. THE MEDIA MAY USE UNSCRUPULOUS TACTICS TO CREATE A STORY. The courts in the United States have made it clear that media may be deceptive and misleading in obtaining information. The fact that reporters lied to an ophthalmologist about their identity in order to obtain access to create a story attacking him did not constitute trespass.[12] The media will not be liable."[13] Although certain journalism is "shrill, one-sided, and offensive," it is deemed to be an important part of the media market.[14] The same principles now apply to information posted on a blog.

One might think that these risks of intrusion are similar to risks from media intrusion in the past. The need for speed and the tendency to publish stories about bloody incidents are not new media characteristics. But the difference today is that technology has enhanced the ability to engage in these intrusions and enhanced the number of media for their publication. An individual with a camera phone can take a video of a crime scene or photograph an auto accident victim, then post that information on his or her Facebook, Instagram, or personal blog so that it is viewed worldwide. Because of the sheer numbers of new media, the likelihood for these occurrences increases dramatically.

While there is great good attributable to new media, there are real risks and real harms to privacy that should be addressed.

The Playing Field for Privacy Rights

The flow of information has increased with the expansion of technology. There is no doubt that even more means of distributing information are on the horizon. Human nature supports an addiction to information, and new technology will feed that desire with more information. The demand for more information will continue even where the information is not verified, not accurate, not useful, and not in the public interest. Human beings crave information, and the new media provide a limitless source of it.

The hunger for information extends to corporations and government. Governments always want more information to legitimately or illegitimately protect their own interests. Corporations crave advertising information, and their ability to monitor thoughts and actions continually expands as consumers trade the ability to keep their purchases and other personal information private for VIP cards, the ability to purchase online, or other commercial incentives.

New intrusions can crowd the intellectual space to think freely. The right to sit in a library, pull a book from a shelf, and read something that only you know you are reading is different from having your searches recorded by Google or Amazon and used to evaluate your taste in books. That type of electronic oversight becomes more dangerous, intellectually intimidating, and Orwellian when the government does it. The disclosures of Edward Snowden in 2014 indicate that the U.S. government was collecting vast amounts of personal information about citizens as part of national security surveillance. Overall, our society tolerates more intrusion, so we should not be surprised that new media participate in the intrusions. There is a marketplace for harmful and even inaccurate information, and the new media are meeting that demand.

Further, the current playing field favors the media publisher of harmful intrusive information over the victim of that information's publication. In a world where almost anyone can claim to be "the media," should the rules be the same as those in use when the printing press was the principal intruder? It may be that the new media are simply the beneficiaries of new technology and a broad definition of free speech. The power of the new media, for purposes of distributing information, is as extensive as the broadest definition of free speech. Some jurisdictions license or regulate media; even the United States regulates broadcast media. But when the new media involve the Internet, they are largely unregulated—and from some vantage points, impossible to regulate.

In addition to direct media limitations, some jurisdictions are willing to actually balance and analyze the magnitude of intrusions against the public value of speech. In the United States, the value of free expression virtually never gives way to the need to protect human dignity.

In other places, such as the European Union, privacy and personal dignity receive more protection than in the United States. There, privacy and dignity are basic human rights. Privacy protections safeguard autonomy, dignity, and the free development of personality. There is no question that in practice and in written law the E.U. countries give far more deference to individual dignity than does the United States. The global variability of legal protections stands in stark contrast to the borderless availability and reach of contemporary sources of information. Both the publisher and the victim of an intrusion exist in this uncertain global setting. Often neither is aware of the consequences or rights that may exist beyond the borders of where they actually live, although their communications and rights may extend beyond their physical location. Acceptance of technological activities varies across borders. The practice of collecting street-level photographic information by Google Earth is directly challenged in Germany but ignored in the United States. The globally diverse playing field is not generally well understood by regular citizens. More efforts to bring some cross-border understanding and even more cross-border agreement would be rational and positive developments in the future.

The playing field involving privacy and the new media certainly does not favor privacy. There are ever-expanding technological means that facilitate the gathering and distribution of information by new media. The value of free expression is lauded over dignity and autonomy. In addition, specific barriers to privacy remedies remain in place and are seemingly intractable.

Barriers to Privacy Protections and Remedies

The deck is clearly stacked against privacy victims and in favor of the new media. The following are the principal factors that must be addressed to reach practical and effective solutions. Some of these barriers can be directly addressed by existing remedies; others are simply a reality that must be considered when crafting new solutions. The growth in technology is not a barrier to be challenged, for example, but rather a factor to be acknowledged and even used to help protect privacy.

Free Speech Is a Dominant and Well-Established Principle;
Privacy Is Not

Free speech is well accepted as a fundamental tenet of good and democratic government. That valid conclusion is not going to change. But in the case of governments that control speech and information, new media privacy invasions are not the issue; government control and intrusion are the issue.

Proponents of protecting privacy interests against new media should not be arguing to diminish free speech rights. The focus must be on accountability for misconduct. In order to expand accountability, the rights of the individual must be articulated and protected without diminishing legitimate free speech rights. A balance is rational and possible. Privacy advocates must respect and acknowledge the power and validity of free speech concerns.

Global Nature of New Media and Inconsistent Laws

Another barrier to creating comprehensive remedies is the international nature of the new press. A blogger in Montana can publish content that is read in France. The laws on privacy, free speech, and defamation are different in different nations. The bases for determining conflicts of laws for information crossing national and international borders are largely inconsistent and often applied unevenly.

A member of the new media may intrude from a remote location on anyone anywhere. Consequences of inconsistent laws include libel tourism, where a person seeks a privacy remedy in a more favorable but perhaps less local jurisdiction. This lack of predictability breeds misunderstanding and a lack of enforcement. As more and more communications are transmitted across borders around the world, resolving conflicts of laws will play a central role in protecting privacy interests. Competing values make global uniformity a high hurdle. But some common principles of accountability for intrusive and harmful communications exist and can foster cross border agreements.

Unbridled New Technology

We know that the last two decades have made each of us vulnerable to intrusion. We now live in virtual glass houses. A GPS device can track a person's actions, movements, and habits twenty-four hours a day. Data formerly obscure are instantly available. These pieces of a life are easily assembled into a complete mosaic—an intimate portrait of our private lives. Camera phones take pictures everywhere and can immediately post them to the world. Drones are now being made the size of a small bird. Modern innovation has increasingly fewer limits, and the new press will use anything available. The law struggles terribly with technology. The law makes a quaint effort to limit intrusive uses by setting loose standards such as determining whether a technology is in "general public use." General public use only shows general awareness rather than whether a telephoto lens, a remote camera, or a GPS is actually intruding on someone's privacy. Who knows what will be in general public use in twenty years? The sum total effect of new technology is that information is increasingly easy to acquire and to publish.

Redefinition of Media: More Sources Than Ever Before

Can anyone be part of the new media? The answer seems to be yes. Defining the media matters in countries where being defined as a member of the media has advantages. In the United States, media may have the privilege of not revealing a source. But the issue of actually defining media for this purpose has been going on for years in Congress. In other countries, the press actually has defined responsibilities. Ultimately, defining "media" for purposes of privacy intrusions should not prohibit the law from enforcing privacy breaches. Individuals who commit the same intrusions should be held accountable as well.

The expansion of new media to include potentially anyone has positive factors, such as the increased availability of accurate on-site reporting. But the simple fact that the number of reporters is indefinable and unlimited means more inaccuracy, more bad with the good.

Gatekeepers Are Obsolete in Many New Media

When the channels for distributing information were few, the traditional media that managed them were the gatekeepers. They were the editors and lawyers who reduced the likelihood of intrusion and defamation. In many parts of the new media, these gatekeepers do not exist. This reality increases the chances of intrusion. Gatekeepers added an element of accountability to mainstream media. If the new reality has no gatekeepers, then accountability must be fixed somewhere. Simply stated, the absence of traditional gatekeepers cannot excuse liability. Any publisher or writer should be accountable for misconduct.

Anonymity in the New Media

Anonymity is another barrier that is also an important aspect of individual freedom and free speech. But like other aspects of free speech, anonymity can be abused, and new technology has made anonymity easier and more prevalent.

Faceless intruders present a new kind of danger in the Internet age. Some of the worst human traits are displayed on the Internet. Psychologists suggest a number of reasons for vicious anonymous intrusions. People lose certain inhibitions and cultural restraints behind the mask of the Internet. There are terms like disinhibition, dissociative conduct, and others that show that when no one is watching, humans can behave cruelly and intrusively. Anonymity is both a legal barrier and a practical barrier to effective remedies. If an intruder's identity is unknowable, then the intruder cannot be held accountable. If the identity is unknown but discoverable, then the law must allow a person who has defamed another to be held accountable. To be effective, remedies to new media intrusions must directly address the issue of anonymous intrusions.

The Liability of Internet Service Providers Is Limited

ISPs are either blank chalkboards or the new gatekeepers. Should service providers that are facilitators of publication on the Internet be responsible for harmful intrusions that others have posted? Ease of access is an asset for free speech and a hazard to personal dignity.

The Internet's ease of access means that publishing information is no longer cost prohibitive. In the United States, ISPs have minimal liability. While the Communications Decency Act was intended to avoid pornography on the Internet, the ultimate impact of the judicially modified provision is to protect most ISPs from liability because the law in the United States does not treat them as publishers of information but as mere facilitators. These immune ISPs provide a perfect vehicle for the anonymous intruders, with no gatekeeper to monitor their conduct. The ISP may be immune, and the anonymous abuser may be impossible to find. There must be reasonable limits to ISP immunity. Other jurisdictions such as the European Union have provided other approaches, such as requiring an ISP upon request to block results that lead to irrelevant and harmful information. Also, it is possible to hold ISPs accountable for either knowingly allowing or encouraging defamation on their websites.

Contemporary Society Has a Lower Expectation of Privacy

Every privacy remedy supposedly contains an objective element: the expectation of privacy must be reasonable, or the intrusion at issue must be offensive to a reasonable person. What does that standard mean and what does it mean today?

John Stuart Mill stated in that "the individual is not accountable to society for his actions, insofar as these concern the interests of no person but himself."[15] While this is an encouraging thought to privacy advocates, it does not reflect current reality. Individuals are certainly accountable for their actions, and in the new open society perhaps they are accountable for even private actions. Privacy scholar Anita Allen describes the new reality as the "new accountability." The thrust of her theory is that contemporary society expects to know more about an individual's intimate life than ever before:

> The New Accountability means strangers may have no compunction about demanding more than you wish to tell and putting

facts about you to uses that offend and hurt you. The freedom and openness of our conduct means just that many more people know of it and perhaps witness it. Just that many more curious, interested, nosey, inquiring people exploit accountability-entitling ties. The links they find may be as attenuated as membership in the public claiming a right to know what is at all interesting, educational, informative, newsworthy, or governmental.[16]

This individual demand to know more reflects a society that expects to know more about everyone. This society obviously has a lower expectation of individual privacy. It often appears that contemporary society is trading personal privacy for a role in one big reality TV show.

An individual living in the twenty-first century does not have the same reasonable expectation of privacy as a person living in the 1700s. The danger is that the trajectory of technology and new attitudes has automatically diminished a personal legal right. In other words, if the new normal includes the knowledge that cell phones are readily monitored, then is there no reasonable expectation of privacy in a cell phone communication? More intrusive technology that is widely available and known to be in public use lowers our expectations—this is what the law deems reasonable. The danger is that new technology and understanding of new realities will actually limit reasonable expectations of privacy. Even worse is the notion that privacy rights will only be reserved for those powerful enough to secure them. Lior Strahilevitz has theorized that privacy protections today are defined by politics and power elites—a positivist theory of privacy law.[17] He believes that privacy has become a commodity available only to the powerful. For example, he points to the protection of celebrity privacy in California. He suggests that privacy law is developing as a distributive right where there are real winners and losers based on who has power.

Technology and human expectations may demand that we continue to disclose personal information and that we be responsible for our actions. Smartphones, iPads, Twitter, and Facebook provide technological means to track or disclose our every move. People are expected to say who they are and what they like on Facebook. Facebook friends talk about where and when they eat and what they read.[18] Does all this lead to the conclusion that there is no longer an expectation of privacy?

That conclusion simply does not make sense. Just because an intrusion is more likely in the new world should not allow it to become a legal act. Just because society at one point accepted racism does not make it acceptable. The majority view should not define fundamental personal rights. A reasonable expectation of privacy for legal purposes need not be equivalent to the prevailing societal desire to know about others. A person can hold a reasonable expectation that others not publicly disclose details held in confidence about an intimate personal relationship. But the fact that society's general view of what is private is changing certainly has an impact on future privacy policies.

Likewise, technical capacity should not automatically redefine what is private. Just because it is possible for someone to use a telephoto lens to see into someone's backyard should not make the backyard a public place. Just because a media person can record a private cell phone conversation should not make it legal. Although the Internet is a very open place, there should be some actions that are personal and private. An intrusion cannot be defined by the ease with which it can be accomplished or the fact that we are aware that the intrusion is easily accomplished.

It is particularly vexing that the barriers to privacy feed off each other and work together to escalate the problem. For example, better technology makes it easier for more individuals to transmit more information in a more global way. The existence of more media outlets with fewer gatekeepers results in an increased amount of information being transmitted without an editorial afterthought. And because this is the state of the new world, the law thrusts the reasonable person into that world without giving the individual the legal tools to remedy the new intrusions that are part of the new reality. The barriers to remedies are indeed high.

Given all these barriers and the importance of free speech, there is a need to explain why we need to protect privacy as essential to the principle of human dignity.

Why We Need to Protect Dignity

Individual dignity is uniformly recognized but unevenly protected. In-crementally, society protects certain physical space, certain types of information (for example, medical information), and certain personal expression—but not always the right to be let alone. There is a danger that accepted intrusiveness of the society in which we live so diminishes our collective expectation of privacy that it will be surrendered forever. However, the values of society evolve, and we may be at a point where individual privacy and dignity have been so visibly diminished that the pendulum will swing back and there will be more support to protect the individual. Change is possible. Police have routinely searched cell phones without a warrant during arrests. After decades of avoiding extending privacy rights in cases involving search and sei-zure, the U.S. Supreme Court determined that a search of a modern smartphone was tantamount to or more invasive than the search of a home. That reversal demonstrates that change in privacy law based on technological evolution is possible.[19]

The importance of dignity is clearly and constitutionally recognized in some jurisdictions and cultures. The debate over dignity and new media is a global discussion; the European Union, for example, identi-fies dignity and privacy as basic rights.

Protection from intrusion is more than a nice thing. Constant ob-servation and intrusion have the effect of suppressing thought, indi-viduality, and creativity.[20] Observation is control, particularly when it has a chilling effect on behavior. In Jeremy Bentham's Panopticon prison, the draped windows of a central tower served to control behav-ior of prisoners by leaving them unsure as to whether they were being observed, but constantly threatened by the possibility. Writings on privacy have alluded to the Panopticon effect as an example of control by an intrusive society.[21] In response to Edward Snowden's disclosure of the National Security Agency's surveillance tactics, political com-mentator Peggy Noonan wrote that ever-diminishing expectations of privacy alter the fabric of America.[22] She argues that while privacy is of-ten thought to conflict with Americans' First Amendment guarantees, they are inextricably codependent. The fear that our most intimate beliefs and communications could be seen by an Edward Snowden or other anonymous government snoops has a chilling effect on thought and speech. These are the core values that the Constitution seeks to protect in both the free speech provision and the protections against search and seizure. But rather than protect privacy, evidence suggests that U.S. government policy actually has gone so far as to discourage technology that would enhance digital privacy.[23]

That chilling effect is a result not just of Big Brother but Big Data and the new media's all-seeing eyes as well. There is a compelling interest to protect free thought. But in the controversy that pits privacy against the new media, privacy still struggles to justify impinging on free speech. Both the broad effects and the more specific harms of intrusions to individuals need to be understood. The public has a general understanding of the ramifications of disclosing falsehoods and lies. Defamation is a well-accepted legal principle. A critical hurdle to protecting privacy in the new world is to achieve an understanding of the need for remedies when disclosure of truthful information causes harm.

Why the Disclosure of True Information Can Be Harmful

The pictures of Nicole Catsouras's mangled body were a depiction of the truth. The royal family did not argue that the pictures of a topless Duchess of Cambridge were inaccurate. The woman who had undergone a sex change operation did not claim that she had not had the operation. In these instances, we feel as human beings that disclosure of information is harming someone because we believe that some information is, by nature of its content, personal and private. Even if an intrusion that captured the information was itself an intrusion, such as in the case of the duchess, the disclosure itself was the greater harm. The capture of information in the Catsouras case was perfectly legal in the course of law enforcement duties. It was the release that was devastating. In response to harmful but true disclosures, the global culture has a split personality: some countries focus on the harm to dignity; others focus on free speech. In the United States, the free press/free speech proclivity is such that courts will acknowledge that the damage to innocent people is virtually not a factor. This conclusion is not consistent with the true history of free speech principles and the reality of current intrusions. Nor is the absolutist nature of this position sustainable in a world in which the increasing number of privacy intrusions will demand accountability.

Even though there are different results in the European Union and the United States when seeking relief for intrusive disclosures, there are common principles and issues. The disclosure must be intentional and offensive and have caused harm. In both the European Union and the United States, free speech principles are considered when balancing interests. The distinction is in the weight accorded to free speech versus the harm to dignity.

In the United States, we need to rethink the deeper meaning of free expression when we weigh an intrusive publication against personal dignity. Personal dignity and the right to think and act freely are part of free expression. Dignity should not automatically lose to a slavish deference to the process of disclosure or definition of newsworthiness without consideration of the impact of disclosure of the content. Of course, as soon as there is a suggestion to look at content, free speech concerns arise. Yet, the suggested balancing of speech versus dignity is done in the United State regularly prior to public release of sensitive materials, for example, in Freedom of Information Act cases. It is a test we know how to administer.

Prior Restraint

One concern about overutilizing prior restraint to protect privacy is that these limitations give too much weight to privacy compared to public access and freedom of speech. Even where prior restraint is not appropriate for these reasons, the law need not restrain release but rather provide for potential liability for horribly intrusive disclosures to a public audience that have virtually no public value. This path will at least compel new media and bloggers to weigh the consequences of a harmful publication. This approach allows the media to acquire and disclose information, but at the same time requires the media to assess the risk of disclosure and be accountable for the consequences.

Intent to Disclose

One possible remedy is to utilize "intent to disclose" as a factor in analyzing these disclosures. In other words, a person can expect information to be available for a limited purpose and not used for another. For example, in the case a court recognized that a model had posed nude for limited purposes but had not consented to be displayed in a newspaper.[24] Similarly, in France, just because a person marched in a gay parade did not mean he consented to be pictured in a national newspaper. These cases allow a person to have some control over what seems like limitless surveillance of personal activities. If a person sends an e-mail to two people, should that be a public display? Just as the analogy of drawing the curtains over an open window indicates intent to be private, can a person designating an e-mail or Facebook posting as private help maintain her privacy? Society recognizes the wrongfulness of some online conduct that parallels conduct in the physical world. For example, cyberstalking is a crime just as stalking in the physical world is a crime. Is it possible for a person to manifest the intent to be private in the online world and be protected from invasion, intrusion, or trespass by new media?

Passage of Time

Another possible remedy for public disclosure of private facts would weigh the passage of time as a factor, where the greater passage indicates elevated protection. If an embarrassing event took place thirty years ago, even if it is part of the public record, should it still be subject to public distribution and wide display? There are isolated cases that have considered passage of time as creating two reasons to protect privacy: the event is of less public interest, and the expectation of privacy is greater. This is the "newsworthiness versus privacy" balancing test viewed through the lens of time. The classic example is the Red Kimono case,[25] involving a movie that described the true life of a prostitute. Those misdeeds had occurred many years earlier, and when the woman who was the subject of the film brought suit, the court decided that disclosure of those facts was an invasion of her privacy, even though the information was true and had been public. Similarly, in a recent E.U. case, the court determined that a Spanish citizen had a right to compel Google, an ISP, to block search results for information about an old unpaid debt that was now obsolete and irrelevant. In both of these cases, the aggrieved person had a new life, and there was little or no public benefit to disclosing the past compared to great personal harm.

Recently, writers and commentators have suggested that there ought to be a right to be forgotten. A right to be totally forgotten and for past deeds to become completely invisible is quite different from a court allowing recovery in the Red Kimono circumstance, although there are some existing analogous circumstances at law—such as with the sealing and expungement of criminal matters.[26] We would not be comfortable with a serial killer or child molester's record being unavailable to the hiring authority of a local high school. However, the passage of time can lessen the public value of smaller wrongs. When combined with good conduct, perhaps we are willing to both forgive and forget. Or, in graver circumstances, forgive without forgetting. In reality, imposing this solution in a privacy context would require placing a statute of limitations on the speech rights of people to raise sensitive matters that are personal to other individuals. For these reasons, this novel solution is unlikely to be a workable remedy, unless the information at issue is no longer deemed to have any value.

Levy a Tax or Fee

Novel remedies have been proposed in this area, such as a proposal to levy a federal tax on data brokers, the revenue of which would be used as a fund for the victims of privacy intrusions. In the same way that some countries tax individual stock market transactions to fund systemic risk insurance, the data brokerage tax would essentially fund a program that would pay settlements to individuals who suffer privacy intrusions. This could possibly be paired with a limited form of immunity for participating data brokers, which might motivate the industry to some degree. However, having spent time as a lawmaker in Florida, I know that there tends to be a strong correlation between novel remedies and remedies that never happen.

Utilize Existing Tort Remedies

Other means of punishing publication in particular circumstances are available but are very narrow. For example, publication of extraordinarily intrusive facts with the intent to harm someone may be an intentional infliction of emotional distress. The proof level here is quite high and would be rare to apply to a publisher. The proof of intent makes this an unlikely basis for a remedy in all but a few instances. Yes, it could apply to someone who intentionally published intimate pictures of someone who had no intent to share them beyond one individual. Unfortunately, such intrusions are becoming increasingly common and their consequences dire, such as when young girls commit suicide because personal photographs that they intended to disclose to only one person reach a wider audience.[27] The malicious classmate or the angry boyfriend or girlfriend publishing a nude photograph may be a candidate for liability. However, the intent standard is a high bar for a media publication in this sort of case.

Appropriation of personality is another available action for disclosure of truthful information. But this property-based remedy will only apply when someone uses the image or identity of another person in advertising or for financial gain. Using an image in a news story is not a violation because of the newsworthiness defense. That conclusion is sensible. Often, this cause of action is considered a celebrity remedy because damages, in part, relate to the enhanced value of utilization of a celebrity's image in advertising. The advertiser is taking something of value and using it for personal gain. If celebrity personalities and copyrights have property value, could the individual dignity of a regular person have value as property? There are suggestions that theft of dignity and privacy is as real a loss and perhaps more harmful than the theft of a wallet or purse. The theory of appropriation could be expanded to include using the identity or image of ordinary people for gain. This type of action is particularly compelling given society's desire to view information that is shocking or that reveals intimate details that are harmful to others. It could be used as a way to force society to pay for the pleasure it takes in others' pain.

As the long list of alternative approaches to harmful yet truthful disclosure indicates, these intrusions are the most difficult for the law to remedy. Conveying the truth is rightly supported. However, the publication of intimate, painful truths that have no value to the public should not be protected. The challenge is in trusting the idea that some information has no public value, or in resocializing ourselves to understand that public interest is not the same as public value. Ultimately, the courts must perform this function. U.S. courts should remodel domestic values to come closer to the dignity values honored in the European Union. We ask our courts to make difficult judgments on life, death, and subtle issues of intent. Why not establish a limit to intrusions into personal privacy?

Creating Remedies for the Future

The remedies I recommend are a combination of common sense and common decency. Courts and legislatures know how to protect some privacy interests better than others. For example, current law will protect against (1) defamation and wrongful statements, and (2) physical intrusions on personal space and privacy. The challenge in responding to new-media intrusions is to expand those principles and to define remedies that can respond to the new world and provide remedies to the broad range of intrusions. Defamation and intrusion upon seclusion, two established legal theories, can serve as the basis for innovative new remedies. Society accepts that telling untruths can be harmful and should be punished. We believe that intruding upon the space of another is a wrong that can be punished. How far can these principles take us? What new remedies are available to protect us more effectively?

The modern media intrude in a number of ways, and, therefore, solutions have to be diverse, creative, and designed to have a real effect. It is the individual who is personally harmed by media intrusions, but the intrusions are very impersonal and come from anywhere. The issue is one of individual rights with global dimensions. The playing field is not level, and there are major barriers to remedies for individual privacy. The options that are available are a combination of old and new remedies with an eye to the future realities of technology. They draw upon bedrock theories of protecting the individual in the face of technology specifically designed to intrude.

A remedy may be designed as a deterrent, a punishment, or both. The punishment can be a criminal or civil penalty. The remedy may be crafted by a legislative body or a court, enabled by legislation or precedent that prevents the conduct or compensates the harmed person. The following are approaches that can protect personal privacy against intrusions by the new media.

Intrusions into Personal Space, Property, or Private Affairs

The laws in most countries protect personal space and property. The remedies of trespass are ancient. Trespass is the theoretical basis for several types of intrusions that media may commit: wiretapping, computer hacking, electronic eavesdropping, breaking and entering, cyberstalking, false imprisonment, and video voyeurism are all wrongs based on intrusive actions. State and federal statutes prohibit many of these intrusions. Intruders may be liable through both criminal and civil means. The eavesdropper who took pictures of reporter Erin Andrews through a hole in the wall of a hotel room was guilty of criminal eavesdropping and voyeurism. The telescopic lens should not lessen the seriousness of electronic eavesdropping on the Duchess of Cambridge. In these cases, the government has determined by statute that certain actions are unlawful because they violate society's standards.

As an alternative to the physical intrusion caused by a trespass, the remedy of intrusion upon seclusion has a potentially broad sweep if its terms are interpreted rationally and applied in a modern context. For these reasons, intrusion-related remedies have some of the broadest potential. The defines an intrusion upon seclusion as an intentional intrusion, physical or otherwise, upon the solitude or seclusion of another or his private affairs or concerns that would be offensive to a reasonable person.[28] Of course, if a person consents, it is not an intrusion.

In the modern world, the media have begun soliciting citizen participation in newsgathering. However, if such solicitations result in physical injury to the participating citizens or others, litigation may result against news organizations that encourage risky behavior that foreseeably caused harm.[29] This type of conduct is another example of a harm caused by newsgathering as compared to publication. The media is not immune from crimes of trespass or immune from intrusions into personal property or space. A major benefit of remedies created around this theory is that they do not rely on punishing the disclosure of information to be successful. Therefore, free speech is not a defense to unlawful intrusions. It is the act of intruding that is wrongful, not the publication of any information.

A logical expansion of intrusion upon seclusion is the protection of a person's digital space and other private matters. A locked door or a fence implies physical seclusion, a wish to be left alone. Why should a pass-code-protected iPhone or password-protected e-mail account be any different? As the case demonstrates, citizens have a reasonable expectation of privacy in the contents of their cell phones. A critical observation of the Court in *Riley v. California* (see 214n19) was that viewing the data in a smartphone could be a greater invasion of privacy than the search of a home. The value of the information contained in the phone is the issue rather than the value of the phone itself. Expanding intrusion upon seclusion to include electronic intrusions is a common-sense adaptation of an old legal remedy to new technological circumstances.

The separation of the issue of intrusion from the issue of publication of information is the key in fashioning remedies in the United States. The E.U. interpretations of privacy allow regulation of truthful but intrusive information in a way that the United States does not—the European Union will regulate information that is intrusive to a person because of its content, rather than how it was obtained. In the United States, a court will find a violation by the paparazzi for crowding too close to Jackie Kennedy or trapping Arnold Schwarzenegger in his driveway, because of the physical intrusion of stalking and false imprisonment. But in these cases, the wrong being punished was not the distribution of intrusive information but rather the acts accomplished to obtain it. By comparison, the British found it a violation to photograph from a remote location and then distribute pictures of Michael Douglas's extremely private wedding—that would not be the result in the United States.

While a continental divide between U.S. and European approaches does exist, California has not waited for an American consensus to develop. Section 1708 of the California Civil Code creates civil liability for "physical invasion of privacy" and "constructive invasion of privacy." The former exists when a person trespasses "in order to physically invade the privacy of the plaintiff" with the intent to capture images or sound of the plaintiff "engaging in a personal or familial activity."[30] The invasion must be offensive to a reasonable person, a traditional tort-based objective standard. The latter cause of action is similar to the first but does not require an actual physical trespass.

Defining intrusions into private concerns in order to anticipate new technology is wise. There are intrusions today that could not have been foreseen twenty years ago. The new media have availed themselves of virtually every new means of intrusion, and there is no reason to think that this tendency will change. Today's world already has readily available commercial photo drones with the ability to fly into private places. When the braver new world of technology moves into science fiction, and technology gives government the ability to scan the thoughts or plans of a terrorist, do we believe the even newer media of that time will reject these new abilities?

Based on a reasonable modernization of the intrusion tort, technologically enhanced observations can be intrusive. In search-and-seizure cases, the courts have recognized advancing technology and struggled to balance what a reasonable person should expect in the swiftly changing modern world with what it has been common and reasonable to expect for centuries. The remedy in search-and-seizure cases is exclusion—the law punishes the government for intruding into the privacy of its citizens by preventing it from using the information obtained as a result. These same courts should be able to recognize that a remedy should also be required when telephoto lenses and computer tracking software are used intrusively by private entities like the media. The law should recognize a civil tort remedy in these cases.

Privacy scholars have suggested that a spin on the traditional remedy of intrusion upon seclusion may be the remedy of the future if the law is prepared to recognize that intrusions can occur by human or nonhuman means. A CCTV device in a locker room or changing room is an intrusion regardless of whether its footage is ever viewed by a human. The key is that the observation itself is the intrusive act; it matters not if the observation is ever published or even viewed.

This point of offensive intrusion is made by Neil Richards in what he terms protection of "intellectual privacy."[31] This concept is best analogized to the old-time researcher sitting in a library, pulling books off a shelf, coming up with ideas, and expressing some of them in writing while not expressing others. In the new world, "pulling books off the shelf" is done online in an "observable" space—the Internet. When researchers are online, buying books or talking with colleagues, their actions are much more observable than they were one hundred years ago. If unfettered observation is permitted with no consequence, free thought is impaired. Centuries ago, our founding fathers would have scoffed at the notion of "freedom to think." The express freedom to do something so private would sound redundant. Times have changed. Perhaps our notions about the freedom to think should change as well.

Jane Yakowitz Bambauer suggests that the new intrusion tort can extend to electronic intrusions that are offensive.[32] Our new concept of personal space can encompass some part of the Internet. Personal space and communications are already considered private in many contexts. For example, hacking private e-mail content is a violation of the law. Why not extend this protection to situations where an individual specifically deems information to be private, or expressly chooses to disclose only to a limited audience? Unlawful intrusions and offensive observations are something we know how to punish and prohibit. Peeping Toms, electronic eavesdroppers, and viewers of child pornography violate our norms and our laws. This is not uncharted territory, at least not on a global scale. Europe is rightly perceived as a stronger protector of human dignity. That is because European laws create a lower threshold to establish actions that violate privacy rights.

What I propose is a domestic model closer to the European model that places greater weight on human dignity. In the new world, an Internet intrusion by new media could be to falsely friend a person on Facebook and then use that person's profile information to publish an embarrassing blog post, detailing that individual's private life. In many U.S. courts today, there would be a finding of no expectation of privacy and therefore no remedy for this harm. But this is a prime example of why courts should redefine personal space in the new electronic world and why intrusions by anyone, including the new media, are wrong. The United States needs to take a stronger position respecting personal dignity and reflect that change in its legal system.

Avoid or Protect against Disclosure of Sensitive Information

The media cannot divulge harmful information it does not have. As a matter of policy, lawmakers have made the collection of certain information illegal. An example in the United States is treatment of an individual's social security number. Because the number can be used to intrude on an individual's life, the law prevents private entities from asking for the number. The list is specific in the United States, but not comprehensive. Statutory protections have been passed to protect video rental records, names of rape victims, and health records. Some states also protect autopsy photos. Even the Freedom of Information Act specifically protects against unwarranted privacy invasions to prevent the release of information held by the federal government.

Consequently, creating policies and precedent that protect sensitive information before it becomes public is a viable and achievable goal. The fact that information is not owned or controlled by the press relates to the second of the privacy matrix: "Who owns or possesses the information?" If the law were to give increasingly strong protection to categories of information before it is publicly released, the answer to this question would weigh in favor of the privacy interest of the individual rather than the media's desire for disclosure.

In addition to the statutes identified, U.S. courts have balanced privacy interests against the public's interest in disclosure. An example is the Dawn Brancheau case. A court determined that the disclosure of a video that contained images of Dawn Brancheau during a fatal attack by an orca at SeaWorld should not be made public. The balancing test by the court was very similar to FOIA cases and even cases in the European Union, where the issue of degree of private intrusion is weighed against the public interest. The balancing test is performed to public release. Since the information is not yet public, free speech arguments do not apply. In the United States, if the information was available publicly, then a restriction on publication would be a prior restraint and unlikely to survive. For example, private individuals filmed their own video during the SeaWorld incident and then released it to the public. Fortunately, that video showed nothing of the attack. The principal point is that the private video was in the hands of private persons who chose to disclose it, rather than in possession of a public entity that could be ordered not to disclose it. Therefore, the courts could not restrict the publication without its being viewed as disfavored prior restraint.

Limitations on making information public are a matter of policy in determining the information that we believe is unsuitable for public release. Defining those issues will be a moving target in terms of our beliefs and norms. But if we protect information from public view, then there are legal limits on disclosure, and there must be concomitant legal remedies for violations of those limits.

Mitigate the Effects of Disclosing Private Information

Once information has been publicized by new media, options for redress are limited. If the disclosure itself is legally wrongful, then there are remedies available. But what if a legal battle for damages is too time consuming, costly, or perhaps ineffective? In fact, for high-profile intrusions by media in the new world, the picture or statement may survive forever in cyberspace, and even the remedy of monetary damages may seem ineffective to address the tangible harm.

The concepts of retractions, apologies, and takedowns exist in current laws and policies. This type of mitigation is a remedy that is a logical option in many circumstances. It also has the benefit of being low cost and immediate—if it can be achieved. The Digital Millennium Copyright Act (DMCA) provides explicitly for takedowns of information posted on the Internet. The central purpose is to protect commercial information; however, sometimes that definition has been expansive. For example, some organizations or individuals issue DMCA takedown notices against works they simply do not like or find embarrassing, or even worse, works to which they have no ownership right.[33] The use of automated software to search for material that violates a copyright has only increased takedown abuses. In any case, the act is an example of utilizing removal as a remedy to fight against distribution of harmful information. This particular remedy is based on the heightened protection of intellectual property. However, it does not solve the problem of the same posting being reposted on multiple sites, which requires site-by-site attention.

Printing or posting a retraction is a long-existing option for media outlets that concede they have made a mistake, a practice that is regulated and governed under the law. However, takedowns or apologies may be possible both through other legal means and simply through requests. Websites are often willing to take down information upon a specific request. These alternatives are viable, but the new world requires fast action and knowledge of the harmful disclosure. Even if the takedown occurs, the information may be permanently circulated on the Internet. One example was the attempt to take down photos of the dead body of Nicole Catsouras. Even though a court concluded the images were wrongfully made public, the nature of the Internet is such that the intrusive photos have been distributed and redistributed so many times that total retraction is impossible, unless the law places the onus on the ISP to scour its sites for the harmful information. So, even if the first wrongful disclosure is punished, future disclosures may continue and may at that point even constitute protected speech. A high-profile disclosure that is passed around the Internet is not a good case for mitigation as a remedy.

A minor inaccuracy or insult by a news source might be remedied by a retraction rather than lengthy and costly litigation. More widespread distributions of harmful information on blogs must first be located and taken down without substantial harmful effect. If those takedowns are accompanied by admissions of inaccuracy, the remedy is even better.

In the Internet world, a piece of information once posted may never go away. However, removal can reduce the impact, and knowledge of an intrusion can provide a victim with the ability to defend and clarify.

Some have specifically advocated the use of apologies and retraction. Apologies as remedies have become more popular in the United States in civil cases where the defendant is a governmental entity, such as a city or state. Apologies are simpler, cheaper, and, particularly when they are public, a more meaningful way for victims to have the wrong redressed.

Safeguard Human Dignity by Punishing Dissemination of Private Facts

The concept of punishing disclosure of facts that are truthful but harmful is the most difficult and yet critical remedy when it comes to protecting against new media. Disclosures of confidential information or untruthful disclosures are actions our culture and our laws know how to punish. We do punish truthful disclosures if they are legally defined as confidential. For example, the rather obsolete protection of video rental records is protected by federal statute. But if not specifically protected, the disclosure of truthful information is broadly protected speech in the United States. There are instances where the rule is absolute, and there are sound reasons to look more closely at blanket protection of such intrusive disclosures. The theory of public disclosure of private facts still exists, but in the United States it has been reduced to almost nothing. These types of statements are viewed as part of free speech and free expression, and in media terms, they are newsworthy.

In the European Union, the standards are different. In punishing the distribution of intrusive but true information as well as punishing defamation, the E.U. approach differs dramatically. The mission is to protect dignity. That mission seems to encompass something more than a right to privacy, motivated by a desire to preserve and protect a "right of reputation."[34] The words "dignity" and the "right to reputation" by their very use raise the question of the United States' limited approach to protecting individuals from abuse and intrusion by the media. Clearly, the standards and burden are much more difficult in the United States. The underlying right to reputation places the individual in a more important place in the legal culture of the European Union.

Another problem is the unsteady evolution of the reasonable expectation of privacy. For virtually all remedies the threshold is a reasonable expectation of privacy. Of course, legal standards cannot be totally subjective to individual whims and preferences, so there must be some objective standard. However, to fashion a remedy for disclosure of private facts, we must confront the conclusions of courts that many private matters, especially those presented on the Internet, do not warrant a reasonable expectation of privacy. Therefore, matters disclosed to friends on Facebook, an e-mail sent to five friends, and a telephone number you dialed on your cell phone are not considered within the ambit of a reasonable expectation of privacy. Should everything you do on the Internet that is exposed to multiple persons or to faceless institutions such as telephone companies be considered public?

An option to expand the reasonable-expectation standard is to understand that the new electronic world must provide some shelter to allow humans to live with dignity. The modern analogy of drawing the blinds must be available. To protect privacy from harmful but truthful new media we need to be creative and realistic. In analyzing a remedy, it is logical at the outset to understand that the U.S. approach is not the only approach. The European Union and others will look at a disclosure of truthful information and weigh the public good of the disclosure against the individual harm of the disclosure. There have been isolated cases in the United States where this formula was used, but they are very isolated. Normally, we place overwhelming weight on the value of the process of disclosure. U.S. courts place so much weight on the value of any truthful disclosure that disclosure in the name of public interest will virtually always outweigh the harm to an individual's dignity, reputation, and privacy. This balance must shift.

In a 2012 concurrence, Justice Sonia Sotomayor suggested that it might be time for the Court "to reconsider the premise that an individual has no reasonable expectation of privacy in information voluntarily disclosed to third parties."[35] Given society's ever-increasing reliance on digital technology and the inherent personal disclosures that accompany such reliance, Justice Sotomayor proposed that mere voluntary disclosure alone should not disqualify that information from Fourth Amendment protection.[36] On a daily basis, digital users disclose phone numbers they contact, e-mail addresses they correspond with, and purchases they make online. Justice Sotomayor's logic is an extension of existing legal theories like attorney-client privilege and doctor-patient confidentiality, where the act of disclosure is not enough to render an expectation of privacy unreasonable. In an age where disclosure has become less truly voluntary, it would be wise to create separation between the act of disclosure and an individual's expectation of privacy.[37] Justice Sotomayor indicates the potential for reexamining some of the fundamental barriers that traditional privacy theory places in the way of new remedies.

Punish False and Defamatory Disclosures

Our culture is perfectly willing to punish false statements. Defamation is a well-established remedy. Although the new media's publication methods present practical and legal barriers, they are not an excuse for escaping liability.

The issue of anonymity is problematic when bringing legitimate defamation actions. The rise of Internet anonymity has generated harmful and abusive communications. Unfortunately, there is no end in sight for this trend. While not a necessary condition for defamation to take place, the shield of anonymity significantly increases the chances of someone disclosing false information about a person. Current law in the United States may require an individual to surmount numerous hurdles in order to redress a defamatory statement by an anonymous blogger. These cases are called John Doe cases because the name of the accused defamer is not yet known. The Internet is not necessarily completely anonymous; online identities can be traced, but they remain anonymous until revealed by a service provider. To prevail, a plaintiff must prove the likelihood of success of the defamation case to even obtain the name of the person who wrote the message.[38]

In seeking to show that defamation is likely, plaintiffs must show that the context of the statement demonstrates that it is actually defamatory. That means that a statement on a notoriously inaccurate blog may be discounted based on the logic that no one should believe it. That standard is unreasonable and completely counterintuitive. Why is it that the more unreliable the blog, the less accountable the bloggers? This standard means that the more reckless publishers are, the more likely they are to be protected. This decision would provide greater protection to an inaccurate source than is provided to one with a reputation for accuracy. Further, the plaintiff may need to reveal his or her identity and retell the defamatory story in the course of seeking a remedy. This is the plaintiff's paradox, in which a plaintiff must expose the facts he or she believes are defamatory in order to seek a judgment. In other words, the plaintiff must be exposed while the defamer remains anonymous.

In Great Britain, there was an effort to solve this paradox. That effort has been termed a superinjunction. The superinjunction was intended to protect the name of the plaintiff from embarrassment by preventing the publication of his or her name at filing. The concept was not a uniform success. The name of British footballer Ryan Giggs was publicized anyway because of a Twitter disclosure of his name. The efforts he made to keep his name secret only made the secret more salacious.

When seeking a remedy for defamation, the victim should not be required to submit to public shaming while the defendant remains anonymous. There are instances where a party to a lawsuit may be anonymous in the United States and elsewhere. In certain instances, minor children may have their name redacted or kept confidential during a proceeding. The law should provide the same privilege to defamation plaintiffs who are already at the mercy of the public by virtue of the misdeeds of another.

Great Britain has considered an incentive for ISPs to discourage anonymity. An ISP is given a higher degree of protection from liability if it encourages or requires postings that are not anonymous. Of course, for such a policy to be effective in the United States, the ISP must have some liability in the first place. Still, there are opponents to increased

ISP liability who are concerned that making ISPs more accountable may make them more restrictive of content or oversensitive to controversial postings. By and large, those opponents are the very ISPs who would be or have been previous beneficiaries of the CDA's Teflon immunity.[39] However, ISPs should have the capacity and resources to at least be responsible for serious intrusions. They are the beneficiaries of a vast flow of information, and they should have some accountability when there is great harm. Cases that have found liability for soliciting salacious and defamatory information are a good start. Defamation is a viable cause of action to protect against media abuses. But the United States needs to rethink the way anonymity is protected for those who defame and for ISPs that publish defamatory material. ISP liability in the European Union is a good model. The ISP should have some reasonable accountability for facilitating and publishing defamatory information. The E.U. standard requires some rational oversight and does not forgive complete ignorance. That standard is a good model for a more global approach to protecting privacy against media defamation on the Internet. Some cases in the United States have moved in this direction,[40] which is an auspicious start. An ISP should not be able to foster and solicit defamatory material and subsequently claim ignorance and immunity.

Encourage Journalists to Establish Ethical and
Professional Standards for New Media

The establishment of ethical and professional standards by and for the new media does not create a legal remedy, but it does help establish practical limits and boundaries for conduct. In fact, there are even instances where journalistic ethical standards may have legal consequences in the context of showing malice or malicious intent.[41] The issue of new media and social media has not escaped the attention of mainstream news organizations. The American Society of Newspaper Editors has issued social media policies for their reporters.[42] Twitter and Facebook have created guides for journalists. Nontraditional media have criticized guidelines as attempts to impose traditional values on the new setting—but what is so wrong with that?

Because of the prevalence of new media and the expanding use of nontraditional modes of communication for news, the issue will not go away. In fact, journalism schools are teaching new media, and there is some impetus to examine ethics in this new context. These journalism schools recognize new media as different and recognize the importance of analyzing the effects and boundaries of new media.[43]

In many cases, traditional media continue to fact-check their publications. Some newspapers have a policy not to publish letters to the editor with factual inaccuracies. This policy supports the saying that everyone is entitled to his own opinion, but not his own facts. Yet factual inaccuracies in new media are plentiful.

Currently there are television shows, such as CNN's[44] that focus on media and on media mistakes. The new media clearly have the attention of journalists and journalism. The leaders in the industry need to focus on ethical standards to protect privacy, and awareness of the need is increasing. One can only hope that it gains traction and support moving forward.

The Argument for Multiple Approaches

A simple approach would be to define an overriding right to privacy and dignity. Based on the barriers and playing field described above, that task is very difficult in the United States. The principle of free expression is justifiably strong and is not going to go away. But we should be willing to say there are limits to free expression when there is real harm. The European Union has accomplished this task and seems to have likewise preserved free speech. There should be circumstances when egregious disclosures give rise to accountability and liability. Both the right to free speech and the right to free expression are based on the First Amendment; unfettered free speech should not trample free expression. Choosing how to express oneself and safeguard one's own concept of personal dignity is the essence of free expression. Surely we have a greater right to protect what is most vital to us—our dignity—than the new media has to exploit intrusions on that very same dignity. The harm to innocent victims is real, traumatic, and deeply personal. I have seen that trauma in the tear-filled conversations with the families of murder victims who want to keep images of their lost loved ones private; shared the agony of wives dealing with intrusive media requests for autopsy reports in a time of private mourning; and talked about the possibility of seeing the video of the actual death of a sister published on a website. Media intrusions are not abstract or hypothetical.

Finally, the conversations on media and privacy conflicts need to be global. I have been part of discussions with lawyers, academics, and media from various nations. These dialogues are useful to gain deeper insight into how different nations and cultures approach these issues. As it turns out, most of the basic goals are identical: preservation of free expression and the importance of personal dignity. There is no doubt that the laws from various jurisdictions reach disparate results. But there is also no doubt there is much to learn from other jurisdictions.

The "multiple approaches" approach provides no single simple solution. There is no simple solution to an old conflict that has taken on so many new dimensions and is often stymied between two critical rights.

Principles for Seeking Privacy Protection in the New Media Age

1. Sanction disclosure of certain intimate private facts
2. Utilize and adapt existing torts
3. Utilize law punishing intrusions upon space, property, and personal information
4. Avoid initial disclosure of sensitive information
5. Punish defamation including outrageous falsity
6. Promote and support media creating self-defining ethical standards that include new media

Conclusion

The future is fraught with danger to personal privacy from the expanding new media. The privacy issue is complex on all levels and competes with the strong interest in free press. The speed of the changes in technology creates difficulty for the law. Remedies are different depending on many variables in the matrix described in chapter 2 including place, identity, and medium of intrusion. The protections for media communications are substantial; the ability to protect privacy is overwhelmed by ever-changing technology and inconsistent global privacy protections.

Realistic policies require forethought and creativity. Some of the principles of older remedies may be expanded to deal with new intrusions. Laws can evolve and adapt. A warrantless search of smart phones by police was routine. Now it is unconstitutional. Wiretaps went from legal to illegal, and by extension, the same can take place with new modes of electronic or computer intrusion. Serious and increased intrusion by new media with new technology is a certainty. Our legal system and contemporary society cannot simply ignore the consequences. The waning societal value at stake is profound and fundamental: basic human dignity.

Acknowledgments

Ron Goldfarb, my literary agent, is an inspiration and a friend. He has advised, reordered, edited, and generally made this book much better.

I wish to thank Tyler Hudson, Emily Snider, and Andrew Starling for their exceptional research and their commitment to making this book the best it can be. I also wish to thank my diligent research assistants over the years of this book's creation: Lorna Cobb, Rachel Malkowski, Samantha Crawford, Heather Reynolds, Joe Kovecses, L. B. Martin, Paul Pakidis, Allison Fischman, Brant McKown, Matthew Christ, and Kelsey Harclerode.

Notes

Chapter 1. New Media, Old Conflict

1. For the convenience of the reader, a glossary of useful terms is provided after the conclusion of this book.

2. Dombrowski v. Pfister, 380 U.S. 479, 487 (1965).

3. Castells, "Cultures of the Internet," 333.

4. Throughout this book I rely on the term "blogger" in the general sense, which encompasses other types of web speakers and web publishers, to include all persons who engage in communications via what we have come to know as the new media. However, the distinction between a speaker and a publisher can have legal significance. When the distinction is important to the analysis, I so specify.

5. "Ecuador: Stop Using Defamation Laws against Critics," Human Rights Watch, October 10, 2013, http://www.hrw.org/news/2013/10/10/ecuador-stop-using-defamation-laws-against-critics.

6. See, for example, Texas v. Johnson, 491 U.S. 397 (1989) (burning the nation's flag at the Republican National Convention is valuable protected speech).

7. See Dow Jones and Co. v. Gutnick, (2002) H.C.A. 56, 2002 (Austl.).

8. Levi, "Social Media and the Press," 1531, 1578–80.

9. Pew Research Center for the People and the Press, "Further Decline in Credibility Ratings for Most News Organizations," August 16, 2012, http://www.

people-press.org/2012/08/16/further-decline-in-credibility-ratings-for-most-news-organizations/.

Chapter 2. Can Privacy and New Media Coexist?

1. For instance, some scholars have argued that obscene material should be eliminated as a category of unprotected speech simply because it is popular, capable of being enjoyed in private, and a permanent feature of our culture, suggesting that free speech should have a very broad application. Calvert and Richards, "Stopping the Obscenity Madness," 8–15.

2. United States v. Abrams, 250 U.S. 616, 630 (1919) (Holmes, J., dissenting).

3. United States v. Rumely, 345 U.S. 41, 57 (1953).

4. See Wonnell, "Truth and the Marketplace of Ideas," 669, 672.

5. Black, "Bill of Rights," 865, 880.

6. Mishkin v. New York, 383 U.S. 502, 518 (1966) (Black, J., dissenting).

7. See West, "Awakening the Press Clause," 1047–48.

8. Ibid.

9. Warren and Brandeis, "Right to Privacy," 193.

10. Ibid., 198.

11. Katz v. United States, 389 U.S. 347 (1967). This is a seminal case interpreting the Fourth Amendment, which deals with government intrusions into privacy. It was the first clear articulation by the Court that citizens hold a "reasonable expectation of privacy" as a matter of right, which should not be invaded.

12. Solove, "Conceptualizing Privacy," 1087.

13. Ibid., 1113.

14. Ibid., 1111, 1114.

15. Ibid.

16. See Richards and Solove, "Privacy's Other Path," 126.

17. See Allen, "Daniel J. Meador Lecture," 1375, 1377–78.

18. Richards, "Intellectual Privacy," 387, 389.

19. Richards, "Dangers of Surveillance," 1934, 1945–46.

20. Bambauer, "The New Intrusion," 205, 210.

21. National Association for the Advancement of Colored People v. State of Alabama ex rel. Patterson, 357 U.S. 449, 466 (1958).

22. See Bartnicki v. Vopper, 532 U.S. 514, 554 (2001) (Rehnquist, J., dissenting).

23. See Whitman, "The Two Western Cultures of Privacy," 1151.

24. Brandenburg v. Ohio, 395 U.S. 444, 447 (1969). ("The constitutional guarantees of free speech and free press do not permit a State to forbid or proscribe advocacy of the use of force or of law violation except where such advocacy is directed to inciting or producing imminent lawless action and is likely to incite or produce such action.").

25. In Germany, *Volksverhetzung* (incitement of popular hatred) is a punishable offense under section 130 of the Strafgesetzbuch (Germany's criminal code) and can lead to up to five years' imprisonment. Section 130 makes it a crime to publicly incite hatred against parts of the population or to call for violent or arbitrary measures against them or to insult, maliciously slur, or defame them in a manner violating their constitutionally protected human dignity. Thus, for instance, it is illegal to publicly call certain ethnic groups "maggots" or "freeloaders." Volksverhetzung is punishable in Germany even if committed abroad and even if committed by non-German citizens.

26. In Texas v. Johnson, 491 U.S. 397 (1989), the U.S. Supreme Court held that the burning of an American flag was protected expression under the First Amendment where there was no threatened disturbance of the peace.

27. See Roth v. United States, 354 U.S. 476, 485 (1957).

28. Solove, "Conceptualizing Privacy," 1087.

29. Ibid., 1146.

30. Ibid., 1154.

31. Ibid.

32. Nissenbaum, "Privacy as Contextual Integrity," 119.

33. Solove, "Conceptualizing Privacy," 1152.

34. Ibid., 1153.

35. While discussed here as a theory, the principles at issue are evolving into law, at least in the European Union. See Google Spain v. AEPD & Mario Costeja Gonzalez, C-131/12 (May 13, 2014).

36. Center for Democracy and Technology, "On the 'Right to Be Forgotten': Challenges and Suggested Changes to the Data Protection Regulation," May 2, 2013, https://www.cdt.org/files/pdfs/CDT-Free-Expression-and-the-RTBF.pdf.

37. McNealy, "Emerging Conflict between Newsworthiness and the Right to Be Forgotten," 120–22.

38. Gordon Rayner, "Duke and Duchess of Cambridge Consider Legal Action," *Daily Telegraph*, September 14, 2012, http://www.telegraph.co.uk/news/uknews/kate-middleton/9542954/Duke-and-Duchess-of-Cambridge-consider-legal-action-over-unjustifiable-publication-of-topless-pictures.html.

39. Brancheau v. Demings, No. 2010-CA-6673, 2010 WL 7971871, *5–6 (Fla. 9th Cir. Ct. 2010).

40. Pell v. Procunier, 417 U.S. 817, 833 (1974), quoting Branzburg v. Hayes, 408 U.S. 665 (1972).

41. The First Amendment does not confer a license on the press to violate valid criminal laws. Branzburg v. Hayes, 408 U.S. at 691. See Dietemann v. Time, Inc., 449 F.2d 245 (9th Cir. 1971), holding employees of magazine liable for gaining entrance to plaintiff's personal office and using hidden cameras and recording devices without plaintiff's permission.

42. The illegality of the acquisition of the information can impose liability on the newsgatherer as well as the publisher, depending upon the publisher's knowledge at the time of publication. See Boehner v. McDermott, 484 F.3d 573 (D.C. Cir. 2007); Peavy v. WFAA-TV, Inc., 221 F.3d 158 (5th Cir. 2000); Quigley v. Rosenthal, 427 F.3d 1232 (10th Cir. 2005); Pearson v. Dodd, 410 F.2d 701 (D.C. Cir. 1969).

43. Peavy v. WFAA-TV, Inc., 221 F.3d 172 (5th Cir. 2000).

44. Bartnicki v. Vopper, 532 U.S. 514 (2001), finding that a stranger's illegal conduct does not remove the First Amendment shield from speech that contains matters of public concern.

45. Desnick v. American Broadcasting Companies, Inc., 44 F.3d 1345, 1351–52 (7th Cir. 1995).

46. Ibid., 1352.

47. Ibid.

48. Ibid.

49. Charter of Fundamental Rights of the European Union, chap. 1, art. 1, 2000 O.J. (C 364) 1 (EC).

50. Douglas v. Hello Ltd., (2005) EWCA Civ 595 (2006) QB 125.

51. See Mills, *Privacy*, 36.

52. 5 U.S.C. §552—Public information; agency rules, opinions, orders, records, and proceedings, http://www.law.cornell.edu/uscode/text/5/552.

53. New York Times Co. v. Sullivan, 376 U.S. 254, 279–80 (1964).

54. See Gertz v. Robert Welch, Inc., 418 U.S. 323 (1974).

55. Photographs were taken of Princess Caroline of Monaco engaging in private activities. A German federal constitutional court, interpreting German law, enjoined the publication of those photographs that included images of her children because of the private nature of the activity. The court did not, however, protect the images of the princess shopping and relaxing on the beach. Von Hannover v. Germany, 2004-III Eur. Ct. H.R. 294, §25.

56. Levi, "Social Media and the Press," 1555.

57. Aniston v. Brandt et al., Case No. BC343896 (Cal. Super. Ct., December 5, 2005).

58. Nissenbaum, "Privacy as Contextual Integrity," 124.

59. Bartnicki v. Vopper, 532 U.S. 514, 535 (2001).

60. Anderson v. Strong Memorial Hospital, 573 N.Y.S. 2d 828, 829–30 (N.Y. Sup. Ct. 1991).

61. Ibid., 832.

62. See CTB v. News Group Newspapers, [2011] EWHC 1232 QB.

63. Edward Gay, "Judge Restricts Online Reporting of Case," *New Zealand Herald*, August 25, 2008, http://www.nzherald.co.nz/nz/news/article.cfm?c_id=1&objectid=10528866.

64. However, it is useful to note that most social media sites restrict such intrusions if there are privacy settings in their Terms of Use agreements.

65. American Law Institute, *Restatement (Second) of Torts*, 1965, §559.

66. Ibid., §558.

67. 376 U.S. 254 (1964). The holding established that a public official suing for defamation must show that the media outlet acted with "actual malice" in order to prevail in the lawsuit.

68. U.N. Human Rights Council Spec. Rapporteur, *Rep. of the Spec. Rapporteur on the Promotion and Protection of the Right to Freedom of Opinion and Expression*, 33–37, 72–73, U.N. Doc. A/HRC/17/27 (May 16, 2011), http://www2.ohchr.org/english/bodies/hrcouncil/docs/17session/A.HRC.17.27_en.pdf.

69. But see Bill Kenworthy and Beth Chesterman, "Criminal-Libel Statutes, State by State," *First Amendment Center*, August 10, 2006, http://www.firstamendmentcenter.org/criminal-libel-statutes-state-by-state.

70. See Dendrite International, Inc. v. Doe No. 3, 775 A.2d 756, 759 (App. Div. 2001).

71. See American Law Institute, *Restatement (Second) of Torts*, 1965, §46.

72. Cal. Civ. Code §1708.8.

Chapter 3. Information, Power, and Intrusion

1. Ariès et al., eds., *A History of Private Life*, 438–39.

2. Hamburger, "Development of the Law of Seditious Libel," 661, 668.

3. Ibid.

4. Manning, "Origins of the Doctrine of Sedition," 99, 111.

5. Ibid.

6. Hamburger, "Development of the Law of Seditious Libel," 668.

7. Ibid.

8. Ibid.

9. Ingelhart, *Press Freedoms*, 17.

10. Ibid.

11. The laws and controls that surrounded the development of the press are discussed later in this chapter.

12. Rosenberg, "Liberty versus Loyalty," 1, 3.

13. Ibid.

14. Ibid., 4.

15. Ibid.

16. Ibid., 6–7. See also Merrill et al., eds., *Twilight of Press Freedom*, 3, 6–7.

17. Ibid., 4.

18. Abrams v. United States, 250 U.S. 616, 630 (1919) (Holmes, J., dissenting).

19. See generally Smith, *Printers and Press Freedom*.

20. Anderson, "Freedom of the Press," 429, 446.

21. De Sola Pool, *Technologies of Freedom*, 11.

22. Schwartz, "The Bill of Rights," vol. 1, 266.

23. See *Madison's Fourth Proposal to the House (1789)* in Gales and Seaton, eds., 451.

24. Berns, "Freedom of the Press and the Alien and Sedition Laws," 109, 113.

25. Ibid.

26. Ibid.

27. See Merrill et al., eds., *Twilight of Press Freedom*, 19.

28. Ibid., 21.

29. Boesche, *The Strange Liberalism of Alexis de Tocqueville*, 179.

30. Ibid., 177.

31. Franklin et al., eds., *Mass Media Law*, 365.

32. Warren and Brandeis, "Right to Privacy," 196.

33. Gormley, "One Hundred Years of Privacy," 1335, 1343–45.

34. Warren and Brandeis, "Right to Privacy," 195–96.

35. Ibid., 195.

36. Ibid., 210–11.

37. Ibid., 211.

38. Ibid.

39. Ibid., 196.

40. "Yellow journalism" refers to a highly publicized feud between rival newspaper publishers Hearst and Pulitzer over a cartoon published in an effort to sell more newspapers. See Milton, *The Yellow Kids*, 40–41.

41. Gormley, "One Hundred Years of Privacy," 1350.

42. Ibid., 1355, citing Roberson v. Rochester Folding Box Co., 64 N.E. 442 (N.Y. 1902).

43. Pavesich v. New England Life Insurance Co., 50 S.E. 68 (Ga. 1905).

44. See, for example, New York in Roberson v. Rochester Folding Box Co., 64 N.E. 442 (N.Y. 1902).

45. Ibid. In 1899 California amended its criminal libel statute, which made it a misdemeanor to publish a portrait of a person in a newspaper or book without that person's consent. In 1903 New York enacted a statute that prohibited the use of an individual's name or likeness, without consent, for advertising or trade purposes. §§1–2, 1903 N.Y. Laws 308. Pennsylvania enacted a statute in 1903 that allowed for civil actions for negligent but nondefamatory newspaper publications. Pa. Laws 265 (1903). Virginia and Utah are similar to New York. See Va. Code Ann. §8.01-40; Utah Code Ann. §§76-4-8 to 76-4-9 (1953).

46. Ingelhart, *Press Freedoms*, 221.

47. Ibid., 222.

48. See generally Federal Communications Commission online, "About the FCC," http://www.fcc.gov/aboutus.html.

49. See F.C.C. v. Fox Television Stations et al., 556 U.S. 502 (2009), holding that the FCC's new policy on "fleeting expletives" was not an arbitrary and capricious standard although the standard could not be implemented in this case because of a lack of adequate notice to Fox and ABC.

50. Cable and satellite communications are regulated differently because the information is not transmitted through public airwaves. Private companies contract with individuals to provide cable and satellite services. Thus, because of the private nature of the communication, the FCC asserts more limited control.

51. In reference to other global satellite communications, the International Telecommunications Satellite Organization (INTELSAT), an intergovernmental consortium that owns and manages a constellation of international broadcast services, largely regulates international satellite communications. For more information regarding INTELSAT, see generally http://www.intelsat.com/. Also see International Media, TV & Broadcasting Regulation Authorities (itve.org) for a list of countries and the governmental organizations that regulate the national media, http://www.international-television.org/regulation.html.

52. United Nations Charter, chap. 1, art. 2, para. 4, http://www.un.org/en/documents/charter/chapter1.shtml.

53. A. Cohen, "The Media That Needs Citizens," 1, 3.

54. See Levi, "Social Media and the Press," 1549.

55. See Colleen Shalby, "Conflicting Reports on Alleged Boston Suspect Flood Social Media," *PBS Newshour*, April 17, 2013, http://www.pbs.org/newshour/rundown/boston-marathon-bombing-sparks-clashing-reports-regarding-possible-arrest/.

56. Ibid.

57. Ibid.

58. Ibid.

59. Ibid.

60. Warren and Brandeis, "Right to Privacy," 195.

61. Red Lion Broadcasting Co. v. F.C.C., 395 U.S. 367, 399–400 (1969).

62. Reno v. American Civil Liberties Union, 521 U.S. 844, 868–69 (1997).

63. See Bland v. Roberts, 730 F.3d 368, 386 (4th Cir. 2013), as amended (September 23, 2013).

64. Ibid., 394.

65. Ibid., 387.

66. United States v. Maynard, 615 F.3d 544, 562 (D.C. Cir. 2010).

67. Ibid.

68. See, for example, United States v. Skinner, 690 F.3d 772, 777 (6th Cir. 2012), stating that the "law cannot be that a criminal is entitled to rely on the expected untrackability of his tools" and implying that such expectation with

regard to a cell phone is unreasonable; United States v. Takai, 943 F. Supp. 2d 1315, 1322–25 (D. Utah 2013).

69. Aristotle, *Metaphysics*, book 1, part 1.

70. See Dunbar, "Gossip in Evolutionary Perspective," 100, 109. Dunbar theorizes that language itself developed as a result of the socially oriented human brain that has a naturally intense interest in the doings of others.

71. Suler, "Online Disinhibition Effect," Abstract, 321.

72. Suler, "Online Disinhibition Effect," 184.

73. See CNN iReport.com, which provides would-be iReporters with a means to upload potential stories, http://ireport.cnn.com/.

74. See Doug Gross, "Survey: More Americans Get News from Internet than Newspapers or Radio," CNN.com, March 1, 2010, http://www.cnn.com/2010/TECH/03/01/social.network.news/.

75. Ibid. Gross points out that "social networking sites like Facebook and Twitter have made news a more participatory experience than ever before."

76. *PRweb*, "Media Advisory: Schools Facing Learning Crises Spawned by Internet," January 28, 2011, http://www.prweb.com/releases/2011/01/prweb5010 934.htm.

77. Ibid.

78. Ibid.

79. See http://zapatopi.net/treeoctopus.

80. *PRweb*, "Media Advisory: Schools Facing Learning Crises Spawned by Internet," January 28, 2011, http://www.prweb.com/releases/2011/01/prweb5010 934.htm.

81. Ibid.

82. Ibid.

83. Ian Parker, "The Story of a Suicide," *New Yorker*, February 6, 2012.

84. Johnson, *The Information Diet*.

85. Ibid.

86. See Levi, "Social Media and the Press," 1572–78.

Chapter 4. The Globalization of Information

1. Rosenberg, "Liberty versus Loyalty," 2.

2. Ibid.

3. Obsidian Finance Group, LLC v. Cox, 740 F. 3d 1284, 1291 (9th Cir. 2014).

4. See Siebert, Peterson, and Schramm, *Four Theories of the Press*.

5. Merrill, *Global Journalism*, 13.

6. Lloyd, "A Criticism of Social Responsibility Theory," 199.

7. Ibid.

8. Merrill, *Global Journalism*, 13, 15.

9. Lloyd, "A Criticism of Social Responsibility Theory," 200.

10. Ibid., 201.

11. Ingelhart, *Press Freedoms*, 346.

12. Whitman, "The Two Western Cultures of Privacy," 1156.

13. Ibid., 1161.

14. Barron, "Book Review: Press Law in Modern Democracies," 434, 447.

15. *Universal Declaration of Human Rights*, art. 12, December 10, 1948, http://www.un.org/en/documents/udhr/.

16. See *International Covenant on Civil and Political Rights*, art. 17, December 16, 1966, http://www.ohchr.org/en/professionalinterest/pages/ccpr.aspx.

17. APEC Elec. Commerce Steering Group, APEC Privacy Framework Factsheet, http://www.apec.org/About-Us/About-APEC/Fact-Sheets/APEC-Privacy-Framework.aspx.

18. Chris Pounder, "Why the APEC Privacy Framework Is Unlikely to Protect Privacy," Out-Law.com, October 15, 2007, http://www.out-law.com/page-8550.

19. Ibid.

20. Ibid.

21. Article I, UNESCO Res. 4/9.3/2.20, UNESCO Gen. Conf. Res., UNESCO doc. 20 C/Resolutions, at 100–104 (1978).

22. Great Britain also withdrew.

23. However, in 2010, President Barack Obama signed legislation intended to promote a free press around the world. Inspired by the murder in Pakistan of journalist Daniel Pearl, the Daniel Pearl Freedom of the Press Act requires the State Department to expand its scrutiny of news media restrictions and intimidation as part of its annual review of human rights in each country.

24. See, for example, Society of Professional Journalists, "Code of Ethics," 1996, http://www.spj.org/pdf/ethicscode.pdf.

25. Reporters Without Borders, press release, October 16, 2007.

26. Kim Zetter, "World's Top Surveillance Societies," *Wired*, December 31, 2004, http://blog.wired.com/27bstroke6/2007/12/worlds-top-surv.html.

27. Compare Von Hannover v. Germany, 2004-III Eur. Ct. H.R. 294, §25, finding a privacy violation when photographs of the Princess of Monaco engaging in private activities with her children were published without her consent, with Moreno et al. v. Hanford Sentinel, Inc. et al., F054138, slip op. (Cal. Ct. App. April 2, 2009), finding no privacy violation for an intrusive newspaper article when the person discussed in the article had opened herself up to criticism when she published controversial information on her MySpace page.

28. Sipple v. Chronicle Publishing Co., 154 Cal. App. 3d 1040 (Ct. App. 1984).

29. Ibid.

30. Whitman, "The Two Western Cultures of Privacy," 1197.

31. Ibid.

32. Cade Metz, "Maradona Rubbed from Yahoo! Web by Argentinean Judge," *Register*, January 15, 2009, http://www.theregister.co.uk/2008/11/13/yahoo_and _maradona/.

33. Ibid.

34. Ibid.

35. Dow Jones & Co. v. Gutnick, [2002] H.C.A. 56, 2002 (Austl.).

36. House of Lords, Judgments—Berezovsky v. Michaels and Others, http://www.parliament.the-stationery-office.co.uk/pa/ld199900/ldjudgmt/jd000511/bere-1.htm.

37. For more information on the Godfrey case, see Mike Ingram, "UK Internet Libel Case Could Set Dangerous Precedent," World Socialist Web Site, April 16, 1999, http://www.wsws.org/en/articles/1999/04/int-a16.html.

38. Lewis v. King, [2004] EWCA (Civ) 1329 (Eng.).

39. Ibid.

40. Ibid.

41. Weaver et al., *The Right to Speak Ill*, 188, 198.

42. Ibid., 198–99.

43. See House of Lords, Judgments—Berezovsky v. Michaels and Others, http://www.parliament.the-stationery-office-co.uk/pa/ld199900/ldjudgment/jd000511/bere-1.ht.

44. American Law Institute, *Restatement (Second) of Conflict of Laws*, 1971, §6, 10.

45. See Internet Solutions Corp. v. Marshall, 39 So. 3d 1201 (Fla. 2010).

46. Associated Press, "Tabloid Retracts Britney Spears Stories," *USA Today*, July 18, 2006, http://www.usatoday.com/life/people/2006–07–18-spears-enquirer_x.htm.

47. See Ian Herbert, "Hollywood Stars Turn to British Courts to Mount Their Fight for Libel Damages," *Independent*, August 8, 2006, http://www.independent.co.uk/news/uk/crime/hollywood-stars-turn-to-british-courts-to-mount-their-fight-for-libel-damages-410972.html.

48. See Mark Stephens, "New Celebrities of the Libel Courts," *Times (U.K.)*, July 18, 2006.

49. Campbell v. MGN Ltd., [2004] 2 A.C. 457, ¶82 (Hope, L. J.), ¶¶132–33 (Lady Hale, J.).

50. Ibid., 36 (Hoffman, L. J.).

51. Mills, *Privacy*, 90–91, citing Florida Star v. B.J.F., 491 U.S. 524 (1989), where a newspaper's publication of information it obtained lawfully regarding the name of a rape victim was protected by the First Amendment.

52. Bin Mahfouz v. Ehrenfeld, [2005] EWHC (QB) 1156 (Eng.).

53. Douglass Lee, "N.Y. Protects Authors against Foreign Libel Judgments,"

First Amendment Center, May 12, 2008, http://www.firstamendmentcenter
.org/n-y-protects-authors-against-foreign-libel-judgments.

54. Beauchamp, "England's Chilling Forecast," 3073.

55. Ehrenfeld v. Bin Mahfouz, 2006 U.S. Dist. LEXIS 23423 (So. Dist. N.Y. 2006).

56. Ibid.

57. Ehrenfeld v. Bin Mahfouz, 489 F.3d 582 (2d Cir. 2007).

58. Ehrenfeld v. Bin Mahfouz, 881 N.E. 2d 830, 831 (N.Y. 2007).

59. Ibid., 835.

60. Weinstein, Korn, and Miller, *New York Civil Practice*, §302(d), stating, "Foreign defamation judgment. The courts of this state shall have personal jurisdiction over any person who obtains a judgment in a defamation proceeding outside the United States against any person who is a resident of New York or is a person or entity amendable to jurisdiction in New York who has assets in New York or may have to take actions in New York to comply with the judgment, for the purposes of rending declaratory relief with respect to that person's liability for the judgment, and/or for the purpose of determining whether said judgment should be deemed non-recognizable . . . to the fullest extent permitted by the United States constitution, provided: (1) the publication at issue was published in New York, and (2) that resident or personal amenable to jurisdiction in New York (i) has assets in New York which might be used to satisfy the foreign defamation judgment, or (ii) may have to take actions in New York to comply with the foreign defamation judgment. The provisions of this subdivision shall apply to persons who obtained judgments in defamation proceedings outside the United States prior to and/or after the effective date of this subdivision."

61. See Bob Egelko, "'Libel Tourism' Bill Passes State Senate," *San Francisco Chronicle*, May 15, 2009, http://www.sfgate.com/cgi-bin/article.cgi?f=/c/a/2009/05/15/BA7I17KKT6.DTL. Also see Douglass Lee, "N.Y. Protects Authors against Foreign Libel Judgments," First Amendment Center, May 12, 2008, http://www.firstamendmentcenter.org/n-y-protects-authors-against-foreign-libel-judgments.

62. Samantha Fredrickson, "Specter Re-Introduces 'Libel Tourism' Bill in Senate," Reporters Committee for Freedom of the Press, February 17, 2009, http://www.rcfp.org/browse-media-law-resources/news/specter-re-introduces-libel-tourism-bill-senate.

63. Free Speech Protection Act of 2009, S. 449 IS, 111th Congress, February 13, 2009, http://www.govtrack.us/congress/bills/111/s449.

64. See *New York Times*, "Libel Tourism," editorial, May 26, 2009, A18.

65. Free Speech Protection Act of 2009, S. 449 IS, 111th Congress, February 13, 2009, http://www.govtrack.us/congress/bills/111/s449.

66. See "Statement of Professor Linda J. Silberman before the Subcommittee on Commercial and Administrative Law of the U.S. House of Representatives, Committee on the Judiciary," February 12, 2009, 5, http://judiciary.house.gov/hearings/pdf/Silberman090212.pdf.

67. See Murphy, "International Law and the Internet," 405.

68. Ibid.

69. See Silberman statement from n66 above, 5.

70. Ibid., 7.

71. Ibid., 9.

72. Ibid., 10.

Chapter 5. The Internet Defies the Gatekeepers

1. For example, anyone can acquire a domain name, so long as it is not already in existence, by paying companies such as Godaddy.com for the service. See GoDaddy.com, http://www.godaddy.com/, discussing procedure and prices for obtaining a domain name.

2. South Korea, for one, requires identification.

3. Reno v. American Civil Liberties Union, 521 U.S. 844, 851 (1997).

4. 47 U.S.C. §230—Protection for private blocking and screening of offensive material, (b)(2) (2006), http://www.law.cornell.edu/uscode/text/47/230.

5. Jennifer Valentino-DeVries, "FTC Hints at Findings in Upcoming Privacy Report," *Wall Street Journal*, September 24, 2010, http://blogs.wsj.com/digits/2010/09/24/ftc-hints-at-findings-in-upcoming-privacy-report/.

6. Solove and Hartzog, "The FTC and the New Common Law of Privacy," 114.

7. Julia Angwin, "Watchdog Planned for Online Privacy," *Wall Street Journal*, November 12, 2010, http://online.wsj.com/article/SB2000142405274870384820 4575608970171176014.html.

8. Weaver. *From Gutenberg to the Internet*, 10.

9. Ibid., 13.

10. Lev Grossman, "Iran Protests: Twitter, the Medium of the Movement," *Time*, June 17, 2009, http://www.time.com/time/world/article/0,8599, 1905125,00.html.

11. See ICT Regulation Toolkit, InfoDev, and International Telecommunications Union, http://www.ictregulationtoolkit.org/en/Section.2189.html.

12. Harbit and Clark, "Shaping the Internet in China," 377.

13. See Goldsmith and Wu, *Who Controls the Internet*, noting, "Search engines like Google routinely block links because of possible government action. Google receives a constant stream of letters in the United States—about thirty a month—insisting that it remove specified pages from its search results. . . . Google complies with most of these requests" (75).

14. Ibid. Usually the government orders ISPs to remove these pages because they are in violation of U.S. copyright or trademark laws.

15. Ibid., 73. For example, if a web page created in France is posted on a U.S. website, the U.S. government has no jurisdiction to order the French creator to take down the site. However, the government can threaten the domestic ISPs that post the web page on U.S. sites with sanctions.

16. Ibid.

17. Ibid., 97. Moreover, the government also controls the Internet internally by requiring Internet café users to register their national IDs prior to their issuance of a computer. Further, these computers are continuously monitored via surveillance cameras and by roaming officers who are ensuring that users are not using the Internet for any prohibited reason. Thus, China has found a unique way to limit its citizens' freedom of speech, which is essentially by violating their right to privacy as well (at least by U.S. standards).

18. The government prevents external information from entering China by regulating the "nine Internet Access Providers that control the physical lines to the outside world." Basically, the Chinese government filters the information traveling through these IAPs, dumping the information it does not approve of and allowing the information that it does. See Alfred Hermida, "Behind China's Internet Red Firewall," BBC News, September 3, 2002, http://news.bbc.co.uk/2/hi/technology/2234154.stm. Thus, the Chinese Internet user could connect to a proxy server in the United States to request information banned by the Chinese government. But the Chinese government had considered the use of proxy servers and therefore implemented proxy-blocking efforts intended to jam or block the use of proxy servers from within the country. See Jonathan Zittrain and Benjamin Edelman, "Empirical Analysis of Internet Filtering in China," Research Publication No. 2003–02, Berkman Center for Internet and Society, Harvard Law School, March 20, 2003, http://cyber.law.harvard.edu/filtering/china/.

19. Kreimer, "Censorship by Proxy," 11.

20. See "Internet Filtering in China," OpenNet Initiative, May 9, 2009, https://opennet.net/sites/opennet.net/files/ONI_China_2009.pdf.

21. For example, the Chinese government is not able to regulate U.S. sites that discuss such topics as democracy, freedom, or liberty, but it may control access to U.S. sites.

22. China's attempt to censor the Internet has also been referred to as the Golden Shield Project. The project was begun by the Ministry of Public Security (MPS) in 1998 and was in operation by 2003. The project cost an estimated U.S. $800 million. See Walton, *China's Golden Shield*; see also Martin J. Young, "Asia's Battle against the Web," *Asia Times*, May 16, 2007, http://www.atimes.com/atimes/asian_economy/ie16dk01.html. With the Golden Shield Project, MPS is

attempting "to build a nationwide digital surveillance network, linking national, regional and local security agencies with a panoptic web of surveillance" with the goal that this firewall will be "a database-driven remote surveillance system—offering immediate access to registration records on every citizen in China, while linking to vast networks of cameras designed to cut police reaction time to demonstrations." Chen, "Legislative Update," 229, 266.

23. See Kreimer, "Censorship by Proxy," 19, 22. For example, in Germany the manager of CompuServe was prosecuted for allowing child porn through German ISP portals from outside nations. Furthermore, European nations are much more likely to block sites that would be lawful in the United States, such as sites relating to Nazism or white supremacy. In fact, in 2002 Google in France and Germany blocked more than one hundred sites that were available on the U.S. Google site.

24. Statutory Instrument 2002, no. 2013, The Electronic Commerce (EC Directive) Regulations 2002, http://www.opsi.gov.uk/si/si2002/20022013.htm. Under the directive, ISPs fall into the broad definition "information society service," which includes "any service normally provided for remuneration, at a distance, by means of electronic equipment for the processing (including digital compression) and storage of data, and at the individual request of a recipient of a service."

25. EC Directive Regulation, 16.

26. EC Directive Regulation, 17.

27. Ibid.

28. EC Directive Regulation, 18.

29. Ibid.

30. See Google Spain v. AEPD & Mario Costeja Gonzalez, C-131/12 (May 13, 2014).

31. Pub. L. No. 104-104 codified at 47 U.S.C. 230 (1996).

32. See Zeran v. America Online, Inc., 129 F.3d 327, 333 (4th Cir. 1997). The *Zeran* court's rationale for immunizing ISPs under these circumstances was based on the fact that while it may be feasible for the traditional print publisher to cipher through all potential defamatory statements prior to publication, "the sheer number of postings on interactive computer services would create an impossible burden in the Internet context."

33. 47 U.S.C. §230(c)(1). See also 47 U.S.C. §230(c)(2) providing:

No provider or user of an interactive computer service shall be held liable on account of:
(A) any action voluntarily taken in good faith to restrict access to or availability of material that the provider or user considers to be obscene,

lewd, lascivious, filthy, excessively violent, harassing, or otherwise objectionable, whether or not such material is constitutionally protected; or

(B) any action taken to enable or make available to information content providers or others the technical means to restrict access to material described in paragraph (1) subparagraph (A).

34. Batzel v. Smith, 333 F.3d 1018, 1030 (9th Cir. 2003), quoting 47 U.S.C. §230(f)(2).

35. Balkin, "The Future of Expression in a Digital Age," 427, 433.

36. Chicago Lawyers' Committee for Civil Rights under the Law, Inc. v. Craigslist, Inc., 519 F.3d 666, 672 (7th Cir. 2008): a plaintiff "cannot sue the messenger just because the message reveals a third party's plan to engage in unlawful discrimination."

37. Ibid., 671–72.

38. See Jones v. Dirty World Entertainment Recordings, LLC, 840 F. Supp. 2d 1008 (2012); Hare v. Richie, 2012 WL 3773116 (2012).

39. Jones v. Dirty World Entertainment Recordings, LLC, 840 F. Supp. 2d 1010 (2012), quoting Fair Housing Council of San Fernando Valley v. Roommates.com, LLC, 521 F.3d 1157 (9th Cir. 2008).

40. Hare v. Richie, 2012 WL 3773116 *17 (2012).

41. Ibid.

42. Jones v. Dirty World Entertainment Recordings, LLC, 840 F. Supp. 2d 1012 (2012), quoting Fair Housing Council of San Fernando Valley v. Roommates.com, LLC, 521 F.3d 1157 (9th Cir. 2008).

43. Jones v. Dirty World Entertainment Recordings, LLC, Case No. 13–5946 (6th Cir.) (June 16, 2014).

44. However, in the United States immunity for ISPs is based on statute, which establishes that ISPs "merely provide the forum for publication." In countries such as the United Kingdom, ISP liability is still largely based on common law principles to determine whether the ISP was essentially a publisher of the defamatory statement and, therefore, liable. See Michael Geist, "UK Court Rules on ISP Liability," blog posting, March 14, 2006, http://www.michaelgeist.ca/content/view/1163/125/.

45. Bunt v. Tilley, [2006] EWCH 407 (QB) [34]. The U.K. test of a "passive publisher" is much like the U.S. standard defined in the CDA.

46. See ibid., [59](2), defining publisher as meaning "a commercial publisher, that is, a person whose business is issuing material to the public, or a section of the public, who issues material containing the statement in the course of that business." See also ibid., (3) defining who should not be considered a publisher.

47. Godfrey v. Demon Internet Ltd., QBD [1999] 4 All ER 342; [2000] 3 WLR 1020; [2001] QB 201.

48. Godfrey v. Demon Internet Ltd., [2001] QB 201, 205.

49. Ibid., 207–9.

50. See discussion in Mills, "Two Contemporary Privacy Issues in Poland," 110.

51. Ibid.

52. Toby Mendel, "Mapping Digital Media: Online Media and Defamation," Open Society Foundation, April 2011, http://www.opensocietyfoundations.org/reports/mapping-digital-media-online-media-and-defamation.

53. Associated Free Press, "Google Fined for 'Paedophile' Libel against Priest," *Herald Sun*, April 26, 2010, http://www.heraldsun.com.au/news/world/google-fined-for-paedophile-libel-against-priest/story-e6frf7lf-1225858177940.

54. Proposition Draft Bill on Civil Rights Framework for Internet in Brazil, sec. 1, art. 9, http://culturadigital.br/marcocivil/2010/05/07/new-proposal-for-section-iv-for-download/.

55. Associated Press, "YouTube Blocked in Brazil," *Los Angeles Times*, January 9, 2007, http://articles.latimes.com/2007/jan/09/business/fi-youtube9.

56. Alan Clendenning, "Judge Lifts Order That Led to YouTube Ban in Brazil," *USA Today*, January 9, 2007, http://www.usatoday.com/tech/news/2007-01-09-brazil-youtube_x.htm.

57. French web users were accessing the Yahoo Auctions site in the United States to purchase Nazi memorabilia. See Goldsmith and Wu, *Who Controls the Internet*, 2. See also Callister, "The Internet, Regulation and the Market for Loyalties," 70.

58. Goldsmith and Wu, *Who Controls the Internet*, 5, internal citation omitted.

59. Callister, "The Internet, Regulation and the Market for Loyalties," 59, 62–63.

60. Goldsmith and Wu, *Who Controls the Internet*, 5, noting that Yahoo's founder, Jerry Yang, stated that Yahoo was not going to take down its site in the United States simply because a French judge ordered them to do so.

61. See Callister, "The Internet, Regulation and the Market for Loyalties," 71–72, citing Yahoo!, Inc. v. La Ligue Contre Le Racisme et L'Antisemitisme, 169 F. Supp. 2d 1181, 1193 (N.D. Cal. 2001).

62. Yahoo!, Inc. v. La Ligue Contre Le Racisme et L'Antisemitisme, 169 F. Supp. 2d 1186.

63. Goldsmith and Wu, *Who Controls the Internet*, 8.

64. Jon M. Garon, "New Legislation Renews Conflict between Content Creators and Content Distributors," *Business Law Today*, December 2011, http://apps.americanbar.org/buslaw/blt/content/2011/12/article-1-garon.pdf.

65. Ibid.

66. Katz v. U.S., 389 U.S. 347, 361 (1967) (Harlan, J., concurring).

67. American Law Institute, *Restatement (Second) of Torts*, 1977, §652D.

68. Ibid.

69. Ibid., §652B.

70. Jonathan Lynn, "Internet Users to Exceed 2 Billion This Year," Reuters, October 19, 2010, http://www.reuters.com/article/2010/10/19/us-telecoms-internet-idUSTRE69I24720101019.

71. Preece, *Online Communities*.

72. Compare the different treatment that the disclosure of one's sexuality received in two different countries. In the United States, Oliver Sipple, who saved President Ford from assassination, was outed in the mainstream media as a homosexual man. Sipple could not show public disclosure of private facts because he had become a public figure due to his role in averting the attempted assassination and because people in his local community (San Francisco?) knew him to be a homosexual. Therefore, his homosexuality was not a private fact. Compare this outcome to France, where a man had his photograph taken at a gay pride parade. In France, the fact that he had revealed his sexuality to a restricted community (the gay community of Paris) did not mean that he had lost all protection before the larger public. See chap. 2, Mills, *Privacy*, 288–89.

73. See United States v. Kilbride, 584 F.3d 1240, 1244 (9th Cir. 2009).

74. Miller v. California, 413 U.S. 15, 20–23 (1973).

75. Ibid., 24.

76. Roth v. United States, 354 U.S. 476, 484–85 (1957).

77. Queen v. Hicklin, [1868] L.R. 3 Q.B. 360, 1868 WL 9940; see also Roth v. United States, 354 U.S. 488–89 (listing relevant cases).

78. Ibid., 489.

79. Miller v. California, 413 U.S. 33; see also Hamling v. United States, 418 U.S. 87 (1974), emphasizing that the purpose of the community standard criterion "is to assure that the material is judged neither on the basis of each juror's personal opinion, nor by its effect on a particularly sensitive or insensitive person or group."

80. See U.S. Federal Communications Commission, http://www.fcc.gov/aboutus.html.

81. 18 U.S.C. §1464—Broadcasting obscene language; F.C.C. v. Fox Television Stations et al., 556 U.S. 502 (2009). Note that current indecency enforcement is between 6 a.m. and 10 p.m. It is a violation of federal law to broadcast obscene programming at any time. It is also a violation of federal law to air indecent programming or profane language during certain hours.

82. The Motion Picture Association of America (MPAA) rates U.S. films. The rating system, created in 1968, is not required by law but rather allows the American film industry to self-regulate by voluntary submission. All six major U.S. motion picture studios are members of the MPAA. The ratings (G, PG, PG-13,

R, and NC-17) are determined by an independent board of parents. The board considers factors such as sexuality, violence, and language in rating the films.

83. Ashcroft v. American Civil Liberties Union, 535 U.S. 564 (2002).

84. Ibid., 569.

85. Reno v. American Civil Liberties Union, 521 U.S. 844, 877–78 (1997).

86. Hamling v. United States, 418 U.S. 87 (1974), dealing with the dissemination of pornographic brochures via U.S. mail; Sable Communications of California, Inc. v. FCC, 492 U.S. 115 (1989), dealing with sexually explicit telephone operators.

87. Ashcroft v. American Civil Liberties Union, 535 U.S. 582 (2002).

88. Ibid., 583 (O'Connor, J., concurring).

89. Ibid., 587.

90. Ibid., 589.

91. Ibid., 590 (Breyer, J., concurring).

92. Ibid., 595 (Kennedy, J., concurring), quoting Red Lion Broadcasting Co. v. F.C.C., 395 U.S. 367, 386 (1969).

93. United States v. Kilbride, 84 F.3d 1240 (9th Cir. 2009).

94. Ibid., 1254.

95. United States v. Little, 365 F. App'x 159, 164 (11th Cir. 2010).

96. Ibid. In 2005 the Third Circuit likewise declined to alter the *Miller* test (see Miller v. California, 413 U.S.) to account for a lack of Internet jurisdiction. See United States v. Extreme Associates, Inc., 431 F.3d 150 (3d Cir. 2005).

97. Ibid.

98. Edward Wasserman, "World of Expression Undergoing a Cleavage," *Miami Herald*, October 11, 2010, http://www.miamiherald.com/2010/10/11/1867315/world-of-expression-undergoing.html.

99. McIntyre v. Ohio Elections Commission, 514 U.S. 334, 342 (1995).

100. Coleman Jr., "A Free Press," 243, 244.

101. Lidsky, "Silencing John Doe," 855, 892–904.

102. Ibid., 888–92.

103. Ibid., 890.

104. Jennifer Steinhauer, "Verdict in MySpace Suicide Case," *New York Times*, November 26, 2008.

105."MySpace Kicks Out 90,000 Sex Offenders, Connecticut AG Says," CNN. com, Feb. 4, 2009, http://www.cnn.com/2009/TECH/02/03/myspace.sex. offenders/index.html?eref=yahoo.

106. Debra Cassens Weiss, "DC Lawyer Pursues Suit to Unmask Authors Who Changed Her Wikipedia Page," *ABA Journal*, September 16, 2013, at http://www.abajournal.com/news/article/dc_lawyer_pursues_suit_to_unmask_authors_who_changed_her_wikipedia_page (last accessed Oct. 3, 2013).

107. Section 230(c)(1) of this act states, "No provider or user of an interactive computer service shall be treated as the publisher or speaker of any information provided by another information content provider." See 47 U.S.C. §230(c)(1), http://www.law.cornell.edu/uscode/text/47/230.

108. Carafano v. Metrosplash.com, Inc., 339 F.3d 1119, 1122 (9th Cir. 2003).

109. Ibid., 1121.

110. Ibid., 1121–22.

111. Ibid., 1122.

112. Ibid.

113. Ibid., 1124.

114. Ibid.

115. Catsouras v. Department of California Highway Patrol, 181 Cal. App. 4th 856, 865 (Cal. 4th Dist. Ct. App. 2010).

116. Ibid.

117. Ibid., 863.

118. Ibid.

119. Ibid., 865. See also Jessica Bennet, "A Tragedy That Won't Fade Away," *Newsweek*, April 25, 2009, http://www.newsweek.com/id/195073/page/3 (last visited October 19, 2009).

120. Jessica Bennett, "A Tragedy That Won't Fade Away," *Newsweek*, April 25, 2009, http://www.newsweek.com/id/195073/page/3 (last visited October 19, 2009).

121. Catsouras v. Department of California Highway Patrol, Minute Order, February 11, 2008, http://www.concurringopinions.com/archives/images/Catsouras Opinion.html (last visited October 19, 2009).

122. Catsouras v. Department of California Highway Patrol, 856.

123. ReputationDefender.com, a company that aims to clean up one's Internet reputation by the removal of negative media and the circulation of positive media, began representing the Catsouras family after the accident. See Jessica Bennett, "A Tragedy That Won't Fade Away," *Newsweek*, April 25, 2009, http://www.newsweek.com/id/195073/page/3 (last visited October 19, 2009).

124. Ibid.

125. A search of "Nikki Catsouras accident photos" on Google.com had returned 74,900 results as of November 22, 2010.

126. Jeffrey R. Young, "JuicyCampus Shuts Down, Blaming the Economy, Not the Controversy," *Chronicle of Higher Education*, February 5, 2009, https://chronicle.com/article/JuicyCampus-Shuts-Down/1506/.

127. Ibid.

128. "Juicy Terms and Conditions," December 11, 2007, http://juicycampus.blogspot.com/2007/12/juicy-terms-and-conditions.html (last visited October 20, 2009).

129. Ibid.

130. Ibid.

131. "Do you really think Juicy Campus is going to stand up to the police on privacy issues, compromise their website, and defend a student like that? Psh-hhhh." See "Juicy Anonymity," December 9, 2007, http://juicycampus.blogspot .com/2007/12/juicycampus-anonymity.html.

132. Ibid.

133. A federal appeals court has held that defamation rules apply equally to the institutional press and to bloggers. See Obsidian Finance Group, LLC v. Cox, 740 F. 3d 1284, 1291 (9th Cir. 2014).

134. See Dendrite International v. Doe, 775 A.2d 756 (N.J. Super. 2001) (setting the standard); Independent Newspapers, Inc. v. Brodie, 966 A. 2d 432, 454–56 (Md. 2009) (adopting the standard).

135. Doe v. Cahill, 884 A.2d 451, 460 (Del. 2005).

136. Doe v. Individuals, 561 F. Supp. 2d 249 (D. Conn. 2008).

137. Ibid., 251–52.

138. Lidsky, "Anonymity in Cyberspace," 1373, 1386–88.

139. Krinsky v. Doe 6, 159 Cal. App. 4th 1154 (Cal. App. 6th Dist. 2008).

140. Ibid., 1159.

141. Ibid.

142. Ibid.

143. Ibid., 1167.

144. Ibid., 1179.

145. Recall the Auto-Admit case, in which the court staunchly refused to view the defamatory statements as nonfactual assertions despite their location on an Internet message board. However, Lidsky suggests that this distinction is explainable by the private nature of the plaintiff and the resulting low level of public concern for the low-value speech. Lidsky, "Silencing John Doe," 1387–89.

146. Cohen v. Google, Inc., 887 N.Y.S.2d 424, 429–30 (N.Y. Sup. Ct. 2009).

147. Ibid., 425.

148. Ibid., 429.

149. Ibid., 425–26.

150. Ibid., 426.

151. Ibid., 428.

152. Ibid., quoting Gross v. New York Times Co., 82 N.Y.S.2d 153 (N.Y. Sup. Ct. 1993).

153. Keith-Smith v. Williams, [2006] EWHC 860 (QB).

154. Owen Gibson, "Warning to Chatroom Users after Libel Award for Man Labelled a Nazi," Guardian, March 22, 2006, http://www.guardian.co.uk/media/ 2006/mar/23/digitalmedia.law.

155. Ibid.

156. Ibid.

157. Ibid.

158. See Ingelhart, *Press Freedoms*, 11.

159. Ibid., 21.

160. Ibid., 23.

161. Ibid., 25.

162. Bezanson, "The Developing Law of Editorial Judgment," 754, 757.

163. Ibid.

164. Ibid., 856.

165. Ibid.

166. Weaver, "Brandenburg and Incitement in a Digital Era," 1263.

Chapter 6. Is Everyone an iReporter?

1. Mark Glaser, "Distinction between Bloggers, Journalists Blurring More than Ever," *Mediashift* blog posting, February 28, 2008, http://www.pbs.org/mediashift/2008/02/distinction-between-bloggers-journalists-blurring-more-than-ever059/.

2. As Scott Gant notes in *We're All Journalists Now*, "The contributions of citizens working outside established news organizations have not been limited to the disclosure of discrete facts and one-time events. For instance, bloggers— including some active-duty military personnel—have provided important coverage of the conflicts in Iraq and Afghanistan, often supplying information that could not be obtained by mainstream journalists" (32).

3. John R. MacArthur, Publisher's Letter, *Harper's Magazine*, October 2013, 8, http://harpers.org/archive/2013/10/publishers-letter/. In his criticism of the populace's embrace of the new media, MacArthur laments at how many people would agree to spend two or three dollars for an espresso but balk at spending the same for reliable news sourced by traditional media, framing the media debate as a question of economics as well as availability.

4. United States v. Associated Press, 326 U.S. 1, 20 (1945).

5. Snyder v. Phelps, 131 S. Ct. 1207 (2011).

6. Ibid., 1213.

7. Ibid., 1217–19.

8. Snyder v. Phelps oral argument, 20–21, http://www.supremecourt.gov/oral_arguments/argument_transcripts/09–751.pdf.

9. George Stephanopoulos, "Justice Stephen Breyer: Is Burning Koran 'Shouting Fire in a Crowded Theater?'" *ABC News Blogs*, September 14, 2010, http://abcnews.go.com/blogs/politics/2010/09/justice-stephen-breyer-is-burning-koran-shouting-fire-in-a-crowded-theater/.

10. See Hustler Magazine, Inc. v. Falwell, 485 U.S. 46, 56 (1988).

11. Obsidian Finance Group, LLC v. Cox, 740 F. 3d 1284 (9th Cir. 2014).

12. Ibid., 1288–94.

13. Don Van Natta Jr. and Jo Becker, "12th Suspect in Hacking Scandal Arrested in London," *New York Times*, August 10, 2011, A10.

14. Raphael G. Satter, "Media Organizations Condemn Wikileaks' Disclosure," *Washington Times*, September 2, 2011. http://www.washingtontimes.com/news/2011/sep/2/media-organizations-condemn-wikileaks-disclosure/.

15. Cable News Network, Inc. v. American Broadcasting Co., 518 F. Supp. 1238 (D.C. Ga. 1981); Lewis v. Baxley, 368 F. Supp. 768 (M.D. Ala. 1973).

16. Consumer's Union of the United States v. Periodical Correspondents Association, 365 F. Supp. 18 (D.D.C. 1973).

17. Sarasota Herald-Tribune v. State, 924 So. 2d 8, 16 (Fla. Dist. Ct. App. 2005).

18. See Gant, *We're All Journalists Now*, 93–95.

19. Ibid., 120–27.

20. Ibid., 127.

21. Branzburg v. Hayes, 408 U.S. 665 (1972).

22. U.S. Constitution, amendment I, http://www.law.cornell.edu/constitution/first_amendment.

23. For a discussion of this theory, see Stewart, "Or of the Press," 631. Potter Stewart felt strongly that the founding fathers intended a "distinction between the two" clauses, a separate meaning for each (634). He reasoned that it is "tempting to suggest that freedom of the press means only that newspaper publishers are guaranteed freedom of expression. They *are* guaranteed that freedom, to be sure, but so are we all, because of the Free Speech Clause. If the Free Press guarantee meant no more than freedom of expression, it would be a constitutional redundancy" (633).

24. Ugland, "Demarcating the Right to Gather News," 113, 155, quoting 1 Debates and Proceedings in the Congress of the United States 690 (1789).

25. First National Bank of Boston v. Bellotti, 435 U.S. 765 (1978).

26. Ibid., 799–800.

27. Citizens United v. Federal Election Commission, 130 S. Ct. 876, 905–6 (2010).

28. Ibid.

29. Ibid.

30. Branzburg v. Hayes, 408 U.S. 665 (1972).

31. Baker, "Are Oliver Stone and Tom Clancy Journalists," 739, 741.

32. Ibid., 741, 744.

33. von Bulow v. von Bulow, 811 F.2d 136 (2d Cir. 1987).

34. Ibid., 142; Baker, "Are Oliver Stone and Tom Clancy Journalists," 749.

35. von Bulow v. von Bulow, 811 F.2d 142 (2d Cir. 1987).

36. Baker, "Are Oliver Stone and Tom Clancy Journalists," 755.

37. Titan Sports, Inc. v. Turner Broadcasting System, Inc., 151 F.3d 125 (3d Cir. 1998).

38. Ibid. See also Swartwout, "In re Madden," 1589, 1601.

39. Ibid.

40. Swartwout, "In re Madden," 1602.

41. Titan Sports, Inc. v. Turner Broadcasting System, Inc., 151 F.3d 129–30.

42. Ibid., 130.

43. Swartwout, "In re Madden," 1607; von Bulow v. von Bulow, 811 F.2d 136, 145 (2nd Cir. 1987).

44. Swartwout, "In re Madden," 1607.

45. Ibid., 1607.

46. Ibid., 1606.

47. See Baker, "Are Oliver Stone and Tom Clancy Journalists," 752. According to *von Bulow* (see n33 above), so long as the authors intend to disseminate information when they conduct newsgathering, they are considered to be press. Swartwout, "In re Madden," 1608.

48. Lovell v. City of Griffin, 303 U.S. 444, 452 (1938).

49. Baker, "Are Oliver Stone and Tom Clancy Journalists," 750.

50. Ibid. The courts have upheld the journalist privilege for classes that serve a public interest, noting the underlying public interest in documentary filmmaking in Silkwood v. Kerr-McGee, 563 F.2d 433 (10th Cir. 1977), and the importance of investigative reporting in Shoen v. Shoen, 5 F.3d 1289 (9th Cir. 1993). See Baker, "Are Oliver Stone and Tom Clancy Journalists," 751.

51. Rukavina, "Re-Pressing the Internet," 351, 371.

52. Too Much Media, LLC v. Hale, 20 A. 3d 364, 379 (N.J. 2011).

53. Rukavina, "Re-Pressing the Internet," 371.

54. Ibid.

55. Harvard Law Review Association, "Protecting the New Media," 996, 999. Further, "Once information is generally available to the news media, the government may not arbitrarily differentiate among members of the media," including Internet journalists. Rukavina, "Re-Pressing the Internet," 355. As the First Circuit Court of Appeals has stated, "Neither the courts nor any other branch of government can be allowed to affect the content or tenor of the news by choreographing which news organizations have access to relevant information." Ibid., quoting Anderson v. Cryovac, Inc., 805 F.2d 1, 9 (1st Cir. 1986).

56. Lidsky, "Prying, Spying, and Lying," 173, 180.

57. Blumenthal v. Drudge, 992 F. Supp. 44 (D.D.C. 1998).

58. Swartwout, "In re Madden," 1610.

59. For example, Joshua Micah Marshal won the 2007 George Polk Award for Legal Reporting. Marshal operates a political news blog and led the media

coverage of the dismissals of the United States attorneys by George W. Bush for political reasons.

60. "CNN Enlists iReporters to Capture 'The Moment' of Obama's Oath," CNN. com, January 16, 2009: "'We're pleased to partner with CNN to bring this historic event to life through the eyes of those attending the inauguration,' said Yusuf Mehdi, Senior Vice President, Microsoft," http://news.turner.com/article_display.cfm?article_id=4207.

61. For cases dealing with bloggers, see Media Law Resource Center online, *MLRC: Legal Actions against Online Speech*, http://mlrcblogsuits.blogspot.com/.

62. Harvard Law Review Association, "Protecting the New Media," 990, 1000.

63. Ibid., 1001–1002.

64. Those states are Alabama, Alaska, Arizona, Arkansas, Connecticut, Delaware, Florida, Georgia, Indiana, Illinois, Kentucky, Louisiana, Montana, Nevada, New Mexico, New York, North Dakota, Ohio, Oklahoma, Pennsylvania, and Rhode Island.

65. Harvard Law Review Association, "Protecting the New Media," 1003; O'Grady v. Superior Court of Santa Clara County, 44 Cal. Rptr. 3d 72 (Ct. App. 2006).

66. Free Flow of Information Act of 2009, S. 448, 111th Cong. §2(a), as introduced in the Senate, February 13, 2009.

67. Ibid. §8(2)(A).

68. Ibid. §8(5).

69. Free Flow of Information Act of 2009, H.R. 985, 111th Cong. §2(a), as referred to S. Comm. on the Judiciary, April 1, 2009.

70. Ibid. §4(2).

71. Branzburg v. Hayes, 408 U.S. 665, 704 (1972).

72. Ugland, "Demarcating the Right to Gather News," 137.

73. Ibid., 138.

74. Kaufman v. Islamic Society of Arlington, Tex., 291 S.W.3d 130, 139 (Ct. App. Tex. 2009).

75. Some journalists resist even labeling their trade as a profession because the term connotes inviting outsiders to set standards for journalism. See Gant, *We're All Journalists Now*, 129.

76. Licensing of the Press Act of 1662.

Chapter 7. New Media, Old Law?

1. Mark Sherman, "Technology? Some Justices Want to Keep Distance," Associated Press, January 7, 2014, http://bigstory.ap.org/article/technology-some-justices-want-keep-distance.

2. George Stephanopoulos, "Justice Stephen Breyer: Is Burning Koran 'Shouting Fire in a Crowded Theater?'" *ABC News* Blogs, September 14, 2010, http://

abcnews.go.com/blogs/politics/2010/09/justice-stephen-breyer-is-burning-koran-shouting-fire-in-a-crowded-theater/.

3. Riley v. California, 134 S. Ct. 2473, 2495 (2014).

4. See Zemel v. Rusk, 381 U.S. 1, 17 (1965): "The right to speak and publish does not necessarily provide for the unrestrained right to gather information." See also Wolfson v. Lewis, 924 F. Supp. 1413, 1417 (E.D. Pa. 1996), holding that "the First Amendment does not, therefore, shield the press from crimes or torts committed in pursuit of a story." Although there is an undoubted right to gather news from any source by means within the law, this does not mean that the First Amendment compels others—private persons or governments—to supply information. See Branzburg v. Hayes, 408 U.S. 665 (1972), and Dietemann v. Time, Inc., 449 F.2d 245 (9th Cir. 1971), holding employees of magazine liable for gaining entrance to plaintiff's personal office and using hidden cameras and recording devices without plaintiff's permission; but see Dyk, "Newsgathering, Press Access, and the First Amendment," 927, arguing that the press should be given more access.

5. Earnhardt v. Volusia County, Office of the Medical Examiner, No. 2001-30373CICI (Fla. Cir. Ct. July 10, 2001).

6. See Fl. Stat. §406.135 (2006).

7. 5 U.S.C. §552, http://www.law.cornell.edu/uscode/text/5/552.

8. See Florida Star v. B.J.F., 491 U.S. 524 (1989): A newspaper is not liable for intentionally publishing the name of a sexual assault victim where the police inadvertently disclosed the name in violation of state law.

9. New York Times Co. v. NASA, 782 F. Supp. 628, 630 (D.D.C. 1991).

10. See Earnhardt v. Volusia County, Office of the Medical Examiner, No. 2001-30373CICI at *1 (Fla. Cir. Ct. July 10, 2001).

11. Brancheau v. Demings, No. 2010-CA-6673, 2010 WL 7971871, at *5 (Fla. 9th Cir. Ct. 2010).

12. State v. Rolling, 91-3832 CF A, 1994 WL 722891 (Fla. Cir. Ct. July 27, 1994).

13. See National Archives and Records Administration v. Favish, 541 U.S. 157, 172 (2004): "As a general rule, if the information is subject to disclosure, it belongs to all."

14. Sarasota Herald-Tribune v. State, 924 So.2d 8, 12 (Fla. Dist. Ct. App. 2005), citing Craig v. Harney, 331 U.S. 36, 374 (1947): "A trial is a public event."

15. Ibid., 17–18.

16. Ibid., 19. The appellate mechanism by which the court reviewed the issue of whether the media were entitled to the photos was a rule governing the court's jurisdiction that enabled it to hear orders excluding the press and/or the public. Because only members of the media sought review, the court limited its holding to the media only, contemplating that their entitlement to the photo-

graphs may be different than that of the public. See Sarasota Herald-Tribune v. State, 924 So.2d 11 (Fla. Dist. Ct. App. 2005).

17. Solove, "Introduction: Privacy Self-Management and the Consent Dilemma," 1879, 1890.

18. See State v. Rolling, 91-3832 CF A, 1994 WL 722891 (Fla. Cir. Ct. July 27, 1994); Catsouras v. Department of California Highway Patrol, 181 Cal. App. 4th 856 (2010).

19. For a survey conducted in all fifty states regarding online access to court records, see Center for Democracy and Technology, "A Quiet Revolution in the Courts: Electronic Access to State Court Records," 2002, https://www.cdt.org/files/publications/020821courtrecords.shtml.

20. Ibid.

21. For articles on states suggesting limiting Internet access to records, see John Greiner, "In Letter, Justice Cites Crime Fears," *Oklahoma News*, March 15, 2008, http://newsok.com/article/3216639/1205570145; Mark R. Schweikert, "Judges Can Balance Online Access to Court Records," *Columbus Dispatch*, January 26, 2008, http://www.columbusdispatch.com/live/content/editorials/stories/2008/01/26/Schweikert_SAT_MUST.ART_ART_01-26-08_A9_RK 95G3I.html?sid=101.

22. Rebecca Riddick, "Computer Glitch Blamed for 'Secret Dockets,'" Law .com, July 5, 2006, http://www.law.com/jsp/article.jsp?id=1151658317132.

23. See, for example, Peck v. United Kingdom, 36 Eur. H.R. Rep. 41 10 (2003), where the European Court held that a man had no expectation of privacy when a CCTV camera filmed him in public while he was holding a knife that he used to slit his wrists.

24. See Solove, *The Future of Reputation*, 162, citing Gill v. Heart Publishing Co., 253 P.2d 441 (Cal. 1953).

25. Ibid.

26. Ibid.

27. Moreno v. Hanford Sentinel, Inc., F054138, slip op. (Cal. Ct. App. April 2, 2009).

28. But see Diaz v. Oakland Tribune, Inc., 139 Cal. App. 3d 118, 127 (Cal. Ct. App. 1983), finding information may not be newsworthy even when that information was contained in a police record. This case is rare.

29. See, for example, Showler v. Harper's Magazine Foundation, 222 Fed. Appx. 755, 764 (10th Cir. 2007), holding that plaintiffs could not sustain a claim for publication of private facts in the photograph of an open casket, the view of which was voluntarily disclosed to twelve hundred people at a funeral.

30. Sudbeck, "Placing Court Records Online."

31. But see Whitman, "The Two Western Cultures of Privacy."

32. Allen, "Privacy Torts," 1711.

33. Ibid., 1762–63.

34. McCullen v. Coakley, 134 S. Ct. 2518 (2014).

35. In relation to the title of this section, see Pearson v. Dodd, 410 F.2d 701, 705 (D.C. Cir. 1969): "In analyzing a claimed breach of privacy, injuries from intrusion and injuries from publication should be kept clearly separate."

36. Von Hannover v. Germany, 2004-III Eur. Ct. H.R. 294, §25.

37. See Mills, *Privacy*, 231.

38. Diaz v. Oakland Tribune, Inc., 139 Cal. App. 3d 118 (Ct. App. 1983).

39. Ibid.

40. See Edwards v. National Audubon Society, Inc., 556 F.2d 113, 120 (7th Cir. 1977).

41. Campbell v. Seabury Press, 614 F.2d 395, 397 (5th Cir. 1980).

42. Ibid.

43. The Tenth Circuit follows the reasoning of the Fifth Circuit. See, for example, Gilbert v. Medical Economics Co., 665 F.2d 305 (10th Cir. 1980). *Restatement Second of Torts* § 652D (1977) asks whether "a reasonable member of the public, with decent standards" would have any concern for the information.

44. See Mzamane v. Huffington Post, *Digital Medial Law Project*, February 26, 2009, http://www.citmedialaw.org/threats/nomvuyo-mzamane-v-huffington-post.

45. See Staten v. Steel, 191 P.3d 778 (Or. Ct. App. 2008), affirming the jury's award of $110,000 for plaintiff when a picture of plaintiff and his wife leaving a nude dancing club was posted on a website along with commentary implying that plaintiff was sexually frustrated.

46. See Cornwell v. Sachs, 99 F. Supp. 695 (2nd Cir. 2000), holding that plaintiff, a world-renowned author of crime novels, was likely to succeed on her tort claim against defendant for posting the plaintiff's name on his website.

47. See Milum v. Banks, 642 S.E.2d 892 (Ga. Ct. App. 2007), affirming the jury award of fifty thousand dollars in compensatory damages to plaintiff, when the defendant alleged on his political blog that the plaintiff had delivered bribes from drug dealers to judges. Also see Wagner v. Miskin, 660 N.W.2d 593 (N.D. 2003), affirming the jury award of three million dollars from the defendant when she alleged on her website that the plaintiff, a professor, had harassed the defendant with sexually provocative phone calls.

48. See Christopher J. Boggs, "Blogs Can Get Insurance Clients 'SLAPP'ed!" *Insurance Journal*, July 14, 2008, http://www.insurancejournal.com/news/national/2008/07/14/91851.htm.

49. Ibid.

50. Kono v. Meeker, N.W.2d 872 (Iowa Ct. App. 2007).

51. Ibid.

Chapter 8. The Future of Dignity and Privacy

1. Clark Hoyt, "Sometimes, There's News in the Gutter," *New York Times*, August 9, 2008, http://www.nytimes.com/2008/08/10/opinion/10pubed.html?pagewanted=all&_r=0.

2. See also Bartnicki v. Vopper, 532 U.S. 514, 535 (2001).

3. See, for example, Cindy Swirko, "UF Veterinary Prof Accused of Secretly Videotaping Students," *Gainesville Sun*, September 21, 2013. The article states that the professor used a camera pen to secretly photograph his female students' breasts and thighs.

4. Shulman v. Group W Productions, Inc., 18 Cal. 4th 200, 209 (Cal. 1998).

5. Ibid., 209–12.

6. Ibid., 242–43.

7. Ibid., 242.

8. See Earnhardt *ex rel.* Estate of Earnhardt v. Volusia County, 2001-30373-CICI, 2001 WL 992068 (Fla. Cir. Ct. July 10, 2001).

9. Perkins v. Principal Media Group, No. 3:03-CV-00578 (M.D. Tenn., May 12, 2005).

10. See Krinsky v. Doe 6, 159 Cal. App. 4th 1154 (Cal. Ct. App. 2008).

11. Steinbuch v. Cutler, No. 05CV00970 (D.D.C. May 18, 2005).

12. See Desnick v. American Broadcasting Companies, Inc., 44 F.3d 1345, 1355 (7th Cir. 1995).

13. Ibid.

14. Ibid.

15. Mill, *On Liberty*, 115.

16. Allen, "Daniel J. Meador Lecture," 1390.

17. Strahilevitz, *Toward A Positive Theory of Privacy Law*, 2010.

18. Allen, "Privacy Torts," 1377.

19. See Riley v. California, 573 U.S. (June 25, 2014).

20. J. Cohen, "Examined Lives," 1373, 1425–26: "Pervasive monitoring of every first move or false start will, at the margin, incline choices toward the bland and the mainstream." We lose, in her terms, "the expression of eccentric individuality."

21. See Slobogin, "Public Privacy," 213, 219.

22. Peggy Noonan, "What We Lose If We Give Up Privacy," *Wall Street Journal*, August 16, 2013, http://online.wsj.com/article/SB10001424127887323639704579015101857760922.html#articleTabs%3Darticle.

23. Froomkin, "'Pets Must Be on a Leash,'" 965, 990.

24. McCabe v. Village Voice, 550 F. Supp. 525 (E.D. Pa. 1982).

25. Melvin v. Reid, 297 P. 91 (Cal. D.C. 1931).

26. See, for example, Fla. St. §943.0585, limiting expungement to crimes that do not involve violence or the commission of a sex offense, and allowing additional expungements for crimes that meet the same qualifications but only if the record had been sealed and the offender committed no new offenses for a period of ten years.

27. Sharon Noguchi, "Preteens and Young Adults Embrace Rude Online Culture," *San Jose Mercury News*, August 30, 2011, http://www.knoxnews.com/news/2011/aug/30/students-embrace-rude-online-culture/?print=1, discussing the self-hangings of Amanda Brownell and Jill Naber after they were harassed online.

28. American Law Institute, *Restatement (Second) of Torts, 1977,* §652B.

29. Rappaport and Leath, "Brave New World." See, for example, Weirum v. RKO General, Inc., 539 P.2d 36, 41 (Cal. 1975), affirming the liability of a radio station to third parties injured by the "competitive pursuit [of its listeners] on the public streets."

30. Cal. Civil Code 1708.8: A person is liable for physical invasion of privacy when the defendant knowingly enters onto the land of another person without permission or otherwise commits a trespass in order to physically invade the privacy of the plaintiff with the intent to capture any type of visual image, sound recording, or other physical impression of the plaintiff engaging in a personal or familial activity and the physical invasion occurs in a manner that is offensive to a reasonable person.

31. See Calvert and Richards, "Stopping the Obscenity Madness."

32. Bambauer, "The New Intrusion," 205, 206.

33. See Schonauer, "Let the Babies Dance," 135, 153–54.

34. Some critics, though, have suggested that a more regulatory approach "may have a substantially regressive distributive impact" on individuals with less money, power or social currency." See Strahilevitz, "Toward a Positive Theory of Privacy Law," 2010, 2017.

35. United States v. Jones, 132 S. Ct. 945, 957 (2012) (Sotomayor, J., concurring).

36. Ibid.

37. See also Solove, "Conceptualizing Privacy," 1152: "Clinging to the notion of privacy as total secrecy would mean the practical extinction of privacy in today's world. In contrast to the notion of privacy as secrecy, privacy can be understood as an expectation in a certain degree of accessibility of information."

38. See Dendrite International, Inc. v. Doe No. 3, 775 A.2d 756, 759 (App. Div. 2001).

39. See Zeran v. America Online, Inc., 129 F.3d 327, 327 (4th Cir. Va. 1997); Doe v. America Online, Inc., 718 So. 2d 385 (Fla. 4th DCA 1998) *approved*, 783 So. 2d 1010 (Fla. 2001).

40. See Jones v. Dirty World Entertainment Recordings, LLC, 840 F. Supp. 2d 1008 (2012); Hare v. Richie, 2012 WL 3773116 (2012).

41. Levi, "Social Media and the Press," 1596n243. See, for example, Murchison et al., "Sullivan's Paradox," 7, 11–12: "By permitting the use of circumstantial evidence of journalistic behavior to prove the journalist's state of mind, the Sullivan rule has spawned a de facto set of judge-made standards that covers all aspects of journalistic behavior. These standards include the use of sources, the quality of writing, the demand for corroboration, the duties of editorial supervision, and the use of quotations."

42. Levi, "Social Media and the Press," 1579.

43. The New York University Journalism School has an undergraduate concentration in media criticism: "This concentration brings a new approach to the study of the mass media, combining analytical strategies associated with press criticism, media theory, and cultural studies with a focus on new media and the radical ways in which they are transforming our social worlds, economic landscape, and cultural environment." See http://journalism.nyu.edu/undergrad uate/concentrations/media-criticism/.

44. See http://reliablesources.blogs.cnn.com/.

Glossary

This book relies on technical and sometimes obscure terms necessary to adequately discuss new media, new technology, and privacy. To assist the reader, key terms are identified and defined below. Please know that the definitions of some of these terms are in flux. Where terms have more than one use or meaning, I so indicate.

Ambient journalism. Reporting environment in which consumers are saturated by information from various media and constantly updating news sources.

Ambient media. Modern communication of information in ubiquitous and pervasive environments, produced in decentralized locations by using various technologies to reach consumers of that information.

Big Data. Buzzword or catch phrase used to describe a massive volume of structured and unstructured data that is so large it is difficult to process; also used to refer to the technology that an organization requires to handle such data. This term is given a secondary meaning in this book that simply refers to the concept of a massive quantity of data about any particular subject now more widely available and accessible as a result of contemporary technology.

Blog. Website or web page on which an individual or organization posts content consisting of commentary and links to other sites and other content, all of which are typically organized around the personality, preferences, and opinions of the person or entity controlling the blog.

Blogger. Person who controls the content of a blog by participating in the posting, organizing, editorializing, or publishing aspects of the blog.

Communications Decency Act (CDA). Title V of the Telecommunications Act passed by the United States Congress in 1996. Purporting to regulate indecency and obscenity, the act was an attempt to curb the availability of pornographic material on the Internet. It also defined Internet service providers and drew a distinction between them and publishers of material online. The United States Supreme Court later struck down the provision of the act regulating indecency.

European Union (E.U.). Economic and political union of twenty-eight member states located primarily in Europe that operates through a system of supranational independent institutions as well as intergovernmental decisions that are negotiated by a majority of the member states.

Facebook. Popular social networking site that allows users to build and control their own personal profile to display on the site for the purposes of connecting with and receiving messages and information updates from other users who have profiles on the site.

Facebook friend. Person on Facebook whom a Facebook user has added to his or her contacts from within her profile by requesting that the other user become a friend and by having that request accepted by the other user.

Facebook like. Option on the Facebook website that allows a user to provide positive feedback on another user's post by clicking on a graphical "Like" option beneath the post to publicly signal approval. After the "Like" option is clicked, the name of the responder is displayed underneath the post as someone who liked it.

Federal Communications Commission (FCC). Independent agency of the U.S. government that was created by Congress and charged with the regulation of the airwaves within the United States. The mission of the FCC has been articulated as one to "promote safety of life and property through the use of wire and radio communications."

Federal Trade Commission (FTC). Independent agency of the U.S. government that was created by Congress and given regulatory power over consumer protection, with a secondary goal of the elimination of anticompetitive business practices within the United States.

Follower. One who subscribes to receive the updates of a particular person on a social media site.

Infotainment. Buzzword for a media device or service that delivers a combination of information and entertainment; this term can refer to content available through traditional media such as television or print, or through more modern media enabled by the Internet.

Information Technology (IT). Broad term for the use of computers and telecommunications systems to store, retrieve, transmit and manipulate data.

Internet. Global network connecting millions of computers that is controlled in a decentralized manner by allowing independent operators, that is, Internet hosts, to determine which Internet services to use, access, and make available to the global Internet community.

Internet disinhibition. Concept that describes the lack of traditional social norms that would constrain human behavior in a face-to-face setting but either do not exist or exist to a much lesser degree when the medium of interaction takes place on the Internet.

Internet host. Computer system that is accessed via modem or telephone line by a computer user working at a remote location.

Internet service provider (ISP). Company that provides Internet services, including personal and business access to the Internet.

iReporter. Participant in a citizen journalism initiative that allows people around the globe to contribute pictures and video of breaking news stories as they witness them through personal experience. The Cable News Network (CNN) originally coined the term "i-Report" when it began to explicitly include such reports as sources of news for publication.

Libel tourism. Term used to describe the phenomenon of plaintiffs who engage in forum shopping, often on a global scale, to determine where to file a libel lawsuit.

Medium (sing.) and **media (pl.)**. Form and technology used to communicate information. As used in this book, if the term is preceded by "the" as in "the media," it is intended as a shorthand method of referring to the modern press.

Meme. Concept expressed in the form of a joke or witty posting that spreads "virally" from one person to another via the Internet.

New media. Generic term for the many forms of electronic communication that have become possible through the use of information technology.

Practical obscurity. Concept that information available in a limited context is obscured by the circumstances required to disclose the information to a wider audience. In the seminal example from the case of *U.S. Dept. of Justice v. Reporters Committee*, 489 U.S. 749 (1989), the information at issue were rap sheets that listed detailed criminal histories of individuals that otherwise would have been obscured by the fact that the pieces of information on the rap sheet were not compiled in any other place.

Press. A term to refer collectively to the traditional entities responsible for publishing news in a public forum, harkening back to the idea and purpose of the original printing press.

Reasonable expectation of privacy. Fluctuating legal concept that delineates the privacy rights of individuals on the basis of whether their individual expectation of privacy is objectively reasonable and therefore cognizable at law.

Right to be let alone. The idea that privacy can, does, or should exist where an individual has not taken personal action that would thrust his affairs into the wider public view, regardless of whether the information at issue was nonetheless disclosed at some time to the public; a concept of dignity that protects privacy outside of the traditional legal sphere in which it is recognized.

Search engine. Program that uses the Internet to search for documents or images available online that contain specified terms. It operates by enabling the user to type in a keyword to guide the search; the program then returns a list of documents or images where the keyword was found.

Search engine optimization (SEO). Methodology of strategies, techniques, and tactics used to increase the number of visitors to a website by obtaining a high-ranking placement in the search results page of a search engine.

Traditional media. A generic term for the many forms of communication that preceded the Internet and were originally used as the primary means for disseminating news, such as newspapers and magazines.

Tweet. Message using 140 characters or less in which an individual expresses what he or she is doing and then posts to an audience of followers on Twitter using Internet technology.

Twitter. Free social messaging tool that enables people to stay connected through brief text message updates by answering the question "What are you doing?" Twitter users can select or deselect other Twitter users to follow, meaning that they are opting to receive messages from that user.

Uniform resource locator (URL). Global Internet address of documents or other resources available on the World Wide Web.

Viral. Descriptive term for the manner in which a popular joke, image, or meme can spread exponentially from one user to the next over the Internet; also used as "to go viral."

Wi-Fi. Trademarked by the Wi-Fi Alliance, term that refers to the wireless networking technology that uses radio waves to provide wireless high-speed Internet and network connections.

Bibliography

Allen, Anita L. "Daniel J. Meador Lecture: Privacy Isn't Everything: Account-ability as a Personal and Social Good." *Alabama Law Review* 54 (Summer 2003): 1375–91.

———. "Privacy Torts: Unreliable Remedies for LGBT Plaintiffs." *California Law Review* 98 (2010): 1711–66.

American Law Institute. *Restatement (Second) of Conflict of Laws.* Vol. 1, chaps. 1–8, secs. 1–221. Philadelphia, Pa.: American Law Institute, 1971.

———. *Restatement (Second) of Torts. St. Paul, Minn.: American Law Institute, 1965, 1977.

Anderson, David A. "Freedom of the Press." *Texas Law Review* 80 (February 2002): 429–530.

Ariès, Phillippe, Georges Duby, Paul Veyne, and Arthur Goldhammer, eds. *A History of Private Life.* Cambridge, Mass.: Harvard University Press, 1992.

Aristotle. *The Metaphysics.* Translated, with an introduction by Hugh Lawson-Tancred. London: Penguin, 1999.

Baker, Kraig L. "Are Oliver Stone and Tom Clancy Journalists? Determining Who Has Standing to Claim the Journalist's Privilege." *Washington Law Review* 69 (1994): 739–64.

Balkin, Jack M. "The Future of Expression in a Digital Age." *Pepperdine Law Review* 36 (2009): 427–74.

Bambauer, Jane Yakowitz. "The New Intrusion." *Notre Dame Law Review* 88 (2012): 205–71.

Barron, Jerome A. "Book Review: Press Law in Modern Democracies: A Comparative Study." *George Washington Law Review* 54 (1986): 434–51.

Beauchamp, Raymond W. "England's Chilling Forecast: The Case for Granting Declaratory Relief to Prevent English Defamation Actions from Chilling American Speech." *Fordham Law Review* 74 (2006): 3073–148.

Berns, Walter. "Freedom of the Press and the Alien and Sedition Laws: A Reappraisal." *Supreme Court Review* 109 (1970): 109–59.

Bezanson, Randall P. "The Developing Law of Editorial Judgment." *Nebraska Law Review* 78 (1999): 754–858.

Black, Hugo. "The Bill of Rights." *NYU Law Review* 35 (1960): 865–81.

Boesche, Roger. *The Strange Liberalism of Alexis de Tocqueville*. Ithaca, N.Y.: Cornell University Press, 1987.

Callister, Paul D. "The Internet, Regulation and the Market for Loyalties: An Economic Analysis of Transborder Information Flow." *University of Illinois Journal of Law, Technology and Policy* 59 (2002): 59–107.

Calvert, Clay, and Robert D. Richards. "Stopping the Obscenity Madness 50 Years after Roth v. United States." *Texas Review of Entertainment and Sports Law* 9, no. 1 (2007): 1–38.

Castells, Manuel. "The Cultures of the Internet." *Queen's Quarterly* 109, no. 3 (2002): 333–44.

Chen, Elaine M. "Legislative Update: Global Internet Freedom: Can Censorship And Freedom Coexist?" *DePaul-LCA Journal of Art and Entertainment Law* 13 (2003): 229–67.

Cohen, Adam. "The Media That Needs Citizens: The First Amendment and the Fifth Estate." *California Law Review* 85 (2011): 1–85.

Cohen, Julie E. "Examined Lives: Informational Privacy and the Subject as Object." *Stanford Law Review* 52 (2000): 1373–438.

Coleman, William T., Jr. "A Free Press: The Need to Ensure an Unfettered Check on Democratic Government between Elections." *Tulane Law Review* 59 (1984): 243–79.

De Sola Pool, Ithiel. *Technologies of Freedom*. Cambridge, Mass.: Belknap Press, 1983.

Dunbar, Robin Ian MacDonald. "Gossip in Evolutionary Perspective." *Review of General Psychology* 8, no. 2 (2004): 100–110.

Dyk, Timothy. "Newsgathering, Press Access, and the First Amendment." *Stanford Law Review* 44, no. 5 (May 1992): 927–60.

Franklin, Marc A., David A. Anderson, and Lyrissa Barnett Lidsky, eds. *Mass Media Law: Cases and Materials*. 7th ed. University Casebook. New York: Foundation Press, 2005.

Froomkin, A. Michael. "'Pets Must Be on a Leash': How U.S. Law (and Industry Practice) Often Undermines and Even Forbids Valuable Privacy Enhancing Technology." *Ohio State Law Journal* 74 (2013): 965–96.

Gales, Joseph, and William Winston Seaton, eds. *Annals of Congress: Debates and Proceedings of the Congress of the United States.* Vol. 1, *Madison's Fourth Proposal to the House (1789).* Washington, D.C.: Gales and Seaton, 1834.

Gant, Scott. *We're All Journalists Now: The Transformation of the Press and Reshaping of the Law in the Internet Age.* New York: Free Press, 2007.

Goldsmith, Jack, and Tim Wu. *Who Controls the Internet? Illusions of a Borderless World.* New York: Oxford University Press, 2008.

Gormley, Ken. "One Hundred Years of Privacy." *Wisconsin Law Review* (1992): 1335–441.

Hamburger, Phillip. "The Development of the Law of Seditious Libel and the Control of the Press." *Stanford Law Review* 37 (1985): 661–775.

Harbit, Eric, and Duncan Clark. "Shaping the Internet in China: Evolution of Political Control over Network Infrastructure and Content." *Asian Survey* 41 (2001): 377–408.

Harvard Law Review Association. "Protecting the New Media: Application of the Journalist's Privilege to Bloggers." *Developments in the Law: The Law of Media. Harvard Law Review* 120, no. 4 (February 2007): 990–1066.

Ingelhart, Louis E. *Press Freedoms: A Descriptive Calendar of Concepts, Interpretations, Events, and Court Actions, from 4000 BC to the Present.* Westport, Conn.: Greenwood, 1987.

International Covenant on Civil and Political Rights. Adopted and opened for signature, ratification, and accession by General Assembly resolution 2200A (XXI) of 16 December 1966 entry into force 23 March 1976, in accordance with Article 4. United Nations, Office of the High Commissioner for Human Rights. http://www.ohchr.org/en/professionalinterest/pages/ccpr .aspx.

Johnson, Clay A. *The Information Diet: A Case for Conscious Consumption.* 1st ed. Sebastopol, Calif.: Reilly Media, 2012.

Kreimer, Seth F. "Censorship by Proxy: The First Amendment, Internet Intermediaries, and the Problem of the Weakest Link." *University of Pennsylvania Law Review* 155 (2006): 11–103.

Levi, Lili. "Social Media and the Press." *North Carolina Law Review* 90 (2012): 1531–96.

Lidsky, Lyrissa. "Anonymity in Cyberspace: What Can We Learn from John Doe?" *Boston College Law Review* 50 (2009): 1373–93.

———. "Prying, Spying, and Lying: Intrusive Newsgathering and What the Law Should Do about It." *Tulane Law Review* 73 (1998): 173–249.

———. "Silencing John Doe: Defamation and Discourse in Cyberspace." *Duke Law Journal* 49 (2000): 855–946.

Lloyd, Scott. "A Criticism of Social Responsibility Theory: An Ethical Perspective." *Journal of Mass Media Ethics* 6, no. 4 (1991): 199–209.

Manning, Roger B. "The Origins of the Doctrine of Sedition." *Albion* 12, no. 2 (1980): 99–121.

McNealy, Jasmine E. "The Emerging Conflict between Newsworthiness and the Right to Be Forgotten." *Northern Kentucky Law Review* 39 (2012): 119–35.

Merrill, John C., ed. *Global Journalism: Survey of International Communication.* 2nd ed. New York: Longman, 1991.

Merrill, John C., Peter J. Gade, and Frederick R. Blevens, eds. *Twilight of Press Freedom: The Rise of People's Journalism.* Routledge Communication Series. Oxford, U.K.: Routledge, 2001.

Mill, John Stuart. *On Liberty.* Oxford, 1859.

Mills, Jon L. *Privacy: The Lost Right.* New York: Oxford University Press, 2008.

———. "Two Contemporary Privacy Issues in Poland: Liability for Internet Publication and the Registration of Communist Party Affiliation." *Przeglad Prawniczy Warsaw University Law Review* 1 (2008): 110–21.

Milton, Joyce. *The Yellow Kids: Foreign Correspondents in the Heyday of Yellow Journalism.* New York: HarperCollins, 1989.

Murchison, Brian C., John Soloski, Randall P. Bezanson, Gilbert Cranberg, and Roselle L. Wissler. "Sullivan's Paradox: The Emergence of Judicial Standards of Journalism." *North Carolina Law Review* 73 (1994): 7–113.

Murphy, Caitlin T. "International Law and the Internet: An Ill-Suited Match Case Note on UEJF and LICRA v. Yahoo! Inc. *Hastings International and Comparative Law Review* 25 (2002): 405–27.

Nissenbaum, Helen. "Privacy as Contextual Integrity." *Washington Law Review* 79 (2004): 119–57.

Preece, Jenny. *Online Communities: Designing Usability, Supporting Sociability.* New York: Wiley, 2000.

Rappaport, Adam J., and Amanda M. Leith. "Brave New World? Legal Issues Raised by Citizen Journalism." *Communications Lawyer* 25, no. 2 (Summer 2007): 1, 28–38.

Report of the Special Rapporteur on the Promotion and Protection of the Right to Freedom of Opinion and Expression. United Nations, Office of the High Commissioner for Human Rights. May 16, 2011. A/HRC/17/27. http://www2.ohchr.org/english/bodies/hrcouncil/docs/17session/A.HRC.17.27_en.pdf.

Reporters Without Borders. *Worldwide Press Freedom Index 2007.* https://en.rsf.org/press-freedom-index-2007,34.html.

Richards, Neil M. "The Dangers of Surveillance." *Harvard Law Review* 126 (2013): 1934–65.

———. "Intellectual Privacy." *Texas Law Review* 87 (2008): 387–445.

Richards, Neil M., and Daniel J. Solove. "Privacy's Other Path: Recovering the Law of Confidentiality." *Georgetown Law Journal* 96 (2007): 123–83.

Rosenberg, David A. 1976. "Liberty versus Loyalty: The Debates over Freedom of Expression in the Philippines." In *Guided Press in Southeast Asia: National Development vs. Freedom of Expression,* edited by John A. Lent, 1–18. Amherst, N.Y.: SUNY–Buffalo, 1976.

Rukavina, Zrinka. "Re-Pressing the Internet: Journalists Battle for Equal Access." *DePaul-LCA Journal of Art and Entertainment Law* 13 (2003): 351–79.

Schonauer, Matthew. "Let the Babies Dance: Strengthening Fair Use and Stifling Abuse in DMCA Notice and Takedown Procedures." *I/S: A Journal of Law and Policy for the Information Society* 7 (2011): 135–69.

Schwartz, Bernard. *The Bill Of Rights: A Documentary History,* vol. 1 of 2, edited by Bernard Schwartz, Leon Friedman, Karyn Gulien Browne, Joan Tapper, Christine Pinches, Betsy Nicolaus, and Jeanne Brody. New York: Chelsea House, 1971.

Siebert, Fred S., Theodore Peterson, and Wilbur Schramm. *Four Theories of the Press.* Champaign: University of Illinois Press, 1963.

Slobogin, Christopher. "Public Privacy: Camera Surveillance in Public Places and the Right to Anonymity." *Mississippi Law Journal* 72 (2002): 213–300.

Smith, Jeffrey A. *Printers and Press Freedom: The Ideology of Early American Journalism.* New York: Oxford University Press, 1990.

Solove, Daniel J. "Conceptualizing Privacy." *California Law Review* 90 (2002): 1087–155.

———. *The Future of Reputation: Gossip, Rumor, and Privacy on the Internet.* New Haven, Conn.: Yale University Press, 2008.

———. "Introduction: Privacy Self-Management and the Consent Dilemma." *Harvard Law Review* 126 (2013): 1879–903.

Solove, Daniel J., and Woodrow Hartzog. 2014. "The FTC and the New Common Law of Privacy." *Columbia Law Review* 114 (2014): 583–676.

Stewart, Potter. "Or of the Press: Text of Address of Associate Justice Potter Stewart of U.S. Supreme Court, at Yale Law School Sesquicentennial Convocation, November 2, 1974." *Hastings Law Journal* 26 (1974): 631–53.

Strahilevitz, Lior Jacob. "Toward a Positive Theory of Privacy Law." *Harvard Law Review* 126 (2013): 2010–42.

Stewart, Potter. "Or of the Press." *Hastings Law Journal* 26 (1975): 631, 633–35.

Sudbeck, Lynn E. "Placing Court Records Online: Balancing the Public and Private Interests." *Justice System Journal* 27, no. 3 (2009): 268–85.

Suler, John. "The Online Disinhibition Effect." Abstract. *Cyberpsychology and Behavior* 7, no. 3 (2004): 321–26.

———. "The Online Disinhibition Effect." *International Journal of Applied Psychoanalytic Studies* 2, no.2 (2005): 184–88.

Swartwout, Daniel A. "In re Madden: The Threat to the New Journalism." *Ohio State Law Journal* 60, no. 4 (1999): 1589–623.

Ugland, Erik. "Demarcating the Right to Gather News: A Sequential Interpretation of the First Amendment." *Duke Journal of Constitutional Law and Public Policy* 3 (2008): 113–89.

Walton, Greg. *China's Golden Shield: Corporations and the Development of Surveillance Technology in the People's Republic of China.* Montreal: International Centre for Human Rights and Development, 2011.

Warren, Samuel D., and Louis D. Brandeis. "The Right to Privacy." *Harvard Law Review* 4, no. 5 (1890): 193–220.

Weaver, Russell L. "Brandenburg and Incitement in a Digital Era." *Mississippi Law Journal* 80, no. 4 (2011): 1263–88.

———. *From Gutenberg to the Internet: Free Speech, Advancing Technology, and the Implications for Democracy.* Durham, N.C.: Carolina Academic Press, 2013.

Weaver, Russell L., Andrew T. Kenyon, David F. Partlett, and Clive P. Walker, eds. *The Right to Speak Ill: Defamation, Reputation and Free Speech.* Durham, N.C.: Carolina Academic Press, 2006.

Weinstein, Jack B., Harold Korn, and Arthur R. Miller. *New York Civil Practice: CPLR.* 2nd ed. New York: LexisNexis, 2005.

West, Sonja R. "Awakening the Press Clause." *UCLA Law Review* 58 (2011): 1025–70.

Whitman, James. "The Two Western Cultures of Privacy: Dignity versus Liberty." *Yale Law Journal* 113 (2004): 1151–221.

Wonnell, Christopher T. "Truth and the Marketplace of Ideas." *UC Davis Law Review* 19 (1986): 669–728.

Index

Cornell University, 73–74

Cornwell v. Sachs, 213n46

Court of Appeals for the District of Columbia, U.S., 59

Courts: on bank and financial records, 20; of England, 73–74, 196n36; federal, 59, 193n68; of Great Britain, 73, 196n36; jurisdiction of, 73–74; online records of, 139–40, 212n17; on phone records, 20; on privacy, 25, 30; trend of, 126, 209n47; U.S., 7–8. *See also specific courts*

Craigslist, 87, 201n36

Crime, 215n26; arrests on, 26; scene photos, 13

Criminals: laws and, 190n41; mugshots of, 26–27

CyberPsychology and Behavior, 63

Cyberspace, 82

Daily Mirror, 76

Daniel Pearl Freedom of the Press Act, 195n23

Data, 9, 69; controllers, 26; digital, 26–27; privacy regulations, 26; tax levy or fee on brokers of, 166–67

Data Protection Regulation (DPR), 26

Defamation, 178–80; bloggers and, 106–11, 119–20, 146, 206n133, 206n145; cross-border, 72–74; findings of, 10; under First Amendment, 33; foreign, 76–77, 197n60; Internet, 8, 74–76; judgments for, 70; as legal remedy, 44; proof of, 38; remedies for, 168–69; tort and, 44–46, 191n67; in U.K., 76; U.S. Supreme Court on, 45, 191n67

Dendrite International v. Doe, 107

Department of Agriculture, U.S., 2–3

Department of Commerce, U.S., 82–83

Department of State, U.S., 195n23

Desnick v. American Broadcasting Companies, Inc., 32

De Tocqueville, Alexis, 51

DeWine, Mike, 152

Diaz, Cameron, 76

Diaz v. Oakland Tribune, 145–46, 212n28

Digital Millennium Copyright Act (DMCA), 84, 174–75, 199n14

Dignity: false light and, 43–44; future of, 148–49; human, 6, 162, 172–73; of individuals, 13; multiple approaches for, 181–83; personal, 9, 13, 164; as privacy, 24, 188n24, 189nn25–26; protection of, 162–63; right to reputation and, 176–77, 215n34; values of, 168

TheDirty.com, 87–88, 150

Dirty Word Entertainment, 88

Disclosures, 178–80; appropriation of personality for, 167–68; falsity of, 178–80; of information, 31–36, 163–68, 189n41, 190n42, 190n44, 190n55, 215nn26–27; intent of, 165; new media and, 2–3, 9–11, 17–18, 31–35, 48, 189n41, 190n42, 190n44; publishers and, 32, 143–47, 190n42, 213n35, 213n43, 213nn45–47; of sensitive information, 173–74. *See also* Public disclosure

DMCA. *See* Digital Millennium Copyright Act

Dolenga, Michael, 73–74

Domain names, 82, 198n1

Douglas, Michael, 34–35, 171

Douglas, William O., 15

Dowler, Milly, 39–40

DPR. *See* Data Protection Regulation

Drudge, Matt, 127

Drudge Report, 127

E.U. *See* European Union

Earnhardt, Dale, 4, 136–37, 152, 211n8

eBooks, 81

EC Directive. *See* Electronic Commerce

E-Commerce Directive. *See* European Electronic Commerce Directive

Edmondson, Ian, 39

Edwards, John, 150

Ehrenfeld, Rachel, 76–78, 197n60

Electronic Commerce (EC Directive), 85–88, 200n24

Electronic eavesdropping, 22, 169

Eleventh Circuit Court of Appeals, 100

"Endangered Pacific Northwest Tree Octopus," 64

"Endemic surveillance societies," 71

England, 132; courts of, 73–74, 196n36; on jurisdiction, 76–77, 197n60

Enlightenment, 50–51

Equal Protection clause, 132

European Court of Human Rights, 86, 144

European Electronic Commerce Directive (E-Commerce Directive), 85

European Union (E.U.), 72, 142–43, 170–73, 176–77, 181, 204n72, 215n34; Charter of Fundamental Rights of, 34–35; ISPs and, 85–86, 91, 180, 200nn23–24; laws and policies of, 5–8, 155; press in, 68–69; on the right to be forgotten, 26–27, 86, 189n35; social-responsibility approach of, 67–69

Facebook, 26, 63–65, 87, 180, 194n75; friends on, 160–61; "liking," 57–58; posting on, 6

Fair Housing Act, 87, 201n36

Federal Communications Commission (FCC), 55, 193nn49–50; licensing by, 82; on obscenity, 198, 203n81

The Federalist Papers (Hamilton; Jay; Madison), 102

Federal Trade Commission (FTC), 82

Fifth Circuit Court of Appeals, 145

First Amendment, 5, 13, 55, 90–91, 132–33, 181, 190n44, 211n4; absolutist theory and, 16–18; on anonymity, 102; on bloggers, 66; defamation under, 33; on free press, 23–24, 27, 50–51, 114, 121–22; goal and intent of, 117–18, 123; on government intrusion, 50–51; incorporation of, 50; interpretation of, 128; on jurisdiction, 77–79, 197n60; on new media, 118–19; printing and, 50; privacy and, 15, 31–33, 40–41, 66, 189n41; protection under, 76, 196n51; SOPA and, 91–92; value of, 144–45

First Circuit Court of Appeals, 209n55

First National Bank of Boston v. Bellotti, 123

Florida, 74–78, 121–22, 136, 138, 167, 196n51, 197n60, 211n16, 215n26

Florida Legislature, 136

Florida Star v. B.J.F., 74–78, 196n51, 197n60, 211n8

Florida Supreme Court, 75, 139–40

FOIA. *See* Freedom of Information Act

Ford, Gerald, 71–72, 203n72

Forum shopping: press and, 74–78, 196n51, 197n60; privacy and, 74–78, 96, 196n51, 197n60, 203n72

Fourth Amendment: on government intrusion, 50–51; on privacy, 19, 188n11; on rights, 13, 27

Fourth Circuit Court of Appeals, 57–58, 86–87

Four Theories of the Press (Peterson; Schramm; Siebert), 67

Fox News Channel, 2, 56

France: ISPs and, 90–92, 199n15, 202n57, 202n60; on sexuality, 72, 142–43, 165, 204n72

Freedom, 195n23; liberty and, 21; of media, 18, 70–71

Freedom of Information Act (FOIA), 35, 136–37, 140, 164, 173–74, 211n16

Free expression, 23–24, 181; privileges of, 120–24, 208n23; theory supporting, 17–18, 27; in U.S., 7; values of, 6–7, 41–42

Free Flow of Information Act (2009), 129–30

Free press: advocates for, 13; First Amendment on, 23–24, 27, 50–51, 114, 121–22; formalization of, 50–51; future of, 8–11; global standards on, 70–71; new media and principles of, 117–20, 207nn2–3; principles and values of, 12, 14–18, 188n1; privacy and, 6–8; rights to, 3–5; speech and, 9–11

Free speech, 149, 156, 181; absolutist theory and, 14, 16–18; in Great Britain, 15–16; marketplace-of-ideas theory of, 14–15; nations and, 5–8; obscenity and, 188n1; principles of, 33–34; rights to, 7; theories of, 12; in U.S., 15–16, 51; values of, 3

Free Speech clause, 123, 149, 208n23

Free Speech Protection Act, 78–80

FTC. *See* Federal Trade Commission

Funding Evil: How Terrorism Is Financed and How to Stop It (Ehrenfeld), 76–77

Gant, Scott, 122, 207n2

Gay parade, 72, 142–43, 165, 204n72

George Polk Award, 209n59

Georgia Supreme Court, 54

Germany, 155; ISPs and, 85, 200n23; on popular hatred, 24, 189n25; on privacy, 36, 144, 190n55, 195n27. See also *Von Hannover v. Germany*

Giggs, Ryan, 41–42, 144

Globalization, 5–6, 8; local community and, 7, 187n4; of new media, 48, 118, 156; perspectives and philosophy on, 66–69

Global Positioning System (GPS), 59, 138–39, 157, 193n68

Godaddy.com, 198n1

Godfrey, Laurence, 73–74

Godfrey v. Demon Internet, 88

Golden Shield Project, 199n22

Google, 26, 86, 155; litigation against, 89; search results of, 72, 154, 166, 198n13

Google Earth, 155

Google Spain v. AEPD & Mario Costeja Gonzalez, 86

Gossip: circulation of, 52, 61–62; college, 105; function of, 48; infatuation and use of, 62–63

Government, 62; control of information by, 49, 83–92, 198n13, 199nn14–15, 199nn17–18, 199nn21–22, 200nn23–24, 200nn32–33, 201n36, 201nn44–46, 202n57, 202n60; intrusion of, 50–51; transparency of, 139

GPS. *See* Global Positioning System

Grant, Cary, 44

Great Britain, 180; on breach of confidence, 21; courts of, 73, 196n36; free speech in, 15–16; mass printing in, 49; on privacy, 34–35; superinjunction in, 41–42, 179

Griswold v. Connecticut, 19

Guantanamo military base, 71

"Guidelines for the Regulation of Computerized Personal Data Files," 69

"Guidelines on the Protection of Privacy and Transborder Flows of Personal Data," 69

Gutnick, Joseph, 73

Hamilton, Alexander, 102

Hamling v. United States, 98–99, 204n86

Hare v. Richie, 88

Harper's Magazine, 117, 207n3, 212n29

Harvard Law Review, 52

Harvard University, 62

Hoffman, Lord, 75

Holmes, Oliver Wendell, Jr., 14–15, 50, 119

Homosexuality, 71–72, 142, 165, 203n72

House of Representatives, U.S., 129–30

Hudson, Kate, 76

IAPs. *See* Internet access providers

Incitement of popular hatred. *See* Volksverhetzung

Individuals, 12–13; privacy of, 3–11, 58–59; technology and, 8–11

Information: access to, 126, 143–44, 209n50; accuracy and fact checking of, 2–3, 10, 64–65, 117, 207n3; anonymity of, 63–65; breach of confidence and, 21; confidential or public, 30–31, 136–38, 211n8, 211n16; control or ownership of, 30–31, 189n41, 190n42, 190n44; disclosures of, 31–36, 163–68, 189n41, 190n42, 190n44, 190n55, 215nn26–27; distribution of, 135, 144; evolution of, 47–49; as false, opinion or true, 33–34; future and overflow of, 60–65, 194n70, 194n75; government's control of, 49, 83–92, 198n13, 199nn14–15, 199nn17–18, 199nn21–22, 200nn23–24, 200nn32–33, 201n36, 201nn44–46, 202n57, 202n60; illegal acquisition of, 190n42; intent of target of, 36–38; on Internet, 1–3, 6, 9–11, 20, 81–82; intrusive, 41–42; legal perspectives on gathering, 135–43,

National Association for the Advancement of Colored People (NAACP), 2, 23, 59
National Broadcasting Company (NBC), 56
National Enquirer, 109
National Public Radio (NPR), 56
National security, 41
National Security Agency, 162–63
Nations: free speech and, 5–8; legal standards of, 71–74, 195n27; on privacy, 5–8, 67–71; regulation of media by, 67–69
Nazi memorabilia, 90–92, 202n57, 202n60
NBC. *See* National Broadcasting Company
New Jersey, 126–27
New media: anonymity in, 158; conflicts of, 1–3, 8–11; consequences of, 149–53; control of, 66–69, 131; disclosure and information of, 2–3, 9–11, 17–18, 31–35, 48, 189n41, 190n42, 190n44; evolution of, 55–59, 193n68; First Amendment on, 118–19; free press principles and, 117–20, 207nn2–3; future of, 8–11; gatekeepers of, 112–15, 158; globalization of, 48, 118, 156; intent of, 36–38; Internet and, 1–2, 13, 55–59, 193n68; privacy and, 12–13, 27–38, 134–35, 189n41, 190n42, 190n44, 190n55; professional standards for, 180–81, 216n41, 216n43; shield laws and, 129–30, 210n64; speed and, 55–56, 150
News, 2, 56, 74, 127–28, 181, 210n60; false, 49; nature of, 9; sources of, 64–65, 117–18, 175–76; as term, 6, 9
News Corp., 39–40, 121
Newsgathering, 125–26, 130–31, 209n47
News of the World, 39–40, 121
Newspapers, 74–78, 112, 180, 196n51, 196n60, 211n8
Newsworthiness, 165–66, 215n26; of information, 14, 16, 141, 212n28; principle of, 15–16

New York, 16–17, 77–78, 109–10, 192n45, 197n60
New York Court of Appeals, 77, 197n60
New York Times, 2, 45, 74, 85, 127
New York Times v. Sullivan, 45
New York University School of Journalism, 216n43
Ninth Circuit Court of Appeals, 87, 90, 100, 104, 124–25
Nissenbaum, Helen, 37
Noonan, Peggy, 162
North Korea, 68
NPR. *See* National Public Radio

Oakland Tribune, 145–46, 212n28
Obama, Barack, 82–83, 127–28, 195n23, 210n60
Obscenity: FCC on, 198, 203n81; free speech and, 188n1; on Internet, 97–101, 203n79, 203nn81–82, 204n86, 204n96
Obsidian Finance Group, LLC v. Cox, 119–20
O'Connor, Sandra, 99–100
Ohio, 188n24
Olmstead v. United States, 19
Orkut, 89

Pavesich, Paolo, 54
Pavesich v. New England Life Insurance Co., 54
Pearl, Daniel, 195n23
Pearson v. Dodd, 213n35
Pedophiles, 103–4
Pennsylvania, 192n45
Pennsylvania Declaration of Rights (1776), 50
Pentagon Papers, 41
Peterson, Theodore, 67
Phones: camera, 157; cell, 23–24, 40, 59, 162–63; hacking of, 39–40, 121; records of, 20; tapping of, 151
Photography: invention of, 53; privacy and, 53–54
Poland, 89
Pornography: child, 65, 101; on Internet, 97–101, 203n79, 204n86, 204n96

Posner, Richard, 32

Press: in China, 7; concept of, 92–93; control of, 66–69, 131; of eighteenth century, 50; in E.U., 68–69; forum shopping and, 74–78, 196n51, 197n60; functions of, 131; intrusion of, 50–55, 192n45, 193nn49–51; in Latin America, 7–8; libertarianism and, 18, 50, 67–69; liberty and, 126; people and, 120–24, 208n23; printing, 49, 81, 112; social-responsibility approach towards, 67–69; soviet communist model towards, 68; special preferences of, 122–23; as term, 6; traditional, 6–7, 9–10; traditional test of, 124–28, 209n47, 209n50, 209n55, 209n59, 210n60; in U.S., 7–8. *See also* Free press

Printing: First Amendment and, 50; mass, 49; press, 49, 81, 112

Privacy, 26; being let alone as, 12–13, 18–19, *19*; breach of confidence and, 21; with contextual integrity, 37; contractual obligations and, 40–41; courts on, 25, 30; dignity as, 24, 188n24, 189nn25–26; of family, 5; First Amendment and, 15, 31–33, 40–41, 66, 189n41; forum shopping and, 74–78, 96, 196n51, 197n60, 203n72; Fourth Amendment on, *19*, 188n11; as free expression, 23–24; free press and, 6–8; future of, 148–49; Germany on, 36, 144, 190n55, 195n27; global standards on, 70–71; Great Britain on, 34–35; of individuals, 3–11, 58–59; informational autonomy and, 19–22; intellectual, 172; intrusion and, 29; multiple approaches for, 181–83; nations on, 5–8, 67–71; new accountability of, 159–60; new media and, 12–13, 27–38, 134–35, 189n41, 190n42, 190n44, 190n55; personal, 1–3, 8–11, 22–23; photography and, 53–54; positivist theory of, 160; pragmatic, 24–25; prior restraint to, 164; protection of, *182*; reasonable expectation of, 177; remedies for, 39–46, 155–62; rights to, 3–5, 52–54, 153–55; society and, 159–61;

statutes of, 54, 192n45; theories of, 12, 18–27, *19*, 188n11; tort, 42–44, 95, 191n64; of trade secrets, 20–21; treaties on, 69–71, 195n23; U.S. Constitution on, *19*, 27; values of, 3

Privacy International, 70–71

Protection, 26, 132; of anonymity, 58; of bloggers, 45; of dignity, 162–63; under First Amendment, 76, 196n51; of privacy, *182*; of speech, 57–58, 78–80; of trade secrets, 21

Publications, 143–47, 213n35, 213n43, 213nn45–47

Public conduct, 141–43, 212nn28–29

Public disclosure: of private facts, 43, 94–95, 176–78, 215n34, 215n37; values of, 15–16

Public information, 30–31, 136–38, 211n8, 211n16

Public interests, 15, 121–22, 126, 145–46, 209n50

"Public is public" approach, 142, 212n29

Public records: accessibility of, 138–40; online, 139–40, 212n17

Publishers, 76, 187n4, 196n51; on disclosures, 32, 143–47, 190n42, 213n35, 213n43, 213nn45–47; ISPs and, 86–88, 200n32; media, 154; technology and, 15–16

Al-Qaeda, 76

"Rachel's law," 77–78

Radio, 56; broadcast of information by, 54–55; invention of, 54, 113

Rape, 107–8, 206n145

Reddit, 91

Red Kimono case, 165–66, 215n26

Rehnquist, William, 23–24

"Reinforcement bias," 62

Reno v. American Civil Liberties Union, 57

Reporters, 17, 70–71

Reporters Without Borders, 70–71

ReputationDefender.com, 205n123

The Restatement (Second) of Conflict of Laws, 75

44–46, 191n67; of intrusion, 42–43, 191n64; laws, 19; of likeness or name, 44; privacy, 42–44, 95, 191n64; of public disclosure, 43; remedies of, 167–68, 215n27; of trespass, 32–33

Trademarks, 84, 199n14

Trade secrets: privacy of, 20–21; protection of, 21

Treaties: on privacy, 69–71, 195n23. *See also specific treaties*

Twitter, 13, 63–65, 87, 180, 194n75; information on, 6, 41–42; users, 7, 187n4

U.K. *See* United Kingdom

U.N. *See* United Nations

U.N. Human Rights Council, 45

U.S. *See* United States

U.S. Code (U.S.C.), 200n33

Ugland, Eric, 130–31

UNESCO. *See* United Nations Education, Scientific and Cultural Organization

Uniform resource locator (URL), 85

United Kingdom (U.K.): defamation in, 76; House of Lords of, 76; ISPs and, 88–89, 201nn44–46; superinjunction in, 41–42, 179

United Nations (U.N.): International Covenant on Civil and Political Rights of, 45, 69; Universal Declaration of Human Rights of, 69–70

United Nations Education, Scientific and Cultural Organization (UNESCO), 70

United States (U.S.), 5–6, 19, 34, 164; anonymity in, 93; collection of information by, 27, 150, 154, 162–63; courts in, 7–8; free expression in, 7; free speech in, 15–16, 51; ISPs and, 84–91, 198n13, 199nn14–15, 200nn23–24, 200nn32–33, 201n33, 201n36, 201n44, 202n57, 202n60; press in, 7–8

United States v. Kilbride, 100

United States v. Rumely, 15

United States v. Skinner, 193n68

URL. *See* Uniform resource locator

Usenet, 73

Volksverhetzung (incitement of popular hatred), 24, 189n25

von Bulow v. von Bulow, 124–25, 127–29, 209n47

Von Hannover v. Germany, 36, 144, 190n55, 195n27

Wall Street Journal, 8, 73

Warren, Samuel, 12–13, 18–19, 19, 52–54

Washington Post, 74, 127

WCW. *See* World Championship Wrestling

Weatherup, James, 39

Weaver, Russell L., 114

Websites: access to, 85; acquiring, 82, 198n1; community-sponsored, 91; domain names for, 82, 198n1; hoax, 64; immunity of, 87; social networking, 103

Web speakers, 7, 187n4

Weiner, Anthony, 150

WikiLeaks, 30–31, 114

Wikipedia, 91

Williams, Pete, 56

Wiretapping, 22, 151; as unconstitutional, 40; U.S. Supreme Court on, 40

World Championship Wrestling (WCW), 125

World Wide Web, 98

World Wrestling Federation (WWF), 125

Yahoo, 90–92, 202n57, 202n60

Yahoo!Argentina, 72, 144

Yahoo Message Board, 110–11

Yang, Jerry, 202n60

"Yellow journalism," 53–54

YouTube, 89

Zeran v. America Online, Inc., 86–88, 200n32

Distinguished law professor at the University of Florida, Jon L. Mills is a former dean of the Levin College of Law and a former Speaker of the Florida House of Representatives. His specialties are privacy and constitutional law, about which he has litigated high-profile cases and written many articles along with the book *Privacy: The Lost Right*.